Accused American War Criminal

*Best Wishes to —
Jeanne
Fiske Hanley II*

Fiske Hanley II

"Special Prisoner"
of the Japanese
1945

ECHO POINT BOOKS & MEDIA, LLC

Published by Echo Point Books & Media
Brattleboro, Vermont
www.EchoPointBooks.com

Accused American War Criminal
ISBN: 978-1-63561-045-1 (paperback)

*This book is dedicated
to the heroic deeds and
the memory of my eight fellow crewmen
who lost their lives on*

27 March 1945

*John A. Brown
Harlan E. Fintel
Baxter J. Love, Jr.
Leroy F. Rose
Charles A. Anderson
Richard E. Donlavy
James E. Griffith
Albert A. Francescon*

*These brave men were killed over
Japan's Shimonoseki Straits
by intense and accurate
Japanese Naval anti-aircraft fire*

*May God Bless them
and
look after them on their last flight.*

Boeing B-29 Superfortress very heavy (VH) bomber.

504th Bomb Group B-29's on way to Japanese target. Note "Circle E" tail markings designating 504th Bomb Group.

Contents

Foreword

General Curtis LeMay's 20th Air Force brought the full fury of warfare to the Japanese homeland and hastened the war's end. The B-29 "Superfortress" war against the Japanese enemy did not last long — just a little over one year. Its role was swift and deadly. The 504th Bomb Group had the distinction of dropping the last weapon of World War II, a mine, on 15 August 1945, the day that hostilities against the Japanese ceased.

As Assistant Chief of Staff for Administration of the Central Fleet, under the command of Adm. William F. Halsey, it was the duty of my section of the staff to prepare a plan to liberate the American prisoners held by the Japanese. When the time came, Admiral Halsey approved our plan and said to Comdr. Roger Simpson and me:

"Roger and Harold, these are our boys. Go get them!"

On 29 August 1945, major battle units of the US Navy sailed into Tokyo Bay. This started sixty-one hours of non-stop liberation. The first camp liberated was Camp Omori, where American, Australian, Canadian, English, New Zealanders, and Italian prisoners were held, and where prisoners in the Kempei Tai Headquarters Prison in Tokyo were transferred after the cessation of hostilities.

The author, Fiske Hanley, was a flight engineer on a B-29 flying the first mining mission to Japan's vital Shimonoseki Straits on

27 March 1945. His B-29 was shot down after its mine load was dropped. He was one of only two survivors of his B-29. His story of survival as a "Special Prisoner" while awaiting trial and execution as an accused war criminal documents the atrocities suffered by a special type of prisoner of the Japanese. Treatment of "Special Prisoners," imprisoned in dungeon cells of the murderous Kempei Tai, is another example of Japanese inhumanity. It is a horror story that must be told.

HAROLD E. STASSEN

Preface

During the night of 27 March 1945, I was shot down on a World War II bombing mission. I was captured, imprisoned by the Japanese, and held as a "Special Prisoner" in a dungeon at Kempei Tai Headquarters in Tokyo. This was a prison for American airmen accused of killing innocent civilians. We were not treated as POWs. We were "Accused American War Criminals." As wards of the brutal Japanese Kempei Tai Thought Police, who were comparable to Hitler's SS and Gestapo, we were guarded by sadistic goons, especially picked for their brutality. Special, deadly rules applied to our imprisonment. The fate of a captive B-29 crewman was to be tried and executed.

"Special Prisoners" had no way of knowing the total magnitude of Kempei inflicted atrocities because of their isolation during imprisonment. Communication with other prisoners was prohibited and could, and often did, lead to execution. Except when locked in our cells, we were blindfolded and handcuffed. The only time we were taken out of our cells was to be interrogated and beaten.

From the date of my capture until 15 August 1945, I watched as fellow airmen were brutalized, tortured, starved, and murdered. Many died of battle injuries, others were beaten to death or died of malnutrition. The few of us who survived were within a hair's breadth of death from starvation and disease when the war ended. "Special Prisoners" received no medical attention. We were considered sub-humans by the Japanese and treated as animals.

"Special Prisoners" were denied soap, razor, toothbrush, comb, shoes, belt, bedding, and medicine. We never saw the sun. We were not allowed to exercise. No baths, no change from our filthy, ragged, vermin-ridden clothing was permitted. We were put on a diet intended to starve us to death in a few months.

Of those B-29 crewmen falling into the hands of Kempei Tai, less than half survived. Prisoner of war survival would have been zero had the Allies invaded the Japanese mainland. Imperial Japanese Headquarters ordered the execution of all prisoners when their shores were invaded. Japanese people were ordered to fight to the death. The atomic bomb saved millions of lives — American and Japanese. Prisoners of war owe their lives to President Truman's decision to drop the atomic bomb. It ended the war!

I was one of the few fortunate survivors! God saved my life many times during my imprisonment. God protected me.

Acknowledgments

The writing of this book was a traumatic experience, bringing back the bad memories of that short period in my life. I based the book on a forty-page document written in 1945 shortly after my return home. I have expanded that story of stark atrocities which will never leave my mind.

A General Dynamics attorney gave me a copy of the *War Crime Report* on the massacre of prisoners at the Tokyo military prison in May 1945. Bob Martindale helped with Camp Omori information. He was the American camp work officer. Marcus Worde helped keep my memory straight on details of our Kempei and Omori imprisonment. Scott Downing and his wife, Bitsy, were helpful with suggestions for the book and data on the prisoners who were in the horsestalls. Scott was ordered back to Tokyo to help prepare war crime charges against the brutal Kempei Tai staff. To supplement my story, Robert Neptune, Tokyo war crimes prosecutor, supplied me with copies of Kempei Tai Headquarters' prisoner depositions and war crime proceedings against Kempei Tai staff members.

I owe many thanks to Rosemary Davis, and Kathryn and Charles Fuquay for their hours of reading and editing the manuscript. My wife, Anna, herself a published author, put up with the many months dedicated to recalling and reliving this awful experience. She not only encouraged me but spent hundreds of hours going over my raw story, using her computer and writing expertise to make it readable.

Chapter 1

What Happened?

Outside the air was smooth. No white caps could be seen on the waters below us. The airplane was functioning smoothly. Everything looked great! Shortly it would be dark, but right now we were enjoying a great view of the sunset, one of the fringe benefits of flying over the beautiful Pacific Ocean.

As the sky began to darken, I could see the many gauges on my flight engineer's instrument panel begin to glow in the rays of the night lights playing over them. I could barely see Harlan Fintel, our navigator, sitting across the cabin from me. He was bent over his table working on his navigational maps.

Over the intercom Harlan announced that the island of Iwo Jima was about 50 miles away and was showing on his radar screen. Small radar blips indicated hundreds of US Navy ships surrounding the island. As we approached the island, many lights, tracers, and explosions could be seen. It was obvious that there was a war going on.

John Brown, our commander, directed the radio operator to tune to Iwo Jima combat channels as we passed nearby. We listened to urgent and heart-rending communications between advancing, hard-fighting marines and navy/marine fighters buzzing over the island like mad hornets. The supporting fighters were urgently asked to direct machine gun fire and bombs to take out enemy strong-point positions only a few feet from their advanced, precarious positions.

After leaving the vicinity of Iwo, which was roughly halfway to our target, we bored our way through the sky to the Japanese mainland. As we approached the Japanese Empire, we began readying our personal-protection gear for whatever danger we might encounter.

Before taking off, each of us provided some kind of extra protection at our crew station. In my case, I placed a small piece of "flak curtain" centered under my dinghy and a two-foot square of "curtain" under my feet. Some crew members placed sections of "flak curtain" around their stations.

To ready ourselves for combat, we removed our parachutes and put on, in the following order, survival vest, "Mae West" life jacket, flak vest. On top of all this personal equipment, we strapped on a parachute and attached a "one-man" dinghy to the parachute harness. The dinghy served as our seat cushion. As the last combat-ready procedure, we strapped the heavy flak helmet in place. We were ready for whatever defenses the enemy could throw at us.

We checked to assure that our individual good luck charms were on duty. Much ingenuity and originality was displayed in choosing these important items. My good luck charm was an 1890 silver dollar which I carried in my pants' watch pocket. Baxter Love had a small rabbit's foot on a string which he tied above his head. Al Andrews attached a small, red Santa Claus to the bulletproof glass in front of him. John Brown had his razor-sharp hunting knife. Other crewmen had personal good luck charms which were the subjects of lively discussions over the intercom.

Each of us felt that if there were casualties on this mission, it wouldn't be one of us. It would happen to some other crew. The feeling among fighting men was, "I won't be wounded or killed. It will be someone else." We were concerned, but never doubted that we would survive the required 35 combat missions and return home safely.

The oddest feeling came over me during the last portion of the long flight to Japan. As usual, a nervous churning in my gut appeared during this part of a mission and stayed until we left the target area. At times, my thoughts gave me the impression that I was standing apart and studying myself seated at my flight engineer's station, illuminated by the dim lights of the instrument panel. How in the world had I gotten myself into this hellish situation? The subject of my thoughts: me — *Fiske Hanley!* How and why was I in this peculiar place at this particular time? Why was I flying over the Pacific in a B-29? How did I get mixed up in this terrible war? A short time before I was a scholar enjoying fraternity life and planning a great future. How had my life changed so drastically in such a short period?

All my life, I had been involved in the world of aviation. Designing, building, and flying model airplanes was the consuming interest of my youth. When I was six years old I rode as a passenger on a Ford Tri-motor airplane. My fare was less than fifty cents, based on one cent per pound of passenger weight. In high school my gasoline-powered model airplane won the National Contest held in Detroit in 1937. It set a new world's record.

After graduating from Paschal High School in Fort Worth, Texas, in 1938, I earned an Associate in Science Degree in Aero Engineering from North Texas Agricultural College (NTAC). In 1943 I received a Bachelor of Science Degree in Mechanical Engineering with an Aeronautical Option from Texas Technological College.

During my junior year at Texas Tech, the Texas draft board contacted me for military service. Instead of being drafted, I volunteered, was accepted into the Army Air Force Aviation Cadet Program, and was granted a deferment until my 1943 graduation. The Army Recruiting Office in Lubbock, Texas, was very efficient. On 31 May 1943, at eight o'clock on the morning after my graduation ceremony, I reported to the Army Recruiting Office. I was expecting to be allowed a day or two to go home with my parents, who were in Lubbock for my graduation, move my possessions to Fort Worth, and prepare for my army service assignment. Instead, I was handed my induction and shipping orders, a train ticket, and was told to be on a train that left in less than two hours.

I sold or gave away most of my college gear and had the rest packed into the family car, borrowed for the previous night's graduation festivities. I asked the recruiting sergeant what I should do about getting the car to my parents, who were visiting relatives in a nearby town. Without concern he said, "Oh, they'll find it." I quickly packed an extra shirt and my razor in a small bag that I had received as a graduation gift, left the car keys with the recruiting sergeant, and boarded the waiting train.

My army induction was so sudden that I was on the train before it dawned on me that I was no longer a civilian. I was a private in the Army Air Force. Thirteen hours after I graduated, I was on my way to Boca Raton, Florida, for cadet basic training. Had I known how to read my orders, I would have known that I had three days "delay enroute" and could have returned to Fort Worth with my parents, visited for a day or two, and then entrained. I would also have learned that I had an adequate dollar per diem allowance. I had a big celebration the night before and very little money was left in my pocket for the four-day trip. Several train changes and an overnight delay in New Orleans occurred. It was a very "hungry" trip. That recruiting sergeant who prepared the orders could have interpreted the army "mumbo-jumbo." He didn't! I have always wondered if he felt some glee in "putting one over" on a college boy going off to become an officer.

CADET TRAINING

On my arrival at Boca Raton a large army truck was waiting. I was to be its only passenger. It delivered me to the luxurious Boca Raton Club. The army requisitioned the club as an Aviation Cadet basic training center for Engineering, Meteorological, and Communication cadets. My orders read "Report to the Commanding Officer." As I climbed off the truck, I was greeted by a smartly dressed cadet officer who informed me that he, not the CO, would process me into the cadet system. He barked orders at me to stand at "Attention," "About Face," and "Backward Marched" me, suitcase in hand, toward the cadet reception center. My one-man, "Backward Parade" led me past about 600 cadets standing in ranks readying for the evening flag-lowering ceremony. The assembled cadets were all smiles and shouted at the top of their lungs, *"YOU'LL BE SOR-RY."* I grinned with them and was immediately ordered by the cadet officer, *"WIPE IT OFF!"* After my backward march to cadet headquarters, my rigid cadet discipline and induction procedure began. Due to wartime shortages. my one set of civilian clothes had to do for all activities until my army-issued uniforms were obtained two weeks later. I looked unkempt and felt worse in Florida's June heat. When an inspecting officer asked why I was dripping wet after a drill period, I told him that I was merely sweating. He quickly informed me that, "Cadets do not sweat. Cadets perspire. Don't ever forget that, Cadet Hanley." I also learned that there are only three acceptable answers to an upperclassman's question: "Yes Sir," "No Sir," and "No Excuse Sir."

About half the cadets were army enlisted personnel. They were carefully selected based on their excellent demonstrated abilities. The other half came from the collegiate world. A superb mixture.

Cadet training regime began in earnest at 0600 each morning. During my two years of ROTC military training at NTAC I knew a lot about army discipline, marching, and rifle-handling. This training now came in handy. The 16-hour day was packed with army basic subjects such as marching, calisthenics, firearms, survival, guard duty, army laws, rules, and regulations, plus special training by upperclass cadets. On occasion, to test our stamina, we marched all night. We bivouacked in swampy and mosquito-ridden forests. We stood guard duty with real rifles and real bullets.

Cadets were constantly under intense scrutiny. Anything and everything that was leather or metal had to be cleaned and shined daily. We militarized (GI'd) the beautiful club fixtures and floors by scrubbing and polishing them. Our shoes and brass insignia were shined at least twice every day. Our bunk beds had to be made so tightly that a dropped quarter must bounce at least a foot above them. Demerits (Gigs) were liberally passed out for minor infractions. Major infractions could lead to "wash out" of the cadet program. Too many gigs and the weekend was ruined by disciplinary periods of marching around the club. Those who didn't measure up to the strict mental and physical standards were "washed out." These unfortunates became instant privates or returned to their previous rank. Survivors were highly motivated to work harder to meet Air Force Aviation Cadet requirements and graduate as "Commissioned Officers and Gentlemen by Act of Congress."

Cadets training together developed an intense sense of comradeship and *espirit-de-corps*. We trained well together and during our meager time off, we visited the nearby Florida towns of Del

Ray, Fort Lauderdale, and Miami. This area of Florida was crowded with thousands of enlisted troops who mistakenly saluted us, thinking that we were officers because of our unique cadet insignia. We were delighted! This was a real morale builder, as usually our life and treatment as underclassmen was lower than a snake's belly. After six weeks as lowerclassmen, we achieved the lofty status of upperclassmen, and for six weeks life was much easier with more privileges and the respect afforded us by the miserable lowerclassmen. We had hardly gotten used to the great feeling of upperclass superiority when we graduated from basic training, and went on our technical training, where we started all over in the cadet classification system. We became lowerclassmen once again.

TECHNICAL SCHOOL

My cadet class graduated from Boca's basic training in early September and entrained for specialized training at Technical School, Yale University, New Haven, Connecticut. At Yale we were segregated into the several cadet technical categories. My Engineering section was housed in Lawrence Hall, one of the oldest of Yale's colleges. The welcoming upperclassmen made sure that we realized, once again, that we were the lowest form of humanity. We were made to press our noses against the bare, ancient walls where we yelled out our name, rank, and army serial number until hoarse. We scrubbed Yale's ancient wooden floors, layered with years of grime, with toothbrushes and GI soap until the old, splintered boards sparkled. Those who lived through the rigid discipline, hazing, and intense academic intruction became hardy upperclassmen once again and made miserable the lives of new arrivals.

Six months were spent learning our technical specialties. Our technical training was superb. Our specialized education by the air force assured top quality maintenance for the growing fleet of warplanes. Because of the large cadet population at Yale, the technical program was organized into a two-shift operation. Reveille sounded at 0400 for one section; for the other it was 0600. While one section learned military subjects, marched, had survival training and calisthenics, the other section went to technical classes. Subjects ranged from engines and air frames to hydraulics and electrical systems. Aircraft maintenance engineering courses were tough and thorough with much "hands-on" instruction. We had to fly in aircraft that we repaired. With the ever-present screening process, the cadet classes became thinner as more and more of our fellow cadets washed out and returned to the enlisted ranks.

Sunday parades on New Haven's town green, located in the center of this beautiful city, were something to behold and enjoy. Cadet precision marching formations swept across the green to the unconventional band music of "Blues in the Night" and "Buckle Down Winsocki" played by the Air Force Band, directed by Capt. Glenn Miller. Captain Miller commanded the Air Force Band Training Center, which was also located at Yale University. His band played for our lunch and dinner hours in the large and beautiful Yale dining room. Our frequent and elegant cadet dances were a delight to attend with Captain Miller and his excellent musicians providing the music. Aviation cadets had the pick of the prettiest New Haven belles as dates.

Near graduation, the cadets were given $250 in cash as a one time allowance to procure officer's uniforms. We were briefed that suitable uniforms could be bought for less than $100 at the Army Quartermaster clothing store. Most of us disregarded this sound advice and blew our total uniform allowance on specially tailored uniforms at the swanky New Haven men's stores. We graduated in beautiful uniforms with no allowance dollars left over. Looking back, these purchases must have been our show of independence and a strike at the rigid cadet discipline and mental conditioning we experienced.

Before graduation, Engineering cadets were given a list of four possible assignments. Our preference for these assignments were to be listed in priority order. I figured that being assigned to be a B-29 Flight Engineer could be dangerous. My Engineering officer preferences were listed in this order:

1. Air Transport Command
2. Fighter Command
3. Bomber Command
4. B-29 Flight Engineer

Had I understood the army's assignment system, which issued assignments in reverse order of preference, I would have listed them differently.

Assignment orders were posted the morning of our graduation,

4 February 1944. We crowded around the bulletin board in cadet headquarters to learn our fate. My orders directed me to report to the B-29 Flight Engineer School at the Seattle Boeing factory.

That afternoon a beautiful young lady from New Haven pinned on my second lieutenant "bars." I was commissioned an Officer and Gentleman by Act of Congress. I became a second lieutenant.

FLIGHT ENGINEERS' SCHOOL

Some twenty of my fellow officers received the same orders. We entrained that afternoon at the New Haven station with New York City as our first stop. By now I knew how to read army orders and recognized the "delay en route" line as well as the "per diem allowance line." Our orders authorized several days "delay enroute" and a meager per diem rate. We had received several hundred dollars in cash as pay for various army allowances. We were rich. In New York our group stayed at the Astor Hotel located on Times Square. We thoroughly enjoyed two days in the Big Apple, strutting around in our new uniforms, returning salutes, and eating "high-on-the-hog."

Our cross-country train trip to Seattle was anything but monotonous. A technical representative of a Boeing supplier company boarded the train in Chicago. He carried as part of his luggage a case of bourbon and a case of Scotch whiskey. Two of my fellow officers and I shared a large compartment on the train. The airplane parts salesman asked if he could join us. We settled on a great arrangement: we furnished compartment space for him; he furnished "spirits" for us and our friends. We made lots of friends on the long train trip. Our party began in Chicago and lasted all the way to Seattle. When our new friend left the train, he had only his suitcase and quite a hangover. We Flight Engineers-to-be carried many happy memories of that delightful cross-country trip.

Boeing B-29 schooling was intensive and thorough. From classroom instructors we learned about the airplane and its systems. Half of our Flight Engineer class were officers, the other half were senior enlisted students. Boeing Factory School lasted for three months. We learned how a B-29 airplane worked and what made it fly. The airplane was huge and complex. We had never before seen such a monster. The Japanese were going to be in for big trouble!

Student officer life was much easier than cadet life. There was no hazing, no strict discipline, and no threat of being "washed out."

Seattle was a beautiful city and a fun place for recreation. We skied in the nearby mountains and visited the Canadian cities of Vancouver and Victoria on weekends. The RCAF (Royal Canadian Air Force) base near Victoria allowed us to inspect their coastal defense capability, including a radar installation. We didn't know what radar was. None of us had ever seen or heard about it, even though we had unknowingly guarded it at the Boca Raton Club. The Canadian radar's primary purpose was detection of enemy submarines preying on coastal shipping, and for air-sea rescue operations. We were honored that the Canadians trusted us with this secret information. We now knew the purpose of the mysterious humming device during our basic training at Boca Raton Club.

We graduated from Boeing B-29 Flight Engineer School and entrained for flight training at Lowry Field located in Denver, Colorado. We arrived on 6 May 1944 during a heavy spring snowstorm. Since all B-29 production aircraft were being delivered to combat units, there were no B-29s at Lowry. Instead we received our flight instruction in B-17 "Flying Fortresses" and specially modified B-24 "Liberators." Ten B-29 Flight Engineer stations were installed in what had been the B-24 bomb bay area. Our class was divided into two sections. One section attended ground training while the other had flight training. We switched sessions every other day.

We began our flight instruction in war-weary B-17 Flying Fortresses to get the feel of large bombers. We practiced engine operation including "feathering" and "unfeathering" propellers. Our final training was received in the special B-24 aircraft.

One day during our ground class period, we learned that the B-24 carrying the other half of our class had made a forced landing in a field near Denver. We had flown on this airplane the previous day. The airplane turned over in the rough field and caught fire. The flight crew and student engineers were trapped inside the stricken airplane by jammed hatches which could not be opened. All aboard the airplane perished in the fire.

Upon completion of B-29 flight training we had another graduation ceremony. This time we received silver air force "Observer Wings" which were similar to "Pilot Wings," except for a large "O" which was placed in the center instead of a shield. We were now "Flyboys."

We were posted to our respective B-29 combat groups. I was assigned to the 504th Bomb Group currently undergoing training at Fairmont Army Air Field (FAAF) in Nebraska. Fairmont AAF was near a very small town located sixty miles west of Lincoln. The airfield was completely surrounded by cornfields.

THE B-29 "SUPERFORTRESS"

The B-29 "Superfortress" airplane was developed to provide long range (4,000 miles) and large bomb load capability (20,000 pounds). The giant airplanes were designed to demolish distant enemy targets from bases in the United States. In 1944 there was still a possibility that Hitler's war successes might deny our bombers use of European bases. This aircraft was never used or needed in Europe. It became the airplane for strategic bombing of the Japanese home islands. The war against the Japanese Empire called for an airplane with the B-29's capability. It could reach Japanese targets from Chinese bases or captured Marianas Island bases.

These long range planes were equipped with four newly developed Curtiss-Wright R-3350 engines. This unproven engine's reliability and safety were suspect. Eddie Allen, Boeing's chief pilot, had been killed during the test program. The new engine suffered many fires and failures. Too many crews lost their lives due to this unproven airplane-engine combination, but our nation needed its capability to bring the war to Japan's homeland.

The airplane was designed to fly at a maximum gross weight of 120,000 pounds. Most missions were loaded to nearly 150,000 pounds at take-off. Specifications claimed that the airplane could fly and bomb at altitudes over 30,000 feet and strike targets up to 2,000 miles from base. We soon found that the airplane had great trouble flying 1,500 miles to the target, bomb at 25,000 feet with 4,000 pounds of bombs, and return to base. Many crews lost their lives when fuel ran out and they had to ditch before reaching home base.

The B-29's awesome defensive armament consisted of five remote-controlled gun turrets, containing a total of twelve 50-caliber guns plus a 20-millimeter cannon located in the tail turret. B-29 bombers were classed as very heavy (VH) as compared to the heavy designation for B-17 and B-24 aircraft. Pressurized cabins, similar to today's airliners, greatly improved crew operating efficiency. The B-29 was such a large and complex airplane that the pilot (called airplane commander) and copilot (called pilot) needed help to manage the mechanical aspects of its operation. A flight engineer's station was provided for this purpose.

COMBAT TRAINING

On arriving at Fairmont AAF in mid-August, I became a member of one of the finest fighting organizations engaged in winning World War II, the 504th Bomb Group (VH), commanded by Col. Jim "Jungle Jim" Connally. I was assigned as flight engineer on 2d Lt. John A. Brown's eleven-man combat crew, one of 398th Bomb Squadron's 15 combat crews. Fairmont AAF was equipped with a few B-29s.

Our crew trained on war-weary B-17 aircraft. Specialists, like myself, were checked out by ranking squadron personnel on B-29 aircraft after flying about ten hours of dual instruction. Due to my intensive training at Yale, Seattle, and Denver, I had no trouble being certified as a Flight Engineer.

Our crew flew frequent gunnery and bombing missions over air force target areas. One of our training missions in a B-29 was a 3,000 mile flight to a small dot of an island in the Gulf of Mexico called Whale Rock. Harlan Fintel navigated our plane so well that we hit it right on the button. We pulverized the island with bombs and bullets.

During a two week exercise, my combat crew flew to Cuba in a B-17 for ocean and island training. For some unknown reason, a flight engineer was not needed. I was left behind at Fairmont AAF. My requested two weeks leave of absence was denied. After carefully checking with the authorities, I detected no plans for my use during the two week period. I decided that I could go AWOL (absent without leave) and no one would miss me. I checked out a parachute and caught a C-47 "Gooney Bird" flight to Fort Worth Army Airfield. I worried the whole ten days while visiting my parents at home that I would be caught and court-martialed and punished. Upon my return to Fairmont AAF, I learned that I had not been missed. Sometimes the army does strange things.

While we were completing our B-29 training, the United States Marines fought bloody battles and captured three important islands in the Marianas Group. These islands were approximately 1,500 miles from the Japanese homeland and would serve as B-29 bases from which to bomb Japanese homeland targets.

John Brown's combat crew was composed of eleven highly trained specialists:

AIRPLANE COMMANDER ....2d Lt. John A. Brown
PILOT ....2d Lt. Albert H. Andrews
NAVIGATOR........................2d Lt. Harlan E. Fintel
BOMBARDIER.......................FO Baxter J. Love, Jr.
FLIGHT ENGINEER ....2d Lt. Fiske Hanley
RADIO OPERATOR................Sgt. Leroy F. Rose
CENTRAL FIRE
      CONTROL (CFC) ....S. Sgt. Charles A. Anderson
RH GUNNER ....Sgt. Richard E. Donlavey
LH GUNNER........................Sgt. James E. Griffith
TAIL GUNNER ....Sgt. Richard Hall
RADAR OPERATOR ....Sgt. Albert L. Francescon

Our combat crew quickly developed close friendships and formed a highly efficient and effective fighting team. We had no "sour apples" or problem crew members. All crewmen were "clean-cut," intelligent young men. Military officer/enlisted man fraternization taboos were ignored. We trained together, partied together, and operated as a family no matter what the situation demanded. We were a tight, well-disciplined fighting team — eager and combat-ready. For weekend recreation during our training in Nebraska, our crew partied in Lincoln or Omaha. We went as one group, officers and enlisted men together. Any disparaging remark from outsiders about one of our people immediately brought forth the wrath of our entire crew. We were one combat team and proud of it!

The airplane commander, pilot, navigator, bombardier, flight engineer, and radio operator flew in the forward cabin. The aft cabin accommodated four crew members: the CFC, RH, and LH gunners, and radar operator. The tail gunner stayed in the aft cabin during non-combat operation but moved to his small, pressurized station in the extreme rear part of the airplane before we entered Japanese defensive airspace.

Our airplane commander, 2d Lt. John A. Brown, was an experienced pilot. He was a born leader of men. John grew up in the

Army Air Corps becoming a sergeant pilot, then a flight officer, and now a second lieutenant. Most B-29 aircraft commanders were much higher in rank. Very few second lieutenants commanded these very heavy bombers. He should have ranked as a captain had he been an aviation cadet. Brown, though one of the lowest ranked airplane commanders in the 504th Bomb Group, was rated one of the 398th Squadron's finest pilots. Our deputy group commander, Lt. Col. Glen Martin, often flew with our crew during training. He had great respect for John's flying ability. Brown was a "pro!" A born flyer! Brown hailed from Oklahoma City. A sort of joke existed between Brown and me. My commission preceded his by six months and I could theoretically "pull rank" when off-duty. I didn't! On the plane, he owned, deserved, and was due *absolute* authority. He was our leader and we were proud of it!

Our pilot, 2d Lt. Albert (Al) Andrews was from Altadena, California. Al was the oldest member of the crew and the only married member. He and his wife, Roberta, had one son and were expecting another child in a couple of months. Al was capable of performing all requirements of an airplane commander. He provided excellent back-up in this extremely important flying function. Al and I sat back-to-back on the righthand side of the forward cabin.

2d Lt. Harlan Fintel, our navigator, hailed from Deschler, Nebraska. Harlan was quiet, studious, serious, and a precise navigator. At no time during any of our flights were we at loss to know exactly where we were. He was positioned on the airplane's LH side just aft of my flight engineer's station. A radar monitor was located at his station. In order for anyone up front to go aft, they had to maneuver between the large, upper forward turret, which intruded into the forward cabin, and Harlan's navigation table which held all his maps. Harlan had to fold up part of the table to permit passage. He was not happy with this situation. I don't blame him. This poor design feature greatly annoyed all crew members, especially Harlan.

FO Baxter Love, our accomplished bombardier, was from Atlanta, Georgia. Baxter occupied the front-most station on the airplane, where the highly secret Norden bombsight was located. He could also aim and fire the two forward gun turrets. Baxter's bombardier skill was much better than most of the group's higher ranking "designated" lead bombardiers. He skillfully exhibited uncanny bombing accuracies during our single-plane training missions.

Baxter was very unhappy with the 20th Air Force's directive to drop bombs based on a lead bombardier's expertise, which made him just a "switch thrower." Our early war experience showed that this 20th Air Force procedure was badly flawed. General LeMay recognized this and eventually directed that each plane's bombardier conduct his own bomb drops.

Our radio operator, Sgt. Leroy Rose, was a very "private person." He was well liked by the crew. He hailed from the Chicago area. He was very professional in his handling of radio communications linking our airplane to our Tinian base and other contacts such as air-sea rescue units and other aircraft. He played an important role in our mission effectiveness. Rose's station was located immediately in front of the bomb-bay entrance hatch and just aft of the upper gun turret on the airplane's RH side. The entrance to the thirty-foot tunnel leading to the aft cabin was located directly above his station.

As Flight Engineer I was nominally in charge of the enlisted men. Except for Anderson, they were all PFCs when our crew formed at Fairmont Army Air Field. As we progressed through training and Tinian operations, I recommended all enlisted crew members for promotion to the next higher rank. Brown did not feel that Rose was due as many promotions as the other crew members. Brown could never figure out how Rose advanced at the same rate as his fellow crew members. I always included Rose on the promotion recommendations and felt that he was as worthy as the others for promotion.

In the aft cabin the central fire control (CFC) gunner, S. Sgt. Charles Anderson, was the command gunner. He was in charge of all gun operations. His panel directed which gunner could fire which turret. He could fire any of them. Charles had almost completed Aviation Cadet navigation training when the war's need for navigators was drastically reduced. Just before receiving his commission and "Navigator's Wings," his entire class was terminated. All the cadets were demoted to enlisted status and posted to gunnery school. He was about twenty-two years old. Our other enlisted men were younger. They had great respect for Anderson. We were fortunate to have Charles on our crew. His excellent navigational skills from his aborted navigation training served as an excellent back-up for Fintel. Being lost over the vast Pacific could be fatal. Many crews paid for poor navigation with their lives. Charles usually relieved Harlan Fintel and navigated the long flight back to base while Harlan logged sack time in the tunnel. Fintel and Anderson were so proficient at navigation that they could predict which end of the small Tinian Island we'd arrive over.

In order to have a back-up flight engineer in case of emergencies, which could easily happen in combat, I carefully considered which gunner might have the best mechanical aptitude. Sgt. Dick Donlavey, RH gunner, appeared to be the most suited. At every opportunity, I asked Dick to come up front, observe, and learn to operate the complicated flight engineer's station. He became very proficient at this task. I felt very comfortable with the fact that, should I become incapacitated during flight, Donlavey could take over operation of the flight engineer's station and assure that the plane would get the crew back to base.

Sgt. Dick Hall's combat position in the extreme rear end of the airplane was an isolated one when we were pressurized. As Tail Gunner, he controlled the tail's massive armament which consisted of two 50-caliber machine guns plus a 20-millimeter cannon. He manned this important station during our flight over enemy-defended territory. In case of "abandon aircraft," there was a bail-out hatch in the tail position. Donlavey and Hall grew up together. They were boyhood buddies and schoolmates from Richmond, Virginia. They joined the army together and were inseparable. Both spoke with slow Virginia drawls.

Sgt. James Griffith, LH gunner, completed the gunnery team. Jim was from the mountains of Pennsylvania. He was shy, quiet, and very competent.

Sgt. Albert Francescon, radar operator, held down a very important position which on many crews was staffed by a commissioned officer. He operated this new high tech system with efficiency. He worked closely with Fintel, our navigator, to assure that our radar bombing was accomplished with precision. Often in the case of high altitude missions, thick clouds covered Japanese targets. Our bombs had to be dropped using radar. Blind bombing was also necessary on many of our night missions. Night incendiary bomb missions were single plane operations. The bombs were accurately placed on target via the radar capability. Naval mine placement from single airplane missions at lower altitudes had to be precise so that before the invasion of Japan the mines could be located and disposed of by our navy's minesweepers.

By early December 1944 our combat-ready 504th Bomb Group was trained and primed for overseas deployment. We did not know where we were to be based, but figured that it would be some place in the Pacific war zone. In October 1944 the 504th's ground crews shipped out for some mysterious overseas base. They left from Seattle via a slow moving troop transport ship, the SS *Sea Star*, and arrived at Tinian's dock on Christmas Eve 1944, just in time for a heavy Japanese bomb raid staged from Iwo Jima. There were some anxious moments when our troops found out that Tinian's top soil went down only about six inches before the solid coral rock began — not the best condition for digging a quick foxhole! They hid under whatever was available and were quite vulnerable. Fortunately, we didn't lose a man.

In early December 1944 Lieutenant Brown's crew flew a B-17 from Fairmont, Nebraska, to Herrington, Kansas, where our overseas staging base was located. Here we were to pick up our combat B-29 and begin the process of readying it for the long flight west. The Kansas winter weather was blue and bitter. Our crew was assigned a brand new B-29 manufactured in Wichita, Kansas. It was a beauty! We admired everything about it. No crew ever felt more pride of possession.

On the first morning, I walked to the flight line to check with the ground crew and inspect our new airplane. As I was approaching the airplane, the ground crew started cranking number three engine (RH engine nearest the fuselage). The propeller turned over about half a revolution, there was a sharp explosion, a puff of smoke, and all four propeller blades vibrated and stopped. The ground crew swarmed out of the warm flight deck and ran to inspect the silent engine. They tried to rotate the propeller. It would not turn. It was stuck in place. They goofed and I had witnessed it! They had not performed one very important and mandatory step always necessary before starting an engine. They had not "pulled the propeller through by hand."

Engine oil can collect in the lower cylinders of a radial-type engine and, if not cleared out by rotating the propeller, can cause a fluid lock-up. Oil will not compress like cylinder gases and can cause catastrophic internal engine failure during engine starting.

Our number three engine had to be replaced. This caused a two-day delay while the *new* crew chief and his frost-bitten crew had the bitter cold job of changing the engine.

At our overseas staging base, our crew went though a standardized processing procedure. We received many shots for exotic diseases, signed wills, gave next-of-kin identifications, set up pay allotments, received clothing, mailed letters, shipped home unneeded gear, and were issued a .45 automatic pistol. The army was very thorough.

OVERSEAS DEPLOYMENT

Finally, we were ready. Our new plane was repaired and signed for. During the late afternoon of New Year's Eve 1944, we took off from Herrington, Kansas, and headed for Mather Army Air Field in California. This was our first flight in the new airplane. We hadn't flown far when we realized that our plane was shaking all over the sky. We tried everything during the flight to get rid of the vibration. We were forced to set down in Albuquerque, New Mexico, during a cold and dark night. This was an overnight stop. We quickly realized that tropical uniforms were not the most comfortable attire for New Mexico in the freezing winter time.

Ground crews at Albuquerque tried to find the trouble. They couldn't locate the problem. The next morning we took off for Mather Field, our APOE (Air Port of Embarkation) located near Sacramento. During the flight, the vibrations were so violent that one of our radio antenna masts was shaken off. After landing at Mather, I told the maintenance people that this airplane was grounded until the cause of the vibration was found and fixed. A vibrating plane in the air is a frightening and dangerous thing. They checked many possible causes and found nothing amiss. Finally, a Boeing service representative was contacted and flown to Mather to inspect our airplane. After two days of searching, he announced that the problem was solved. He discovered that the "Victory Workers" at the Boeing plant had not properly installed two heavy springs which held the upper engine cowl flaps toward their closed position. The engine cowl flaps were blowing open in flight, causing turbulent airflow over the horizontal stabilizer — thus the severe vibrations. In order to assure the problem solved, a skeleton crew consisting of Brown, the Boeing representative, the crew chief, and

I took the plane on a short check flight. Sure enough, the Boeing rep had fixed the problem. Our airplane flew as smoothly as it should.

The Boeing rep returned to the Boeing plant with the recommendation that this problem and its solution be passed back to the "Victory Workers" at B-29 factories and throughout the air force maintenance circuit.

During our stay at Mather, the weather was perfect. The entire crew spent many hours wiping down and polishing our beautiful aircraft. We were proud of our giant bird and wanted it to be in the finest condition for our overseas flight and combat missions to follow. The airplane couldn't have had more tender loving care than if we had spent our own money to buy it.

At Mather Field we were given our sealed orders, not to be opened until after our take-off from John Rogers Field, Hawaii. Until then, we would not know our final destination. On 4 January 1945, with Major Dwyer our 398th Squadron Operations Officer as a passenger, we departed Mather Field for the first overseas flight leg. After a ten-hour flight, we landed at John Rogers Field on Hawaii's Oahu Island. We taxied to our parking spot, shut down the engines, and secured the airplane.

By the time that I climbed out of the cabin and glanced around, there were many mechanics swarming around all four of our engines. Even though the engines were still hot, they were pulling off engine cowling panels with a vengeance. I found the crew chief and indignantly asked what in the devil he was doing to our airplane without permission. He said, "Lieutenant, you have no say in this. We have orders to change your complete engine exhaust system. Orders from headquarters." He continued his work as if I were not there. I assumed that this was routine on overseas flights, backed off, and joined our crew on a truck which drove us from the flight line to our quarters.

Major Dwyer, due to his rank, was assigned VIP quarters. He was a great officer and was well liked by our crew. He stopped by our officer quarters to "shoot the bull." While we were visiting, a couple of our crew started vigorously scratching their privates. The rest of us wondered what their problem was. We had all been together since leaving Kansas and there was no way that the scratchers could have caught something. They did have a problem, though. They discovered that they were hosting a population of irritating small creatures sometimes called "Crabs" or "Motorized Dandruff." They were greatly embarrassed and immediately took off to visit the medics. In a short time the unfortunate victims returned with tubes of "blue ointment," an anti-crab salve. The major left for his quarters after kidding the vermin victims. He laughed at their discomfort and delivered them a lecture on clean living.

Within minutes he returned with an agitated and irritated look on his face. He asked if our victims had some extra ointment. We all had a big laugh at his expense. He did not seem to think his own predicament was so funny and left in a huff with his medicine. We finally decided that some of the beds in the Bachelor Officers Quarters (BOQ) at Mather Field were infested with these tiny creatures. Those of us not contaminated were lucky.

While at John Rogers Field I remembered that one of my college buddies, Reverdie Ater, was stationed somewhere on the island and called the army's Island Locator Service. Their efficiency was impressive. Within minutes they gave me my friend's rank, location, and telephone number. (With this kind of capability how could we lose the war?) I called my friend who worked in General Richardson's office. The general was in command of all army forces in the Pacific Ocean area. Reverdie came over to John Rogers Field in an army staff car. We had a fine visit. He had been in service about two years and had done quite well for himself as evidenced by his assignment to the general's staff. In the course of our conversation he told me that we were going to be stationed on Tinian Island in the Marianas. *The Marianas? Tinian?* I had never heard of the Marianas or Tinian Island. He also told me a *TOP SECRET:*

He told me the invasion date for the Japan home islands, Operation Olympic, called for the invasion of Kyushu on 1 November 1945. Operation Coronet called for the invasion of Honshu on 1 March 1946.

My knowledge of these dates would haunt me during my Japanese imprisonment and caused me *much* anxiety.

We cleared out of Hawaii on 11 January 1945, and flew to a fuel stop on miniscule Johnston Island, located some 1,200 miles southwest of Hawaii. During the flight to Johnston Island, Major Dwyer opened our sealed orders and found that we were directed to fly to

Saipan Island. This destination didn't agree with my friend's confidential information. He had said we were to be based on Tinian Island. Our orders were to go to Saipan. How did the two fit together?

We took off from Johnston Island and headed for Kwajalein Island located in the Marshall Island Group where, on 11 January we landed just at dusk. The small island seemed completely clear of all vegetation. It was obvious that tremendous fighting had recently occurred there. We watched as marine Corsair fighters continually took off and landed. We were well aware that Japanese occupied islands were nearby. We had entered the Pacific War Zone.

Our gunners spent most of the night preparing their guns for action. This meant stripping the greasy cosmoline preservative from the guns and checking their operation. They helped the ground crew load the ammunition. I was busy with the crew chief and his maintenance operations assuring that our airplane was fully prepared for its long flight through enemy skies to Saipan. Our fine airplane had performed admirably from Mather Field in California to Kwajalein. The flight discrepancies were minor. A good sign!

The next morning, 12 January 1945, we carefully pre-flighted our now combat-ready B-29 and took off for our wartime operations.

The long flight to Saipan was uneventful. We landed at Isley One Air Field and were told to take off and fly a couple of miles to Isley Two Air Field. On landing the second time, our plane was immediately surrounded by several jeeps loaded with senior Army Air Force officers.

OUR TREASURED AIRPLANE CONFISCATED

We lost our beautiful, well-groomed, perfectly maintained, lovingly cared for airplane on Saipan.

We were fighting mad! Major Dwyer went to Saipan's 73d Wing Headquarters and put up a fight to retain our airplane, but he was outranked. Seems that the 73d's losses had been heavy from Japanese bombings and planes shot down or missing. They needed replacement B-29s. They needed and got *ours!*

We were commanded to remove our gear from the airplane and transfer everything to a B-24 which was standing by to fly us to our permanent base. We stripped the airplane of everything we could carry. I "liberated" the fine tool kit that every airplane carried. Our unhappy crew boarded the B-24 for a three-mile flight over to Tinian Island which we could see across the bay. Reverdie had been right after all. Tinian was to be our base.

We had had visions of emerging from the clouds on a beautiful day, making a perfect landing, and rolling to a stop amid crowds standing and admiring this fine aircraft that we had polished to perfection. Instead, we bumped to a stop, as passengers, in a war-weary B-24 which had seen better days.

After landing on Tinian's North Field, we were trucked to the 504th Bomb Group housing area located on Tinian's west side and assigned living quarters. The five officers were placed in a quonset hut; our enlisted people were given a large tent. All combat crews lived in quonset huts, while the ground people, both officers and enlisted men, were assigned tents until the Seabees could finish building the quonset huts.

B-29 ORDER OF BATTLE

B-29 bombardment squadrons were normally assigned 12 to 15 aircraft and the same number of combat crews. The 504th Bomb Group had started training with three squadrons, the 393d, the 421st, and the 398th, of which we were a part. In September 1944 during combat training at Fairmont, Nebraska, the 504th Bomb Group had been reduced from the normal three squadrons to two squadrons. The 393d Bomb Squadron was suddenly detached and transferred to Wendover, Utah. There, it became the cadre of the 509th Composite Group commanded by Col. Paul Tibbets, who became famous for his delivery of the first atomic bomb over Hiroshima. B-29 Bomb Wings were made up of four groups. Our wing, the 313th, was composed of the 6th, 9th, 504th, and the 505th Bomb Groups. When the 509th Composite Group arrived in June, it was assigned to the 313th Bomb Wing. The 21st Bomber Command, headquartered on Guam, was composed of five Wings: the 58th which arrived on Tinian in March 1945 and flew out of West Field; the 73d, which began operations from Saipan in October 1944; our 313th Wing on Tinian flying out of North Field; and the 314th and 315th Wings based on Guam. The last three wings started operations in early 1945. Our crew was part of an enormous fighting machine when you figure 15 aircraft per squadron, 45 aircraft per group, 180 aircraft per wing times five wings. This equates to almost 1,000 B-29 aircraft each capable of carrying ten tons of bombs. Awesome!

Maj. Gen. Haywood S. "Possum" Hansell was commander of the 21st Bomber Command until he was replaced, in February 1945, by Maj. Gen. Curtis E. LeMay. LeMay joined the 20th Air Force as commander of the 58th Wing while it was based in India. He had earlier earned a reputation in Europe as a fierce and innovative war fighting aerial commander. He was the Army Air Force's equivalent of the army's Gen. George Patton. Army Air Force commander Gen. Henry "Hap" Arnold, commanded the 20th Air Force from his Pentagon headquarters in Washington, DC. This organization was truly a strategic air force. It was formed to assure that the B-29s, with their special capabilities, were used for strategic bombing and not subject to service by local commanders who might be tempted to use them for day-to-day tactical bombing missions. Separated from the commands of the two Pacific War Area commanders, Admiral Nimitz and General MacArthur, its operational role was unique. It was to carry out Pentagon war plans to bomb the Japanese Empire into surrender, hopefully avoiding a bloody, high-casualty invasion of the Japanese home islands. Pacific island bases were not available for the first B-29 missions against the Japanese Empire.

The 58th Bomb Wing began bombing operations in mid-1944 from India and China bases. Major logistic and operational problems resulted while using these bases. A move to better bases was needed to provide improved logistics for arms, fuel, and maintenance supplies. To provide the Pacific island bases within range of Japan, Admiral Nimitz's forces, aided by the army, captured three main islands of the Marianas Group. In mid-1944 Saipan, Tinian, and Guam were taken. As soon as these islands were secured, large B-29 airfields were speedily constructed by skilled and hardworking navy construction battalions popularly known as "Seabees." The Marianas airfields became operational toward the end of 1944. In November the 73d Bomb Wing's B-29s began Japanese Empire bombing missions from Saipan bases. The Marianas Islands were located roughly 1,500 miles from the Japanese home islands, well within the B-29's striking range.

Tinian's North Field with its four parallel 8,500-foot runways was the largest airfield in the world. Tinian's West Field had two parallel 8,500-foot runways.

On 6 and 9 August 1945, from this Tinian Air Field, the 509th Composite Group would take off for Japan and drop two atomic bombs. This new and awesome weapon ended World War II. Since the need to invade the Japanese homeland was avoided, millions of Allied and Japanese lives were spared. The dropping of the atomic bombs *definitely* saved the lives of the prisoners of war in Japan. It certainly saved mine!!

Chapter 2

Tinian Island Beginning

Our combat crew arrived on the beautiful island of Tinian during the late afternoon of 12 January 1945. We deplaned from the B-24 at Tinian's North Field after the short three-mile flight from Saipan and dejectedly unloaded our gear. Our morale couldn't have been lower. We had just lost our cherished B-29.

The loss of our airplane was a blow not only to its crew, who had so lovingly cared for it, but to the entire 504th Bomb Group, already short one entire squadron, which was separated from the group in Fairmont, Nebraska. Our battle effectiveness was seriously crippled. The 504th organization, with its two squadrons, had about 1,800 personnel assigned, including over 30 well-trained and battle-eager crews. There were not enough aircraft to fly. Other crews' aircraft had been confiscated on Saipan. The 504th began operations with less than 30 airplanes. We needed at least 45 B-29s and crews.

Our camp site was located about a mile south of the airfield on the island's west side. The camp was ideally situated on a plateau adjacent to a steep cliff which dropped off to the Pacific Ocean. Tinian's Hilo and Earle points jutted out to sea on either side of our camp area. Our camp site was one of the finest spots on the beautiful island. If a war hadn't been underway, our locale would rate as a resort area (as it does today). The climate was first-class. Even though it was mid-January, a balmy tradewind was gently blowing over the island.

The airfield and island were swarming with construction equipment. Navy Seabee troops had bulldozed and cleared out what had been a large Japanese sugar cane plantation. They started runway construction while the marines were still fighting for the island. They were working feverishly, 24 hours a day, seven days a week, to finish the third and fourth of North Field's 8,500-foot runways.

Since Tinian Island resembled New York's Manhattan Island in size and shape, Seabees named the island's areas and roads for New York's features. The island's network of roads had the Big Apple's street names. Riverside Drive passed the 504th's camp area on the seaward side. A major north-south road, called Eighth Avenue, was routed just inland from our housing area.

Most of the camp area consisted of tents erected in orderly rows. A few quonset huts were ready for occupancy. These quonsets came in kits and were rapidly assembled by the Seabees. The huts were half-cylinders, about 20 feet across by 50 feet long, with corrugated sheet metal roofs and plywood floors. Simple outdoor latrines were in place. Encouraged with gifts of several bottles from our meager liquor supply, Seabees built us a theater with a stage, dressing rooms, and footlights. Seabee troops were mostly older men who had been professional builders and technicians in private life. They deserve special commendation. *They were the best!*

504th specialists built a large electrical generation plant out of salvaged parts from heavily damaged Japanese equipment. Our technicians were almost as versatile as the Seabees. They could build or repair almost anything . . . using "borrowed" Seabee tools and materials. Seabees politely complained about the steady disappearance of their construction supplies and tools, but with good grace charged off the losses to freewheeling air corps flyboys. They looked the other way and accepted the losses as operational hazards.

504th volunteers worked on facility enhancements such as an enlisted men's club, an officer's club, professional-quality baseball diamond, and skeet range. Landscaping improvements were made using lawn grass, papaya trees, white-washed rock walkways, and picket fences. The group conducted contests, selected the most beautiful landscaping, and awarded citations. Our quonset group somehow never placed.

We were issued arctic sleeping bags which were inappropriate for the tropics, but worked great as mattresses over our standard army cots. Furniture such as chairs, shelves, and desks were crafted as individual projects. We built windmill-powered home laundries. Great ingenuity was exhibited in the varied designs and efficiency of these washing machines. The general idea was based on a propeller turning a crankshaft which raised and lowered an agitator in a tub. Even though the clothes did not turn out very clean, we were proud of our inventions. It was amazing how quickly the group's area became a comfortable and livable home away from home.

Seabees became our good friends and made Tinian life more bearable. Some Seabee units "adopted" 504th crews and provided them with hot food trays for their flights. Their professional artists applied many of the nose art emblems displayed on most of our B-29 airplanes. These artists were expert at painting beautiful, shapely, and scantily-clad bathing beauties. Some were so risqué that clothing had to be painted on.

A wooden mess hall which provided food service for the entire 504th was finished and in operation. Our crew quickly learned that this mess hall served the worst food we'd ever eaten. GIs were notably dissatisfied with army food, but our food quality was especially bad. It was hardly edible! The main staple seemed to be mutton from New Zealand which was served almost daily. Whenever this delicacy was on the menu, most of us went to the 504th's small post exchange and subsisted on snacks.

Whenever possible, our crew visited Seabee mess lines to enjoy their excellent navy cuisine. Our mess hall was provided with dried or tropical resistant foods such as grease-like butter, powdered eggs, Spam, and New Zealand mutton. Their mess hall somehow obtained fresh eggs, steaks, and ice cream. Air force quartermasters were not the match of their navy equivalents. Navy ships carried all supplies to the island and disbursed it to the various commands. The navy looked after its own. I could understand this! About the only way we could repay the Seabees for their generosity was to fly them as passengers on short local test flights. They enjoyed these flights immensely. I recall one instance where a Seabee chief petty officer was taken along on a combat mission to the Japanese homeland and fortunately returned home safely.

We had no access to refrigerators or ice, but our local flights to proof major maintenance repairs provided a good opportunity to procure cool beer and other beverages from the PX. Our talented "chemists" brewed alcoholic concoctions using "liberated" dried fruit and local sugar cane. In spite of the high quality control exercised during the fermenting and distillation processes, many hangovers resulted from the partaking of this potent beverage.

Movies were shown almost every evening after sundown. Portable chairs made out of bomb crates made viewing the shows on the dirt field more comfortable. Movie attendees were warned to be armed at the shows because food-scrounging Japanese hold-outs were known to infiltrate B-29 unit camp areas while GIs watched movies. We suspected that Japanese infiltrators sometimes clandestinely watched our movies, then slipped away before being observed. Personal possessions and food scraps turned up missing from time to time. Tinian Island was declared secure from the Japanese defenders in early August 1944. It had been invaded by the Marines on 24 July. There were about 500 holdout Japanese troops on the island who were isolated and sealed off in the wild and hilly southeast corner of the island.

Battlefield debris was everywhere. Carrying Colt .45-caliber automatics issued to all crew members, we prowled and explored the heavily wooded areas below the cliff near our camp area. We discovered caves and pill boxes still containing stores of enemy artillery shells, battle debris, and remains of defeated Japanese defenders. We searched through stockpiles of enemy weapons such as torpedoes and artillery shells. We dumbly dismantled some of these dangerous Japanese munitions to salvage interesting brass cases, projectiles, and torpedo propellers. While exploring, we were sitting ducks for battle-hardened Japanese troopers who probably observed our idiotic wanderings. Looking back on these activities, we were very fortunate to have survived our ground activities. We learned that many B-29 crewmen were killed doing exactly what we had done.

Between missions, besides prowling the island, we made our quonset hut more liveable and waited for mail deliveries. We wrote letters on V-Mail stationary. V-mail was a World War II invention which used a form on which the writer wrote his letter. The form was photographed on microfilm, sent to the United States via airplane, reproduced full-size, and mailed to the addressee. This process cut down on mail bulk and was much faster than slow surface shipping. It was an effective mail delivery system. Rigid censoring of mail was enforced to prevent giving away helpful information to the enemy. As an example, "sugar cane" was snipped out of letters because it could indicate the Marianas Islands.

Our quonset housed officers from three combat crews. Sadly, in just a few weeks, both the other crews were lost in combat. This high combat loss rate did not foretell a rosy picture for the five of us remaining in the quonset. Replacement crews were constantly arriving to make up combat and operational losses. Familiar combat crew faces from Fairmont, Nebraska, were rapidly disappearing.

The 504th's ground crews were the best! Our flight and ground crews maintained very close and friendly relationships — good indication of a healthy and efficient combat unit. Flyers' lives and mission success depended on the excellence of airplane maintenance. Three-thousand-mile missions over broad Pacific waters, flying to and from Japanese Empire targets, demanded absolute airplane reliability.

THE B-29

On the flight line our crew had a problem not experienced by most B-29 crews. We didn't have our own assigned B-29. Since our airplane commander's rank was that of a mere second lieutenant, he rated "low man on the totem pole" for airplane assignments. Our low-ranking crew usually flew the "dogs," the least desirable airplanes. We were assigned a different airplane each time we went on a mission. More fortunate crews, with assigned aircraft, selected distinctive nose art names and logos such as *Lucky Lady, Sitting Duck, Pappy's Pullman, Tamerlane, Omaha One More Time, Island Queen,* and *Gamecock.*

We constantly studied the B-29's operating systems and visited airplanes on the flight line to help the ground crew with maintenance. We hoped that by becoming more familiar with the airplane, our chances for longevity were better. We knew that the B-29 was a trouble-prone aircraft and could be a killer *without* Japanese help.

The unproved and developmental nature of the B-29 caused

many losses. Built by Boeing in Seattle and Kansas, Bell in Georgia, and Martin in Nebraska, the *Superfortress* had been rushed through design and placed in production before being "debugged." It was being assembled by hastily trained factory workers such as "Rosie the Riveter." The B-29 started flying combat missions before most of the design problems had been identified and eliminated.

Just a few of the B-29's chronic and deadly problems:

1. Engines overheat and lose vital power at crucial times (mostly during take-off).
2. Propeller speed control unreliable .
3. Fuel consumption unpredicatable.
4. Bomb doors fail to open or close and slow to operate.
5. Electrical system malfunction.
6. Overloaded structural failure.
7. Exhaust system failure causes nacelle fires.
8. Bombs jam in their racks.
9. Aerodynamic problems (one airplane speed from two different engine power settings).

Too many 504th aircraft losses were caused by aircraft operational problems and not by enemy action. Many B-29s, especially those with serious operational problems, did not make the return to Tinian. B-29s combat crews in trouble — and there were many of them — had to ditch or bail out over the Pacific, hoping that navy air-sea rescue units could find and recover them. Though the excellent navy air-sea rescue service searched day and night, they could not possibly locate and save all of our troubled crews who were forced down. Unfortunately, most downed crews were never found. Crews just disappeared with no cause ever determined for their loss. The 504th lost 21 crews during combat missions. Many of these losses did not occur over the target. An emergency landing field was critically needed near the halfway point of our flights to Japanese targets. Iwo Jima was ideally located, but it wasn't captured by the US Marines until 21 March 1945, one week before our last mission.

Marines suffered more than 20,000 casualties during the Iwo campaign. It was a heavy price to pay for an emergency landing field. Its capture hastened the end of the war and saved thousands of B-29 crew lives. Iwo became an emergency haven. Two thousand seven hundred B-29s made emergency landings at Iwo Jima. Some crippled planes landed there as many as five or six times. Iwo also became the base for P-51 long-range fighters which provided much needed escort for B-29s over Japan.

MISSIONS

Our crew flew several interesting missions before being shot down. On one mission, we were almost shot down by our own navy fighters. During the bitter fighting for Iwo Jima, B-29 crews flying on an Japanese Empire strike were ordered to avoid flying near the island. Since the waters around Iwo were covered with US Navy ships, the whole area was declared off limits to B-29 traffic. The navy had authority to shoot down *any intruding aircraft.* Our plane took off late due to pre-flight engine trouble. We were to rendezvous off the coast of Japan with other B-29s to bomb in formation over the target. In order to make up for lost time and assure our timely arrival at the rendezvous point, we decided to ignore the navy warning and fly a straight path, instead of flying the briefed dog-leg flight path around Iwo Jima. We figured that since we would pass over Iwo in bright daylight navy fighters and ships would recognize and identify our B-29 as a "friendly."

Ignoring the restriction, we flew through the "no fly" zone at our cruise altitude of 5,000 feet. As we approached Iwo, we studied the impressive mass of ships surrounding the island. We listened to messages on the busy combat channel as the struggle for Iwo continued. About this time, our gunners reported seeing a flight of unidentified fighters several thousand feet above us. This didn't bother us. Our navy controlled the sea and air around Iwo. Next, we heard a report that US Navy fighters had sighted a large, unidentified aircraft flying below them. The navy pilots thought it was a large Japanese patrol plane such as an *Emily* and the *Kate*, which were similar in size to the B-29. The Japanese used these seaplanes for long-range reconnaissance patrol.

Our gunners kept a close watch on the fighters overhead and reported that they were certainly "friendly" fighters. Our crew continued to listen to the continuing drama of the terrific and heartbreaking struggle to capture Iwo. We came to attention when we heard the navy flight leader say, "Okay, gang, let's go down and get that Jap bastard." Immediately after hearing this tranmission, our gunners reported that the fighters began diving toward our airplane. *We were in trouble — bad!* We couldn't communicate with the navy fighters. We were in a "no fly" combat zone. We were not supposed to be there! We were subject to any action the attacking US Naval Forces deemed necessary. *They had license to shoot us down!* All we could do was hold our course, pray, and hope that the navy recognized our B-29 as friendly.

As the diving fighters neared our plane, a timid voice was heard saying, "Sir, I think that's one of our B-29s." The flight leader replied, "It sure is. Okay, gang, let's get back upstairs and let this big bird go do his thing."

As we watched in awe, the fighters surrounded our airplane, carefully looked us over, wiggled their wings, waved, and returned to their patrol altitude. Our crew let out a sigh of relief and resolved *never* to disobey a flight path order again.

We had flown the B-29, *The Stork Club Boys*, before. It was assigned to Captain Edgerton. *The Stork Club Boys* looked after us pretty well on that earlier mission, except that two 500-pound bombs jammed in the forward bomb bay racks and didn't drop with the other bombs while flying at 27,000 feet. Baxter Love, at great risk to his life, used a portable emergency oxygen bottle and made the hazardous trip into the bomb bay to free up the bombs. After a great strggle, he unjammed the two bombs. They fell through and badly damaged the forward bomb bay doors. Due to B-29 bomb door design, both the forward and aft bomb doors were forced open and could not be closed. After the plane was flown to a lower altitude, I went into the open bomb bays and tried to close the doors with our emergency door actuator. Design limitations of the door actuation system did not permit this. We flew all the way back to Tinian with all bomb doors open. Excess drag caused by the open doors made our return to base marginal. Our cruising airspeed was reduced about 30 mph by the increased drag. We made ready to ditch before reaching Tinian and alerted Air-Sea Rescue Service. It took us almost two hours extra to return to base. Our engines were almost "running on fumes." As we made our landing, Brown and I worried that the open bomb doors would not clear the runway. *They did!* Brown expertly landed that airplane as if he always did it that way. The extra fuel used was the amount we would have used had we flown an additional 240 miles. We made it with only a few gallons of fuel remaining. Close, real close!

On another flight, after dropping our bombs, the nacelle on

number three engine, which I could easily see through my small window, turned a brilliant blue color. I immediately feathered the engine. The trouble-prone exhaust system failed and spewed red-hot exhaust gases onto the cowling. We were lucky the engine did not catch fire. We flew toward Tinian on three engines, hoping that the remaining three engines would continue to perform. They did and we made it! On a mission flown on 4 March 1945 to bomb the Musashimo aircraft factory in the Tokyo area, we arrived at the rendezvous point where we were to join a large 313th Bomb Wing bombing formation consisting of almost 200 B-29s. After cruising at 5,000 feet most of the way, we climbed to the 30,000-foot rendezvous and bombing altitude and started circling the small dot of an island assembly point. We observed about 30 other B-29s maneuvering over the island. Their distinctive bomb group tail symbols showed a mix of all four of the 313th Wing's bomb groups. Our 504th tail symbol was a circle with a big "E" in the center. We observed Sixth Bomb Group *"Circle R,"* Ninth Bomb Group *"Circle X,"* and 505th Bomb Group *"Circle W"* aircraft milling around at 30,000 feet burning up precious fuel "like mad." The B-29s orbited the small island for over 40 minutes. Much of our fuel reserves were consumed. High altitude flying requires great engine power and uses excessive amounts of fuel. Formation flying engine power adjustment adds to excessive fuel usage. We couldn't stand many more minutes of this waste.

WHERE WERE THE WING'S OTHER B-29s?

Other navigators missed the small island designated as the 313th Wing assembly area. Fintel and the navigators on the other milling B-29s found the correct island. The 313th that day flew two different, but unbriefed missions.

Brown turned around and asked me how our fuel supply looked for making home base after all this high altitude maneuvering. I advised that we should immediately head for the target — alone if necessary. We had used up all of our fuel reserve. If we experienced any airplane problems, our safe return to Tinian would be questionable. We would probably have to ditch the airplane!

Brown gritted his teeth, made a command decision, and announced over the intercom, "Prepare for combat. We are heading for the target—by ourselves." A bold decision for a mere second lieutenant. Fintel gave the heading to the Tokyo area target. Brown broke away from the circling airplanes and turned toward the Japanese coast. When we did this, all of the other milling aircraft turned and fell into a tight bombing formation behind us. *We were the formation leader!* Our formation was about group size. This was a real distinction for our low ranking crew. Off we flew toward the Japanese mainland.

Our crew's bombing team was finally going to get its chance to assure accurate bomb placement onto a strategic Japanese target. Love would have his chance as the lowest ranking lead bombardier to direct the bomb loads of 30 B-29s carrying 60 tons of high explosive bombs on the Tokyo target.

We hit Tokyo *on the button.* We approached our IP (initial point), turned toward the target, and began our bomb run. Unfortunately, heavy clouds beneath us covered the target area. We were so short of fuel that we elected to drop our bombs, using radar capability. Fintel and Francescon, with their radar scopes, directed the bomb drop. Love triggered our bomb load on their command. He was disappointed to miss the honor of using his bombsight to direct the formation's bomb load. Other B-29s in the formation dropped their bombs based on our lead action.

Our lead crew mission went off without a hitch, even though we encountered much flak from the heavily defended Tokyo target during the bomb run. Black flak bursts missed our formation but were right on our altitude. We didn't see any fighters, but figured that at least one was somewhere in the vicinity to give our exact altitude to Japanese ground defenses. Fighters were used to precisely fix flak burst altitudes. Japanese radar was primitive at this point in the war.

After the bomb run, the formation broke up. Each plane flew singly back to its Tinian base. We tried to minimize formation flying since such flying required much greater fuel consumption. Jockeying throttles caused engines to gulp precious fuel.

Where were the other wing aircraft? The 313th Wing lead navigator and most of the missing B-29s must have been circling the wrong assembly point. I'd stake my life — and always did — on Fintel's navigation to the correct rendezvous point. Someone had to take the initiative. *Brown did!*

A few months later during one of my POW interrogations in

Tokyo, the Japanese interrogator expressed surprise that our bombers had been able to accurately bomb his city during a heavy snow storm on 4 March 1945. He apparently didn't know about radar. He was talking about our *Lead Mission* but I didn't tell him the story of how this came about. It gave me great satisfaction that our mission success had been confirmed by an eyewitness. History of air force operations in World War II also confirms our crew's bombing success on this particular mission.

We never wanted to waste bombs. On an earlier, single airplane practice mission, we were directed to drop our load of twenty 500-pound bombs on two unoccupied Marianas islands, about 200 miles apart. We were to fly from one island target to the other island target, and on each turn around point of our flight path one bomb was to be dropped on the target island until our bomb load was exhausted.

Halfway between these designated targets was an island called Pagan with a small Japanese military garrison. Our flight path between targets took us right over Pagan Island. Baxter Love asked Brown's permission to ignore the end island's drop points. Instead, he suggested that we drop our bombs on the Japanese Pagan Island installations. Brown said, "Permission granted."

We made dry-run passes at the target islands and dropped our bombs, one at a time, on Pagan Island. The bombs hit with excellent precision and caused a great deal of damage to the enemy military installations. We hadn't exactly followed our briefing directions, but felt great satisfaction with our crew's contribution to the war effort. Japanese victims did not reveal our secret!

My *most* memorable mission was our seventh mission, our first mining mission, over the Shimonoseki Straits. But that's another story . . .

BOMBING PROCEDURES

Prior to March 1945, very poor bombing accuracy had been achieved. Expensive missions were being flown at great loss to aircraft and lives. Capabilities of the new B-29 "Superfortress" were being wasted. Meager bomb damage results from the high altitude raids were not acceptable. Immediate improvement was demanded. General Arnold and other Washington leaders were extremely disappointed.

Maj. Gen. Curtis E. LeMay replaced Maj. Gen. Haywood

"Possum" Hansell in the 21st Bomber Command in February 1945. Hansell had used lead crew, high altitude bombing strategy with daylight missions flown at altitudes up to 30,000 feet. Targets were not hit. Bombs were wasted. The enemy war effort was not damaged.

General LeMay reasoned that if B-29s bombed individually at night while flying at altitudes of 5,000 to 10,000 feet, bomb accuracy would drastically improve. Excessive fuel consumption could be avoided — fuel weight saved meant greater bomb loads could be carried.

At lower altitudes, the B-29 was capable of carrying four to five times the loads carried on earlier daylight, high altitude missions. Night missions should be safer from Japanese defenses. More bombs dropped at lower altitudes would result in increased damage to the enemy and quicken the end of the war. At lower altitudes, planes would not have to cope with the newly discovered problem of "jet-stream" winds. These high altitude winds gave a lot of trouble. It had been determined that "jet-stream" winds over Japan could reach almost 200 mph. The super-secret Norden bombsight was not designed to cope with such high winds and resultant ground speeds which might exceed 500 mph. During "up-wind" bombing, ground speeds could drop to almost zero. The B-29 would hover over the target area, susceptable to fighter and flak attack. The phenomena of these "jet-stream" winds was discovered during B-29 high altitude bombing of Japan. Today they are a major part of weather forecasting.

General LeMay decided to initiate the new bombing strategy. Combat crews in his 21st Bomber Command thought his plan was sheer madness. He ordered that bombing altitudes of less than 10,000 feet be used with full bomb loads. This meant that our planes would be "sitting ducks" subject to enemy anti-aircraft fire ranging from infantry rifles to large caliber flak. Japanese defenses couldn't miss! We knew that this would double and triple our already high aircraft losses. No crew wanted to fly such dangerous missions.

The general directed that the introduction of this new look in bombing be started in early March 1945 with five incendiary "Blitz" missions targeting four major Japanese cities. The project was code-named *"Meeting House."* Tokyo's urban area was to be the first target, followed by the cities of Kobe, Nagoya (twice), and Osaka.

Missions were to be executed as quickly as possible and the results evaluated as a basis for future mission planning.

Our crew flew three of the five "Blitz" missions. On the night of 9 March 1945, 279 B-29s flew the first mission to Tokyo at the very low altitudes of 6,000 to 8,000 feet over the heavily defended enemy capital city. B-29s flew individually toward and over the targeted area of the city. In spite of misgivings about the increased danger of this new concept, crews selected to participate felt a sense of pride.

Japanese civilian population areas were not singled out for these savage attacks without reason. Aerial reconnaissance revealed that home cottage industries were hard at work supplying vital parts for war industries. Post-mission reconnaissance revealed burned-out machine tools proliferated the destroyed portions of the city. If major city areas were targeted for the incendiary bombs, it was to wipe out the civilian production of war materials that went on in the flimsy wooden homes.

During that first "fire-bomb" mission, our B-29 flew by itself at 6,000 feet over the burning city. The hundreds of B-29s striking the city were timed to hit from many directions and staggered altitudes to avoid mid-air collisions. We arrived toward the end of the bomber stream. Tremendous fires were burning all over the target area. We selected a dark area to drop our incendiary bomb load. Our radar indicated that it was a populated area.

The 504th Bomb Group, with only two squadrons, performed the job of three squadrons. Twenty of our group's B-29 "Superfortresses" made it over the target that night. Japanese defenses were caught completely by surprise. Our group lost no airplanes. A total of 14 B-29's were lost by the 20th Air Force. LeMay was proved correct! Losses were no greater than during high altitude missions. Japanese searchlights and flak guns were confused. No fighter aircraft were observed.

Japanese urban area buildings were largely constructed of highly flammable wooden materials. Structures in the target area were completely burned to the ground. Sixteen square miles in the city's center were totally destroyed in the raid. Japanese enemy killed that night was estimated at 100,000.

As our airplane flew above the inferno below, we observed a fire storm so intense that it looked as if we were flying over Hell itself. Rising thermal currents bounced our B-29 all over the sky. Debris soaring on the air currents filled the sky. The sickening stench of burning flesh penetrated our crew compartment. During our earlier high altitude missions, we had been insulated from the awesome effects of our bombing. I was able to look out of the small window beside my station and witness the awful demolition and devastation below. *War is hell!*

LeMay's theory had been put to the test and it worked. The key to B-29 mission success had been found. Airplane and crew losses were acceptable.

Our crew flew two more incendiary "Blitz" missions using LeMay's low altitude/full bomb load strategy. We fire-bombed Kobe and Nagoya. The result was the same: *Total destruction of the bombed area!*

The "Blitz" campaign, begun on 9 March 1945, was completed on 18 March 1945. In just a little over one week, we ran out of incendiary bombs. The navy's seaborne supply system could not keep up with our demand for incendiary bombs. The determination and stamina of both air and ground crews was demonstrated during this maximum effort project. Hard-working ground crews toiled around the clock to assure maximum aircraft availability for these awesome, incendiary missions. The 504th Bomb Group's maintenance people were the finest in the 20th Air Force! They never let us down! Our two squadrons did the work of three squadrons!

Fire-bomb missions were not vengeance. Japanese civilians were not singled out for these savage attacks for no reason. Aerial photographs of burned-out target areas showed machine tools used by the cottage industries were evident throughout the destroyed area. The destruction and loss of Japanese lives from our fire raids did not compare to the terrible atrocities inflicted by Japanese troops on captured civilian populations, on our troops, and hundreds of thousands of suffering prisoners of war. Japanese leaders had to be convinced that unconditional surrender was their only option. Why didn't Japanese military leaders and the Emperor get the message that their cause was lost?

OPERATION STARVATION

B-29 aircraft possessed the range and weapon-delivery capability to carry and accurately place mines in any designated Japanese shipping area. The enemy's mine-sweeping technology did not have the capability to detect and sweep our navy's newly developed sophisticated mines. These deadly naval mines had not been used before to sink Japanese shipping. Our 313th Wing was selected by the 20th Air Force to be the "lead group" and made responsible for *Operation Starvation*, the mining of Japanese waters. Ours was the only B-29 wing directed to carry out this vitally important project. Our wing, possessing over 200 "Superfortresses" were capable of carrying out any assignment that the wing commander, Brig. Gen. Jim Davies, ordered. We were elated that he selected our 504th Bomb Group to lead *Operation Starvation*.

Placement of these mines in the Japanese ports and waterways meant that any enemy ship foolish or daring enough to venture through the mined area would be sunk. Strategic waterways would be blocked. Navy tests on 504th Bomb Group B-29s proved that the airplane with its APQ-13 radar capability could precisely position the mines in carefully selected Japanese waterway areas. Prominent adjacent land features were used as radar-scope reference points. Precise mine location was very important because many of these mines would have to be cleared before the planned invasion of the Japanese home islands.

Operation Starvation was created to deny shipborne supply to the Japanese homeland, which depended almost entirely on imported goods, including food. Our navy's new family of naval mines were to be used. They came in two sizes: 1,000 and 2,000 pounds. The mines contained a new and very powerful explosive called TORPEX. Explosive content was powerful enough to blow the bottom out of thin-skinned Japanese cargo shipping. The mines were devilishly designed to prevent Japanese counter-measures.

The mines were to be laid on the bottom of vital ports and waterways. All mines had a small parachute attached which deployed after leaving the bomb-bay. The parachute slowed the mine's descent and prevented premature explosion on entering the water. Mines were not activated until a water-soluble washer melted after immersion in water.

Mine triggers could be set for the first ship passing overhead, or any later count. Mine explosion was triggered by three different modes: sonic, pressure, and magnetic. Sonic mines exploded by sensing the sound of a ship overhead. Pressure mines triggered by pressure waves generated when a ship passed overhead. Magnetic mines, similar to older mines, were set off by magnetic fields surrounding steel ship hulls. Navy specialists trained air and ground crews on proper handling procedures for these highly sensitive mines. Ground crews were skeptical about handling the mines. Everyone was well aware of the loading and handling dangers. Flight crews were concerned about flying safety with the TORPEX explosive.

The 20th Air Force's field order directed that the first mining mission would be to *"Minefield Mike,"* located in the Shimonoseki Straits. This strategic waterway separated the main Japanese islands of Honshu and Kyushu. It was a major shipping artery that led out of the Japanese Inland Sea toward the west. It was a strategic first choice for *Operation Starvation.*

Our group was hard-pushed to provide 20 aircraft as directed out of the meager 30 assigned to our group. These B-29s had just finished the back-breaking incendiary "Blitz" missions only a few days before. Most of our crews were becoming weary. Our aircraft sustained much damage from the tough "Blitz" missions concluded on 18 March. In spite of many maintenance difficulties, operations were humming along on the flight line. Fuel trucks serviced airplane tanks. Mechanical and structural repairs were rushed along. Armorers prepared and loaded mines, which was the last ground operation performed before take off. Each airplane was to carry twelve 1,000-pound mines.

We heard that no flak and no fighters were expected to defend the target area. *This was to be a cinch mission!* Our crew was pleased to have been selected. It would be an easy count toward our 35 mission requirement.

BRIEFING

On 27 March 1945 our crew attended the mission briefing held in the 504th Bomb Group's war room. We knew we were flying the mission after seeing our names posted on the group operation's bulletin board. The briefing was scheduled to start at 1400 hours. The war room building was a large, roughly built wooden structure with an assembly room large enough to accommodate 30 crews on wooden benches. The room had a raised platform at the front with places for large war maps on the wall behind it. Crews sat together on crude board benches. Twenty crews had been selected: ten from the 398th Squadron and ten from the 421st Squadron.

Most crews were present when our crew arrived. We sat down on our usual rear bench. The assembled combat crews appeared to be in great spirits and gung-ho to fly the upcoming "safe" mission. We veterans of the hairy "Blitz" missions felt that this one would be a breeze. The incendiary missions had been so rough that our plane almost bounced upside down.

Staff briefing officers sat on the front row. At 1400 sharp, Col. Glen Martin, our 504th group commander, entered and rapidly walked up the aisle. We greatly admired our colonel. When he entered the room, the taut command "Ten-hut" rang out. We jumped to our feet and snapped smartly to attention. He mounted the platform and faced us. Behind him on the wall was a black curtain which we knew covered the large briefing map which showed the target and mission route. Colonel Martin commanded, "Rest." We relaxed and sat down.

The curtain was removed, revealing a map of the western Pacific Ocean with the Marianas Islands to the east and the China coast to the west. The flight route to the target and return to Tinian was marked on the map by a red string.

The colonel announced, "Your mining target for this mission, designated Mission Number 16, will be the Shimonoseki Strait. The mine drop area is *Minefield Mike* near the Japanese city of Kokura." He pointed to the map and to the target for this strike. There were gasps from the assembled crews — we knew that Kokura was near the Yawata steel plant which was one of the most heavily defended Japanese targets. Studying the map, we saw that the targeted area was the Shimonoseki Strait's narrowest part and uncomfortably close to Yawata.

Colonel Martin gave us a pep talk on how important this first mining mission was to the war effort and that our 504th was to be the lead player. He expressed confidence that we could place all mines precisely as directed. Our mining area had been carefully selected by Admiral Nimitz and his staff to support the Okinawa invasion, set for 1 April 1945. Blocking the only shipping lane to the west out of Japan's Inland Sea would make the enemy's re-supply of Okinawa very difficult and would be a major blow against the

Japanese war effort. After the colonel finished his inspiring remarks, the group operations officer jumped onto the platform.

He began by saying that the mission was the beginning of *Operation Starvation* whose purpose was to sink shipping, particularly those ships bringing food supplies to the home islands. *Operation Starvation* would bottle-up and isolate the Japanese Empire from overseas supplies, and thus, hopefully hasten the war's end. Twenty group aircraft would be flying the mission, each would carry twelve 1,000-pound mines, amounting to six tons per aircraft, making a total of 120 tons for the group. The mines would be dropped under cover of darkness from 5,000 feet altitude. The mines would be placed by radar direction based on nearby land features displayed on the radar scope. He went over the complete target description, assigned route, aircraft and crew assignments, IP (Initial Point), mining altitude and direction, flight path, and cruise altitude. The need for precise placement accuracy was emphasized.

The armament officer briefed that minimal ammunition would be carried because no enemy fighter defenses were expected. He directed that tail gunners would not fly with us. I glanced over at Dick Hall. He scowled and muttered something under his breath. Flying to Japan without bullets did not seem too wise.

Our navy had been impressed by mine laying accuracy demonstrated during earlier test flights by the 504th. The 504th had been selected to lead this mining operation because it rated as one of the finest organizations in the air force. General LeMay was proud of our capability, as evidenced by our selection as the wing's lead group.

The weather officer briefed that good weather was expected to and from the target and over the area to be mined. There were many howls and cat-calls because weather predictions in the past were usually wrong. The weather officer was at a disadvantage because the air force was not able to fine-tune weather forecasting over Japan. Most of the weather in this part of the Pacific originated north and west of Japan, but neither the Chinese nor the Russians sent weather data. Had this vital data been available our mission planning would have greatly improved.

The navigation officer gave an overview of the route to be followed to and from the target, and gave vague information on air-sea rescue arrangements. He informed us that there were a few US

"Lifeguard" submarines located along our flight path. He pointed to the map and indicated their general locations and gave us their radio frequencies.

The armament officer's briefing was short and to the point. Since this was a mining mission with little enemy opposition expected, tail gunners would not fly the strike. Only a minimal 200 rounds for the remainder of our guns would be carried. Emphasis was placed on maximum pounds of mines to be carried to the target.

The group flight engineer, Capt. "Judge" Gwathmey, briefed us on the fuel and oil load, and engine power settings. He gave us words of wisdom to assure us that there should be no "out-of-gas" ditching during our return to Tinian.

"Be extra careful with the weary engines" said the Judge, reminding us that our aircraft had just finished the March 1945 "Blitz" fire-bomb missions and were not in the best mechanical shape. We were to carry 6,750 gallons of fuel and sixty gallons of oil instead of the usual 80 gallons for each of our four engines. Our cranky R-3350 Curtiss-Wright engines practically drank oil. Reduced oil supply could cause a problem. Engines do not run long without oil. Propellers do not feather without engine oil.

The group bombardier briefed us on the radar procedure to be used to assure precise mine placement accuracy. The bombardier, navigator, and radar operator worked as a team; they couldn't miss, following his directions.

The intelligence officer cheerfully briefed what a cinch mission this was to be, saying, "no flak and no enemy fighters expected." We were to stay over the water and away from the heavy flak concentrations at Yawata. He assured us that it was to be "peaches and cream." All we had to do, he said, was merely fly to the target area, drop the mines, and fly home. It sounded easy. *Too easy!* He announced that there was still no information on Japanese policy for the capture and treatment of bailed-out crew members. If captured, we were to boast of the thousands of airplanes, ships, weapons, men, and battle victories. This didn't sound like too good an idea. He bravely said that he would like to go with us.

We sat there, dumb and happy, and believing it all.

While imprisoned by the Japanese I learned from another POW shot down that same night, that Brig. Gen. Jim Davies, our wing commander, was scheduled to fly the mission as an observer with the Sixth Bomb Group. My confidant told me of the big flurry of excitement on the Sixth Bomb Group flight line, shortly before take off, when a late report was received that many Japanese naval ships were reported moving into the target area. General Davies cancelled his participation! The Japanese *must* have learned what we were going to do! I learned from my captors, the Kempei Tai, that Japanese intelligence was much better than we gave them credit for.

The briefing took less than an hour. At the termination of the briefing Chaplain Raitt, the group chaplain, said a prayer for those going on the mission. Chaplain Rait was ever-present and important to our war-fighting morale. He wrote many kind letters to the next-of-kin of missing crews. We hoped he would never have to write our folks.

We were dismissed and spent the next hour or so doing the many things necessary to get ready for the fifteen-hour mission. We had another hearty meal at our army mess hall. The gourmet cuisine included Spam, tropical axle-grease butter, stale bread, and strong lemonade, better known as battery acid.

TAKING OFF

The selected crews assembled at the sides of a long line of trucks. These six-wheel-driven trucks and the C-47 "Gooney Bird" airplane, according to Gen. George C. "Blood and Guts" Patton, were the main reasons the Allies won the European war. Transportation is of major importance in war fighting. Our side had the best! We climbed aboard our assigned truck and were driven to the 504th's North Field flight line a little over a mile down an excellent coral road named Eighth Avenue.

The short drive to North Field was always interesting. Tinian's vegetation was lush and green. Tropical growth was interlaced here and there with beautiful and colorful flowers. We drove past rusting enemy vehicles, blasted concrete pill boxes, and other battle litter. The marines had attacked the Japanese defenders from the north shore; their battles followed the reverse of our route to the airfield. Evidence of their hard fighting could still be seen. Lush sugar cane fields were still growing alongside the road. The heavy growth was criss-crossed with bulldozed fire lanes so that hold-out Japanese troops, who foraged over the island for food, could be seen and shot or captured before they sabotaged B-29s parked at North

Field. Occasionally we passed an open spot where a Japanese farmer's house had been bulldozed into oblivion during the fierce fighting for the island.

Our truck jerked to a stop and parked in front of a B-29 which we would fly on this mission. We had been assigned the aircraft *The Stork Club Boys*. It had been named for the favorite New York night spot of its airplane commander, Captain Edgerton. Painted on the nose was its Stork Club logo and serial number 42-24864. The serial number meant that it was manufactured under a contract awarded in 1942. We flew in number 864 during a couple of past missions. It had looked after us after two bombs jammed in the forward bomb bay and when we had to return to Tinian without the help of number three engine. *It brought us home!*

The ground crew helped us take our flight gear from the truck. Each man's equipment was placed in a neat pile on the coral hardstand in front of the airplane. We were issued a lot of personal gear for combat which included parachute, survival vest, flak-vest, flak-helmet, leather helmet with attached headphones, .45-caliber automatic, Mae West life jacket, and a small deflated rubber boat called a dinghy which served as a seat cushion. We lined up behind our gear as Brown inspected each man and his equipment to assure we were combat ready. *We were!*

Each crew member began pre-flighting his particular part of the airplane to assure tip-top readiness for the mission. Dick Hall, Charles Anderson, Dick Donlavey, and James Griffith ground-checked the armament system operation. Albert Francescon and Harlan Fintel checked the radar system. The success of this mission depended on precise mine placement using their radar prowess. Harlan Fintel satisfied himself that our navigation equipment was operating properly. Getting lost over the Pacific could be fatal. Many B-29 crews had lost their lives this way.

Baxter Love pre-flighted his Norden bombsight. Even though our mines would be dropped by radar direction, the bombsight would be used to set mine spacing and trigger the mine release. John Brown and Al Andrews went through their pilot check lists while Leroy Rose fussed with his radio communications equipment.

I was responsible for most of the aircraft operating systems, such as engines, fuel, flight controls, auxiliary-power, propellers, and electrical. The crew chief and I discussed the status and readiness of these systems and thoroughly pre-flighted each system visually and functionally to assure proper operation. Nothing was left to chance. Assisted by an understanding and cooperative crew chief, I performed an unauthorized and necessary flight insurance operation. To insure that we had adquate fuel, we added a little reserve to our fuel supply. With the fuel tank caps screwed on, I used the center fuel tank's booster pump to transfer about fifty gallons of fuel to each of the four, supposedly full, wing tanks. I called this "bootleg" procedure "stuffing." It added an extra two-hundred gallons to our fuel reserve. The crew chief then re-filled the center tank. We now had 6,950 gallons aboard. I didn't worry about the added 1,200 pounds of weight. We always flew greatly overloaded above the airplane's designed gross weight. With our added reserve we had another hour or so of insurance for our return to Tinian.

The four-blade propellers were rotated a couple of revolutions to assure that there were no oil accumulations in the lower cylinders. I visually checked the entire outside of the airplane with the crew chief. We inspected the bomb bays and their deadly load of TORPEX-filled mines. Ground crew armorers had done a fine job of loading these treacherous weapons.

About this time our flight lunches arrived. There was nothing here to look forward to. Our flight food usually consisted of peanut butter sandwiches. Sometimes, if the cooks were feeling good, they magnanimously added jelly. A tropical chocolate bar was usually included which swelled in your stomach and made you think that you were full. The B-29s had warming ovens. They were designed so that special trays could be plugged in and keep the food warm. Our mess cooks lost the trays. The ovens were never used.

Just before we entered the airplane, a jeep pulled up with Chaplain Raitt aboard. He wished each of us the best of luck. We clustered around him as he offered a prayer for our safe return. This was the first time the chaplain had visited our crew on the flight line before a mission. We appreciated his coming to see us off and felt better about our chances for a safe flight.

Our crew climbed aboard *The Stork Club Boys* and settled into our respective crew stations. Six of us were located in the forward cabin and four in the aft cabin. At Brown's command, I started the four engines in the sequence two, one, three, and four. The engines emitted white oily smoke, which was normal for these cranky

Curtiss-Wright engines, then settled down to a smooth purr. The crew chief, visible from my small side window, gave me a "thumbs up," meaning that everything looked good from the ground. The ground crew waved goodbye. Dick Hall, our tail gunner, who was in the small group gathered outside, looked dejected. It had been ordered that tail gunners would not be needed. He was not happy about being left out and missing "easy" mission credit. He gave us a snappy salute! Dick was an important member of our crew and we would have preferred to have him with us. I am *so glad* he wasn't.

The bomb doors closed. We taxied to the take-off position on the northern most runway of North Field. B-29s were taking off at one-minute intervals on all four runways; four airplanes at a time. For a 60 plane mission, all aircraft could be airborne in fifteen minutes. We lined up at the end of the runway for take-off. I checked our engine ignition system carefully. Our engine performance had to be perfect in order to take off with our 245,000 pound gross weight. Our engines looked good!

Brown received the take-off signal from Tinian's Lotus Tower. Pacific Theater radio call signs used words containing "L" in their signals because Japanese couldn't properly pronounce words containing the letter "L." We made a running turn onto the runway's center in order to provide as much forward momentum as possible for our dangerous take-off. The end of the runway was at the water's edge. If, during take-off roll, one engine malfunctioned and the take-off could not be aborted quickly enough, the airplane would crash into the water and blow up. Commander Parsons from the 509th atomic bomb outfit witnessed four runway crashes during his short visit to Tinian to determine its adequacy for atomic bomb missions. He was not impressed with B-29 performance and safety. Our crew had witnessed several such crashes in the short time we'd been there.

I rapidly closed the engine cowl flaps during the initial take-off roll. Closing them before the take-off roll resulted in dangerous and excessive engine overheating. Wide open cowl flaps caused so much drag and buffet that a B-29 could not take off. As our plane accelerated toward the runway's end, it slowly staggered into the air and mushed toward the Pacific Ocean. We saw the water a mere 20 feet below us. The airplane struggled to gain airspeed. We started a gradual climb to our cruise altitude while turning toward the target on a northwesterly course. We made it again!

We climbed a little above our 5,000 foot cruise altitude and nosed down for level flight so as to get the B-29 to fly "on-the-step." The B-29 had an interesting design deficiency. It would fly a given speed with two different power settings. If the airplane was not flown "on-the-step," it was not aerodynamically clean and consumed excessive fuel. Many crews paid with their lives for being careless with this deficiency! If you ran out of fuel, you ditched! We were flying "on-the-step." We were on our way!

The time was 1630 hours on 27 March 1945. It was a beautiful day with white, puffy clouds all around us. Saipan Island lay about three miles to our right. We could see very little activity on Saipan by the 73d Wing's B-29s. All around us we observed B-29s flying toward the same target 1,500 miles ahead of us. Up to this point, everything had gone right. We felt good about this mission. This would make number seven of the required thirty-five combat missions.

THEN WE COULD GO HOME!!

Chapter 3

To the Target

Outside the air was smooth. No white caps could be seen in the waters below us. The airplane was functioning smoothly. Everything looked great! In a few hours it would be dark, but right now we were enjoying a great view of the sunset, one of the fringe benefits of flying over the beautiful Pacific Ocean. Our ten-man combat crew relaxed and settled back for the long and boring seven-hour, 1,500-mile flight to the target. Some of our crew logged sack-time. Some caught up on their reading.

Engine power was gradually reduced to provide maximum miles per gallon during the cruise. *The Stork Club Boys* was being controlled by what we called "Iron George," the auto-pilot. It was my responsibility to assure the overall operating safety of the airplane. If there were no fuel smells in the cabins, I could announce, "the smoking lamp is LIT." I didn't smoke, but most of the crew did. When cabin air became too contaminated, I could announce, "the smoking lamp is OUT," which resulted in many unkind remarks.

Until we entered the Japanese defense zone, Brown allowed relaxed intercom discipline. Trivial conversations occupied the intercom. During this trip, chatter was that of a relaxed and satisfied crew who were happy to be completing one more of our required thirty-five missions. We were all pleased that this was a low-risk mission.

We were proud of our crew. Our compatibility had built close friendships. Our front cabin team of Harlan Fintel, John Brown, Al Andrews, and I worked smoothly and efficiently together. We always knew where we were, what we were doing, and that we would make it back to home base!

One of my flight engineering tasks was to maintain a "How Goes It" chart. It was an extremely important aid to our operation. It plotted flight mileage to the target and back versus fuel usage. Fuel reserve was shown. A heavy horizontal line was drawn across the top of the chart showing our beginning fuel load which was usually around 6,750 gallons of high-octane aviation gasoline. A heavy vertical line was drawn at the chart's right edge which showed total mission distance to be flown, usually around 3,100 miles. Before flight, I had calculated hourly fuel usage points based on airplane performance curves. These points were plotted and joined by a line which indicated our planned fuel usage versus distance travelled. This predicted performance line intersected the total fuel line somewhere beyond the 3,100 mile mission line which I noted as the "Tinian Line." The distance we could fly beyond the "Tinian Line" was very important. It was our insurance for safe return to base.

As the mission was flown, I plotted the actual fuel used versus the actual distance flown. This number was furnished to me by Fintel. If our fuel consumption line was too steep and intersected the total fuel line short of the "Tinian Line," we were in deep trouble and could look forward to ditching the airplane.

Brown and I were very sensitive to the implications of the "How Goes It" chart. After our six previous missions, measurement of the meager amount of fuel remaining in our tanks correlated with my fuel usage plot within a few gallons.

Flight engineers who became sloppy with the "How Goes It" chart and their crews paid dearly. Missing Aircrew Reports (MACRs) were prepared for these unfortunate crews. The air-sea rescue service found a few of the crews, but not all. Those not found perished!

On an earlier mission, Fintel gave me some erroneous mileage figures to use in plotting the fuel usage line. I cautioned him several times to be more accurate. Our safe return to Tinian depended on the figures he provided. During that mission, I plotted his distance flown figures on the "How Goes It" chart. The line connecting his distance flown points indicated fuel burn-out *two hundred miles short of Tinian*. I knew that his figures had to be in error because we were flying essentially the same flight path and engine power settings as other missions. Our flight had been routine and our aircraft performed beautifully. I was not overly concerned about what the chart showed. I passed the chart to Brown without comment. There was a brief silence while he studied the chart. Suddenly, Brown exploded! "What do you mean? Your chart shows that we're going to run out of fuel?" With exaggerated casualness I told him, "That's right! You'd better make plans for ditching." He spluttered and asked Fintel to recheck his mileage figures. Fintel glared at me and recalculated the mileage we'd flown. He found a 400-mile error. His new distance figure, when plotted, showed that our return to base was no problem. Harlan gave me precise navigation figures from then on.

After four hours of flying, the sky began to darken. I could see the many gauges on my flight engineer's panel begin to glow in the rays of the small cockpit lights playing over them. I could barely see Fintel across from me. He was bent over his table working on his navigational maps. He was largely hidden from view by the upper forward turret which took up most of the aft part of our cabin. It contained four .50-caliber machine guns. The other turrets contained only two guns. Rose, our radio operator, was completely hidden from my sight. His station, behind the turret on the right side of the cabin, was just forward of the pressure bulkhead separating us from the forward bomb bay. I could not see the entrance hatch to the bomb bay.

Fintel announced that Iwo Jima was about 50 miles away and was beginning to show up on his radar screen. He announced that he could see many small radar blips which indicated hundreds of US Navy ships surrounding the island. Iwo Jima had been declared "secure" a few days before on March 18. It appeared Japanese troops had not heard the news, as we could see lights and explosions on the small island below our plane. There was a war going on below. It seemed strange to be flying over Iwo at 5,000 feet. We had previously flown at 30,000 feet while bombing the island to avoid enemy flak.

Brown directed Rose to tune to Iwo Jima combat channels as we passed nearby. We had listened, during recent Iwo flybys, to urgent communications between hard fighting marine troops and navy and marine fighters buzzing over the island like mad hornets when supporting fighters were urgently asked to direct machine-gun fire and bombs to take out enemy strong points just a few feet away from their precarious positions. We felt sorry for the poor marine "Leathernecks." They deserved our utmost sympathy and gratitude.

Capture of Iwo Jima was vital to continuing 20th Air Force operations. As long as the Japanese held this halfway island, it served to give early warning to Tokyo that our bombers were headed toward the Japanese mainland. Japanese fighter planes based on Iwo attacked B-29s. Crippled and fuel-starved B-29s badly needed this island for emergency landings. P-51 fighter planes could be based on the island and escort our bombers all the way to Japan.

After leaving the Iwo Jima conflict, Love went into the forward and aft bomb bays to check the mines to assure reliable installation and readiness. While Love worked in the bomb bays, Rose watched him from the forward cabin and Donlavey from the aft cabin to assure his safety. All mines checked okay! Inspecting our bomb load before entering into Japanese airspace was a ritual we followed to assure no unpleasant surprises over the target.

Well before approaching the Japanese mainland, we began checking our combat gear. Earlier high altitude missions required that we carry bomb bay fuel tanks hanging from bomb racks. Protective, armored flak curtains were installed around the tanks to minimize the risk of puncture by flying flak fragments. Flak curtains were heavy cloth blankets containing five by ten-inch steel armor plates sandwiched between two layers of heavy woven cloth. Our crew "liberated" a couple of these curtains and cut them into pieces and used the pieces to improving the safety around our crew stations. I centered one plate directly under my seat cushion and another section under my feet. This precaution saved my life!

Each crew member wore a flak helmet and vest over the Japanese mainland. Most crew members wore flak vests with all-around flak protection. Since Brown, Andrews and I had a large piece of armor plate at our backs, our flak vests had armor protection in front only. Each crew member sat on a deflated rubber dinghy which was attached to his parachute harness. The dinghy served as a seat cushion.

An unwelcome thought raced through my head. We flew Major Riley's airplane on an earlier mission. On the next mission, that crew had been lost. On the next mission, we had flown Captain Shaffer's airplane. On the next mission, their crew had gone down. I didn't like these thoughts and tried to concentrate on getting ready for our run to the target.

I concentrated on assuring that my personal equipment was in order. My flak vest and helmet were on. My parachute was securely buckled. My Mae West life preserver was in place over my parachute. I was as ready as I'd ever be for combat. I patted the heavy .45-caliber gun nestled in my survival vest and the long hunting knife fastened to my belt. I purchased the marine-type knife at Marshall Field in Chicago on my way to Seattle after graduating from Yale Technical School.

I had a complex assortment of clothing and safety gear. Layered outside my body, I wore suntan shirt and pants instead of flight coveralls worn by most crewmen. Combat dress codes were pretty loose on Tinian. Flight coveralls could be uncomfortable. On top of my uniform was a survival vest, a back-pack parachute, Mae West life preserver, and outside all of this, my flak vest.

I had a nervous feeling in my stomach which always came during this part of a mission and stayed with me until we left the target area. During battle I sometimes seemed to stand apart and observe myself, illuminated by the dim cabin lights, working like a robot doing the things I had to do mechanically. It was a strange feeling. I watched my many instruments in fascination and tried to concentrate on what they were telling me about our airplane's performance. I am sure that my other crewmates had their own way of coping with combat dangers. My thoughts jumped back to reality when I heard Brown announce that we were approaching the Japanese mainland.

I glanced around and could see through the nose windows the Japanese coastline in the bright moonlight. Waves were shimmering as they broke onto the beach. There was a slight overcast. We were flying almost due west. We passed over the Japanese coastal plain.

Headlights of vehicles could be seen below. Japanese drivers had not realized that the enemy was overhead. The coastline rambled off to our right. Mountains could be seen to the left. The countryside looked peaceful. People must be sleeping without knowing of the war, death, and destruction that we were bringing to their homeland.

Brown ordered every crew member to recheck personal equipment and assure that everything was ready. Fintel and Francescon fine-tuned their radar scopes and announced that the Japanese coastline was illuminated on their radar screens. I increased engine power to give us an airspeed of 250 mph for the mining run. Brown had turned off our navigation lights many miles back. The intercom was very quiet. From here on, it was to be used for emergency messages only. All airplane systems were "Go!" We were ready!

The engines purred smoothly and no sparks were coming out of the exhausts as often happened with these cranky Curtiss-Wright engines. I moved the engine mixture controls into "auto-rich." This fuel mixture shift caused engine exhaust color to go from being an almost invisible output to emitting long blue flames from each side of the engine nacelles. I didn't like this situation, but the engines had to be ready for immediate application of war emergency power for escape and evasion maneuvers once we dropped our mine load. Japanese ground observers could easily see our exhaust pattern. I remembered the briefing and relaxed. *No flak and no fighters!* Our gunners reported that the engines looked okay except for the blue exhaust plumes.

We made landfall at one of the major Japanese islands, Shikoku. It was a rugged, mountainous island. As we flew over its southern area, Fintel finished his preparation for dropping our lethal mines. He and Francescon discussed with Love the coordination needed for precisely placing the mines in their designated part of the Shimonoseki Straits. Love was told that he must open the bomb doors and hit the bomb-drop switch when directed based on the radar image of the Strait and nearby prominent land features. The mines would drop in the exact spacing sequence set into the bomb-sight. The mines would descend under their small parachutes, splash into the waters below, and sink to the bottom of the shallow and narrow channel where they would lie ready to rip the bottoms out of enemy shipping.

We had quite a bit of enemy country to fly over before reaching our target area. Our briefed flight path kept us from flying too near Yawata with its deadly flak protection. Yawata was the location of one of Japan's largest steel mills and was heavily defended. Many B-29s had been shot down while trying to bomb this strategic target.

As we flew over the waters of Japan's Inland Sea, we saw many Japanese ships under us. It was a busy shipping area. The target had been well chosen. The Shimonoseki Straits could become a bottleneck blocking vital shipping into the Inland Sea. As we passed beyond Shikoku, we approached Kyushu on our left and Honshu on our right. We had seen three of Japan's major islands. The Shimonoseki Straits separated Kyushu and Honshu.

We were now flying over the Straits. Why were there so many ships traveling though the narrow straits? Our intelligence briefing had not mentioned this. We were not far from our target area. As we flew westward over the Straits, they began to narrow. Honshu and Kyushu were very close to each other. The Shimonoseki Straits became a narrow ribbon of water.

Fintel announced that his radarscope showed that we were approaching our initial point (IP). Bombing procedure dictated that we fly to an exact point, the IP, then turn to the precise heading for the target. Airplane speed, altitude, and heading were carefully maintained during the bomb run in order for the bomb sight or radar to accurately place the bomb load. The bomb run to the target was held for several minutes. The airplane had to be flown straight and level. During this period the aircraft and its crew were vulnerable to enemy defenses.

On this mission there was not supposed to be any enemy interference. We were not worried as we began our flight to the target. I set engine power to give Brown the bombing airspeed. Our airplane altitude was "right on the money."

The selected IP was about 50 miles northeast of our target. We headed for *Minefield Mike*. We flew along the Shimonoseki Straits. Land could be seen on either side.

As we approached the target area, we observed *a big surprise!* In the far distance, ahead of our plane, we saw: *Searchlights sweeping the sky and flak explosions bursting! Our intelligence officer was wrong. He was badly wrong!* He assured us: "No flak, no fighters, no problems."

We were flying directly into the flak and searchlight defenses. This was *not* going to be a "cinch" mission. The intelligence briefing was all wrong! General Davies made a smart decision not to go on this mission.

I firmly believe that Japanese intelligence knew about this mining mission to the Shimonoseki straits before it was launched. The Japanese were waiting for us! They were ready!

As we flew toward the holocaust ahead of us, Fintel directed necessary B-29 course corrrections. All was *"go"* on board our airplane for the mine drop. The armor plate behind me felt cold, but it gave me confidence. I busily watched my many instruments. I learned not to look out my window while over Japanese targets. Scenes of combat were better if I avoided looking at them. My instruments were much better to look at. I felt sorry for Love and the pilots. They had to face the whole wild scene. I didn't envy them. I hoped that we would reach our mine drop area before reaching the heavy flak ahead. Our intercom was ominously quiet. I couldn't help but glance forward from time to time. I saw one of the nervously roving searchlights capture a B-29 in its beam not too far ahead of us, then 20 to 30 searchlights centered on the poor airplane. Flak bursts immediately concentrated on the victim. The airplane was taking murderous punishment. It was hit many times with terrific explosions. It flamed and went down! I was sorry that I saw that event.

Our intercom came alive with the excited reports from our gunners.

"Flak and searchlights near us!"

We had not dropped our mine load yet. We had to fly into the jaws of death. We had to place our mines in the middle of what appeared to be a solid sea of flak and searchlights!

Chapter 4

Shot Down

We bombed land targets on previous missions which were defended by Japanese Army units whose defensive flak was good, but not as good as that of the Japanese naval anti-aircraft units we were to encounter. Naval flak had to be good in order to assure ship survival at sea. Many ships were plying the Inland Sea and Shimonoseki Straits. As we approached the target area with its searchlights and flak, we could see many large ships blasting away with their guns at airplanes ahead of us. We were about to find out the hard way how fast the Japanese could concentrate mighty defenses *based on good intelligence. And their intelligence was good, as I was to find out from my captors, the notorious Kempei Tai.*

It was obvious that the Japanese moved naval assets from all over northern Kyushu and southern Honshu Island to protect their vital Shimonoseki Straits. They could not afford to have this major waterway blocked by mines.

As our airplane approached to within a couple of miles of its mine drop point, most of the searchlights had been turned off. Flak guns had quit firing. The straits below us looked almost peaceful. One or two blue-tinted searchlights stabbed the night skies ahead of us.

We knew from our Tokyo fire-raid experience that these tinted searchlights were directed by radar and used to pin-point a enemy airplane. Once a B-29 was illuminated, other searchlights came on and directed their beams at the victim. Anti-aircraft artillery rained flak on the illuminated target. Little evasive action by a targeted B-29 could be done during a bomb run. After dropping his bomb load, the pilot, by violent evasive maneuvering, might escape. Not many B-29s were that fortunate. The B-29 that we had just observed had *not* been lucky. It had "bought the farm."

We were almost to the target. Fintel's eyes were glued to his radar set. He had already directed Love to open the bomb doors and ready his bombsight for triggering the mines into the waters below. Fintel, speaking calmly in a measured voice, alerted Love that on a ten-second countdown, he would signal, "Drop." The ten seconds passed like hours before Fintel gave the command, "Drop." The airplane shuddered a bit as the 1,000-pound mines dropped from their racks.

Our mission was accomplished. Our mines had been placed precisely in the directed locations, but we were in bad trouble!

A tinted searchlight beam swept across our airplane during the ten-second countdown. We were briefly illuminated, and then in the dark. The searchlight wandered around the sky looking for us. Its radar must have been defective. It swept the area around us and finally caught us in its beam. It held on us and tracked our airplane through the sky. Almost immediately, a cone of many searchlights concentrated on our airplane. We were caught in the lethal cone of lights.

Brown tried to escape the lights by pushing his throttles wide-open and violently maneuvering the airplane while trying to climb into the haze above us. I studied the instruments on my flight engineer's panel. They were brightly lit by the enemy searchlights. Brown and Andrews, as well as Love, must have been blinded by the lights. We had never been illuminated by searchlight beams before. We were caught in what could be a fatal situation. Other airplanes trapped by enemy searchlights were almost always blasted out of the sky. This time we were the victim.

Enemy flak batteries from the many ships below us concentrated their fire on our airplane. We couldn't evade them! They zeroed in! Our airplane was rocked by nearby bursts of large and small caliber flak. Some projectiles were making direct hits on our B-29. Sounds of exploding flak were ear-shattering. Shrapnel hitting the airplane sounded like we were in a heavy hailstorm. We had never experienced such a dangerous situation before. Our giant airplane was being tossed around like a cork in a stormy sea.

We knew there were other 504th aircraft in the air within sight of us and that our plight helped them evade detection. The enemy naval flak batteries below were concentrating on destroying *our* B-29. We had the full and undivided attention of every Japanese gun within range, and there were plenty of them. Our low altitude guaranteed that the enemy could hit us with any caliber gun in the fleet.

I began to pray. As I prayed, I recalled the words of Sir Jacob Astley's prayer with his troops before he led them into battle in 1642:

> *"Oh Lord! Thou knowest how busy I must be this day.*
> *If I forget Thee, please do not forget me."*

My words of prayer strengthened and prepared me for whatever my fate was to be. My life was in God's hands.

There was little traffic on the intercom. Its stillness seemed sinister! I sensed that the entire crew was uptight and keeping their thoughts to themselves. Seconds seemed like hours. Brown concentrated on saving our crew and airplane. Though we were directly over major units of the Japanese naval defenses, up to this time we had received no disabling hits. The searchlight beams never left our airplane. The lights were blinding us. Colored machine gun tracer paths centered on our airplane. The inside of our cabin was brighter than daylight. This must be what Hell must be like.

Our gunners began to report flak hits all over the airplane. All caliber of flak were hitting us. Enemy gunners were not missing us. All the fire power the enemy possessed was coming at us. The flash of heavy flak explosions could be seen and heard. We were in the center of one big explosion. The bursts were rocking our airplane. We bounced around like a cork in a rough sea. Flak noise was deafening.

Our engines were straining at maximum power. The throttles were jammed forward. Our airspeed and altitude slowly increased. I didn't like what I was seeing on my instrument panel. The gauges were going crazy. The needles were spinning like tops. Instrument readings meant nothing.

Gunners reported flak damage. Crew members had been hit in the aft cabin. Wounded gunners were fighting fires with their fire extinguishers. There were four people back there. What was the extent of our casualties? With all the flak hits, everyone was vulnerable. What about our forward cabin crew? I could see Fintel across the cabin. He appeared to be okay. Many fires were reported by the gunners. Suddenly, our intercom went dead, apparently hit by a flak burst. With our communication system shot out, each crew member knew only what was happening at his individual crew station. We were in bad trouble!

Our survival depended on what our airplane commander could do to evade the seachlights and flak and get us out over the Pacific Ocean so that we could either ditch or bail out. Air-sea rescue "Lifeguard" submarines were out there waiting for us. Many questions were running through my head. How was Brown doing? Where were we? What shape was our airplane in? With the intercom out, no one knew.

I configured my body into as small a target as possible and tried to figure out what my instrument panel was trying to tell me. It told me that my flight engineer's station was out of control. No gauge reading made sense. The gauges looked like I'd hit the jackpot at Las Vegas. Flak must have hit vital wiring somewhere causing electrical shorts and stray signals. I had no idea what was happening to our engines or electrical or hydraulic systems. All major electrical wiring passed through the bomb bay which probably was on fire. Damage to these cables could wipe out control of anything operated by electricity. The B-29 was an electrically operated airplane. God only knew what our plane's mechanical situation was.

I knew it was not good!

I wanted to do something, anything, to help our situation but there was nothing I knew to do but await Brown's orders. I felt helpless and useless.

Every now and then I'd raise up and take a quick look out the small window beside my station. My position faced aft so I was spared the terrible view out front. A look forward would reveal horrendous sights that our bombardier and pilots had to face. What I could see out of my window was bad enough. I could see what was happening to the right side of our airplane and it was not good. Our right wing and its two engines were on fire. The last intercom report from our gunners indicated that all *four* engines were on fire. If wings, fuselage, and aft cabin were on fire, our whole airplane was on fire! Totally on fire!

I triggered fire extinguishers to all four engines with no observable effect on the fires. I tried to avoid looking at the hideous sight outside my window. I prayed.

I heard a flak burst outside the airplane near my station. Shrapnel pounded the airplane's side. An explosion went off under my seat. Cabin insulation beside my seat was shredded. I felt no pain and assumed I had not been hit. My prayers and my 1890 silver dollar good luck charm seemed to be working!

Due to the violent maneuvering and maelstrom of flak bursts, I had no idea what our altitude was. As best I could tell, our airspeed was about 250 mph. Our engines were running and pulling us through the air. Vital systems seemed to be operating. I knew that we'd never make it back to Tinian. Our airplane was too badly damaged. Our only hope was to hang on long enough to clear the Japanese coast, ditch the airplane or bail out over water, and hope that a navy "Lifeguard" submarine would pick us up.

I wondered if the airplane's violent bouncing around was a result of Brown's evasive maneuvers or if it was caused by the heavy flak turbulence. Andrews told me after the war that it was from flak explosions. The heavy stuff was throwing us around like a toy. Brown was trying to climb into the cloud layer above us. He didn't seem to be able to make it.

Another terrific explosion erupted right under my seat and raised me upward. This explosion had been very close. *Too close!* There was the acrid smell of exploded gunpowder in the cabin. I moved my feet around and the movement hurt. I knew that this burst had scored. I'd finally been hit! At least I could move my feet.

Suddenly, we were out of the searchlight beams and the flak moderated. It became very dark in the cabin. Cabin air began to heat up and become almost unbreathable. I glanced across the aisle toward Fintel. His face had a look of horror. He was trying to shout something at me. I couldn't understand him. He pointed toward the fire extinguisher mounted on the side of my station. I surmised that either he or our radio operator, Rose, had seen a fire in the bomb bay. I reached over, got the extinguisher, and handed it to Fintel. He grabbed the fire extinguisher and disappeared from sight behind the turret. Almost immediately a burst of super-heated air blasted toward my station from behind the turret. Apparently Fintel opened the bomb bay entrance hatch to fight a fire with the extinguisher and when he did, flames and heat from the fire were sucked into the cabin. Since this was a sealed cabin, the heat coming in had to be sucked forward by openings up front caused by either flak damage or open windows or both. Whatever the cause, the slipstream was sucking the flames and hot air forward. When Rose and Fintel opened the entrance hatch, they sealed their fate. They were incinerated by the bomb bay flames sucked into the cabin. These two brave crew members went to meet their Maker trying to help our crew survive. God bless them!

I was isolated and alone in the super-heated cabin. I raised my arms and frantically tried to pull air into my tortured lungs. My mind raced to figure out a way to survive. What could I do to cool the super-heated cabin air and breathe again? Instinctively, I reached over and wrenched open the nose gear hatch cover, located beside my station. Cool, outside air flowed into the cabin pushing the flames and hot air back into the bomb bay. I could breathe again. The hatch cover wouldn't stay open by itself. I held it open with my right arm and tried to figure out my next survival move.

Our cabin had two escape routes for bail-out. One was through the bomb bay which was now totally on fire. The other route was through the nose hatch beside me which was blocked by the retracted nose gear. The two nose tires were visible under the open nose hatch. The landing gear was electrically actuated. Electrical cables ran through the bomb bay. The wires must have been burned through by now. I doubted if electrical power was available to extend the gear. With the intercom inoperative, the airplane commander would have to use the alarm bell to signal the order to bail out. If the alarm was working, which I doubted, it couldn't have been heard over the flak noise and bedlam present in our airplane. Even if Brown gave the bail out order, everyone in the forward cabin was trapped! The two escape routes were blocked. Our situation looked hopeless.

I turned and looked forward toward Brown's position, but I could see nothing. The darkness and smoke blocked my view. I looked in fascination at the nose gear blocking escape through the hatch. I looked back toward the bomb bay which I knew was burning. The possibility of escaping through my small 14 x 20-inch side window occurred to me. I couldn't squeeze through it with my backpack parachute and dinghy strapped to my body. Even if I could get through, it would be suicidal because the right inboard engine's propeller-tip swung to within a few inches of the fuselage just aft of the window. The propeller would chop me to pieces. That possibility was out of the question. I learned from two captive B-29 flight engineers that the escape route I had rejected had been used by them. These flyers escaped through the flight engineer's window. One received a bad cut on one of his feet from the rotating propeller; the other was unscratched. Hard to believe! Miracles happen!

Our airplane was now flying in a downward spiral, rapidly headed for the ground. I stared at the nose gear as if hypnotized. I was trapped in the airplane, unless it could be extended. It was my only escape route. There was a mechanical hand crank to lower the nose gear, but even if I could find the crank it would take at least five minutes to do the job. We didn't have five minutes left. Whatever I did had to be done in the next several seconds! I turned around in my seat and tried to get Brown's or Andrews' attention and ask them to extend the landing gear. I was still holding the nose hatch open. There was such bedlam and smoke in the cabin, that I couldn't get their attention. I prayed.

A miracle happened! My prayer for help was answered! The nose wheels started moving downward. The nose gear was being extended! I couldn't believe my eyes. My escape route was being unblocked! I was amazed that electrical power still existed. Next, from out of the smoke, an unrecognizable figure came from up front and plunged through the open nose hatch. Someone up front knew a whole lot more about what was going on than I did. He bailed out. Who was he? He had to be either Brown, Andrews, or Love. I knew that it was time for me to go!

When the unknown figure jumped out of the airplane, the hatch cover slammed shut. Flames, smoke, and heat again entered the cabin. I reached down and wrenched the hatch cover open. I didn't hesitate. I climbed out of my seat and jumped through the open hatch into the night air. My flak helmet flew off my head as I hit the slipstream.

I was swept underneath the flaming B-29's fuselage. In just the short instant that I passed through the flames, my hair was burned off and my exposed head and hands suffered burns. A thought occurred to me as I floated into the night air. I'd violated B-29 escape procedure, which was, "Position yourself on the aft side of the hatch and bail out forward so as to clear the airplane structure." I bailed out the quickest way possible. The unknown crew member had bailed out from the front side of the escape hatch. Two wrongs make a right? We both made it! I was lucky again! My Maker was looking after me!

My thoughts were working in a super-charged mode. I didn't know how far above the ground I bailed out. It couldn't have been very high as our mining altitude was only 5,000 feet. I knew that we had lost altitude during the seemingly eternal time period during which we had been under continual flak attack. The ground couldn't be far below me.

After clearing the burning airplane, I reached for my parachute's rip-cord handle which should have been on my left chest area.

The ripcord handle was not there!

Where was it? Did I have my parachute on? Of course I did; our crew always assured that our emergency gear was present, connected, and in working order. I *knew* I had my chute on. But where was the ripcord release handle?

My mind was racing a mile-a-minute! In those split seconds, I recalled a story about an airman who bailed out with a slightly different configured parachute than he normally used. This chute had the ripcord handle located on the other side of his chest. When his *dead* body was examined, it was found that he had scratched through several layers of clothing all the way to his rib bones. He never tried the other side.

I realized the problem! My flak jacket covered the ripcord. If I had followed correct procedure, I should have pulled the little flak jacket tab which released my jacket and it would have fallen away exposing my ripcord handle. I goofed and forgot this feature. I reached under the flak jacket, found the ripcord handle, and gave it a yank. Fortunately, my flak jacket had a fabric panel in back. My parachute opened because the flak jacket panel must have been blown out of the way of the opening parachute. My parachute deployed and the canopy snapped open. There was dead silence as I floated down. I looked all around me. In the distance, I observed our airplane engulfed in flames and spiraling toward the ground. It appeared as a fiery cross in the sky. While I was descending in the parachute, I saw the fiery plane hit the ground and explode in a sea of fire. I offered a prayer for any of my brave fellow crewmen who perished in the flames. Most of my fellow crew members had not been as lucky as I. Eight of them perished! God bless them! They made the ultimate sacrifice for their country. I asked that their souls might find peace in Heaven and thanked God that I was still alive. I prayed for the safety of the unknown crewman who jumped ahead of me. The next day, I learned that the only other survivor was Al Andrews, our co-pilot, the only married crew member.

Many months later, Al told me what he remembered of those final moments of our tragic flight.

Love was hit by a flak burst and killed instantly. Brown was mortally wounded by another burst. Andrews told me that he passed out from the flames, smoke, and heat in the cabin. Al told me how the nose gear miracle occurred. After I opened the nose-hatch cover, he regained consciousness. He saw that Brown and Love were dead. The plane was in flames and spiraling toward the ground. He determined the situation to be hopeless. Instinctively, he hit the landing gear "extend" switch. When the nose gear cleared the hatch, he bailed out. All this must have taken place in a matter of seconds.

If I hadn't opened the hatch, Andrews would not have revived. The nose gear would not have been extended. We saved each other. Our "will-to-live" instincts resulted in the right actions done at the right time.

As I floated downward in the still night air, the world seemed at peace. Deafening sounds of terrible flak bursts, crackling flames, and death rattles of the wounded airplane were completely gone. Utter silence surrounded me. It was eerie. For some strange reason, as I floated down, the latest popular song heard, via Armed Forces Radio, kept banging through my head at top volume. *"Accentuate the positive, Eliminate the negative"* ran though my mind — over and over and over again. It was maddening.

Our airplane flew about four miles inland before crashing. I descended near a small Japanese village called Ueki, located southwest of Yawata, near the Japanese city of Kokura. My parachute's 28-foot canopy gently lowered me toward ground, which was brightly lit by moonlight. I estimated that I was about 1,000 feet above the ground when I bailed out. I was surprised that I was not over water.

It occurred to me that coming down over land instead of water was good, because the flak explosion which burst directly under me probably shredded my dinghy. My Mae West life vest was also probably holed. I wouldn't have lasted long in the water landing.

Below me was a rice paddy with a road running along one side. A telephone line ran along the opposite side. There was little or no wind. I grabbed my parachute's shroud lines and manipulated them to steer away from the telephone lines. By twisting the shroud lines I was able to turn the chute around. I pulled on the lines toward the direction I wanted to move so I could slip the chute in that direction. I maneuvered so as to land in the center of the rice paddy.

As the ground approached, I was aware of a very strange, peculiar odor. It was a nasty, putrid, ancient smell which seemed to rise from something that had lain dirty and decaying for centuries. It was the smell of Japan! I was to learn that this odor was common to Japanese farm areas and resulted from the use of human waste as a fertilizer.

I could plainly hear excited voices and shouting below me. I observed figures moving toward the rice paddy where I was about to land. The natives obviously were very upset and apparently trying to figure out where I was going to touch down. They were forming a ring around my impact point. There were about 40 or 50 angry, excited, and shouting people down there. They were not going to be an ideal welcoming committee. All appeared to be armed with farm implements which they vigorously waved in the air. I looked for guns but saw none. There was much shouting and pointing in my direction. I could hear them jabbering in a strange sing-song language.

I suddenly realized . . . *I didn't know how to surrender!*

Of all the many things we had been taught, we had never been told how to surrender. This was a serious omission. It could prove deadly! A fleeting thought crossed my mind. When I get back to Tinian I must remember to tell someone to add a lesson on "surrender."

Many questions were running through my head. How do I get captured? Do I really want to be captured? What do I do now? I figured that if I pulled my gun to defend myself, I'd surely be a "dead duck." I decided I'd better leave my gun in its waterproof container.

Combat crews had many discussions on whether or not we

would give ourselves up if shot down. We didn't know if the Bushido Code followed by Japanese warriors allowed taking B-29 crewmen alive. We were told that the Japanese considered it a disgrace to surrender. There had been zero feedback from missing crews. We finally decided that we'd "play it by ear" if we ever got into this predicament. It was my time to "play by ear!"

Finally, my feet touched Japanese soil. I hit a soft rice paddy. My impact was cushioned by the damp soil and rice crop. I toppled onto my backside but rapidly got back onto my feet. My parachute settled down on top of me. I was all tangled up in the canopy and shroud-lines. I fought my way out from under the mess, unsnapped the harness, and stepped free. I was bare headed. My frontal flak protection was still in place. I turned a complete circle and looked around me. I was totally surrounded by a mob of vicious looking Japanese people. The mob cautiously advanced toward me from all directions. They made angry and threatening sounds and shook their weapons at me.

I hunched my shoulders, tightened my fists, swallowed hard, and stood my ground. I waited to see what would happen next. . . .

Chapter 5

Captured

I landed on my feet. I moved my arms and legs and felt no pain. I figured I wasn't too badly wounded. It seemed like I was operating in slow motion. The maddening music, **"Accentuate the Positive, Eliminate the Negative"** was still pounding through my head. My flak suit was still in place. My flak helmet was gone. I felt under my jacket to assure that my gun was still secure in its holster. My mind began to struggle with the decision. Do I use the gun or don't I? If only the intelligence officer had been able to tell us about capture and treatment by the savage Japanese. I quickly decided that the gun would be used only as a last resort. Do I allow myself to be captured or take my own life? I was about to find out.

The threatening, screaming Japanese mob closed in. They were shouting in a language I could not understand. The shouts came to my ears as a weird, eerie, out-of-this-world, crazy babble. The high-pitched jabbering was frightening. I believed that I'd found Hell! Savage faces were contorted into fiendish masks. In the bright moonlight I could see men and women dressed in baggy peasant clothing. I suspected that they were rice farmers. They were armed with bamboo spears, clubs, and strange looking farm implements, coming toward me like wild animals ready to pounce on their victim. Their weapons were held at the ready.

I saw no uniforms. We had been briefed that we would have a better chance of survival by surrendering to military troops. Civilians were likely to avenge relatives killed during our bombings. Military and police were more disciplined. We had heard rumors that civilians killed airmen before they could be rescued by uniformed Japanese authorities. There was absolutely zero information feedback from Japan on the fate of missing crews.

We suspected the worst! Thoughts were flooding my mind. I had to make the most important decision that I'd ever make.

Do I surrender and take my chances?
Do I pull my gun and kill as many of the mob as possible?
Do I put a bullet in my brain?
Do the Japanese take B-29 crew members captive?
How do I surrender?

I slowly turned a complete circle, trying to decide which way was best to face the advancing crowd. I looked again for a uniform in the mob. There were no uniforms visible, only crazed, weirdly dressed civilians. I was at their mercy. My chances to live did not look good. My instinct to survive told me to leave my gun in its holster and take my chances with the mob.

My survival depended on what I did in the next few seconds. If I drew my gun I would surely die, even if others died with me. I wanted to live. I decided to leave my gun in its holster.

I told myself, **This is it.** I threw my arms in the air and shouted: **"I surrender! I surrender!"**

I could tell that no one in the mob understood me or even wanted to understand me. I wondered what were the Japanese words for "surrender". . . I didn't know the words!

Why weren't we told the words? How could I make them understand?

One of the Japanese men, holding a bamboo spear, charged at me from my right front. His spear was leveled at my head. At his signal the others joined in his charge. The man with the spear was the first to reach me. I reached out and deflected his spear over my head. He lunged past me! Then the excited horde was upon me.

They were like a pack of crazed and starved animals after raw meat. They were so close that they couldn't use their larger weapons. They became a mass of jammed humanity as they milled around me. I was hit with fists and clubs. They hit me from every direction.

Their main target seemed to be my head. They didn't miss. My flak suit and survival gear gave me some protection and probably saved my vitals from severe wounds. Lack of a helmet made my head fair game. I tried to parry the vicious jabs at my eyes. Fortunately no one had a knife.

The women were especially vicious. They were biting and applying brutal super-pinches which I'd never seen before. They used the fingers of one hand, reinforced by the other hand, to apply extremely powerful and painful pinches. It took a bestial Japanese to figure out how to inflict such painful injury.

There was no reprieve from the attack. I was being clubbed and beaten to death. These savages had no thought of allowing me to surrender. Capture was not in their minds. They were out to kill me! The mob was in a frenzy and out of control. No one seemed to be in charge.

There must have over 50 Japanese savages surrounding and beating me. Their shouting increasing in tempo as they — men, women, and children — were fighting to get in lethal blows. I used my bloody hands and arms to protect my head which was already burned from my bail out from the flaming airplane. I was bleeding profusely. My shirt became soaked with blood. My instinct to live was foremost in my mind, but I was losing that battle.

I have seen movies of shark frenzies. This mob would put the sharks to shame! I tried to move out of the mob's center. I couldn't move through the attackers.

A figure several rows back in the mob managed to severely poke my face on the right cheekbone with a implement shaft of some kind. An inch above and it would have put out an eye. An inch to the left and it would have smashed my nose flat. An inch down and it would have knocked my teeth out. My face was swollen for days from this one injury. I was knocked down countless times and each time struggled back to my feet. I never lost consciousness during the beating.

I kept yelling, **"I surrender . . . I surrender . . . I surrender!"**

They did not understand what my upheld arms and words of

surrender meant. They didn't want to know. Their excited screams drowned out my yells. It was chaotic! A bedlam! It was a nightmare! **I was in Hell!**

My only chance for survival depended on the immediate arrival of uniformed, disciplined soldiers or police.

This was a horrible way to die! I made the wrong decision. I should have shot myself.

I kept yelling **"I surrender,"** and prayed — oh, how I prayed! **Help me, God, please help me!**

He did!

Suddenly, a tall, impressive looking black-uniformed figure waded through the mob toward me. He was much taller than I. He was big and powerful, and towered above the small peasant figures. He fought his way through the crazed savages and reached my side. Then he shouted some guttural, animal-like orders to the mob. They ignored his interference. He grabbed me and began pushing me from the center of this mayhem. The mob continued their murderous attack as we squeezed our way out of the milling mass. They were now beating both of us. He was knocked down several times. I was knocked down beside him. He put his arms around me and tried to shield me with his body. The mob didn't appreciate his interference. He received his share of vicious blows.

His lone presence seemed to have little influence over the mob, but his powerfully built body and his persistence finally won out. He finally dragged me free of the attackers. He barked curt orders to the mob. They began to move back. He and I were finally separated from them. He was not a soldier. He must have been a Japanese policeman because he wore a black uniform.

I kept repeating, "Soldier, soldier, soldier," over and over.

The crazed peasants watched us closely, jabbering amongst themselves, pointing at me, and waving their weapons. They were not happy to have had their murderous attack interrupted. I learned that the Japanese peasants have no love for their policemen. Police are feared by their own people.

My rescuer pulled my arms behind my back and snapped handcuffs on my wrists. He showed no hostility. He behaved very professionally. I reasoned that he was one of the local policemen, known and feared by the natives. He was bleeding from scratches on his face. His uniform was torn from our struggle. He risked his life to save me. I was very grateful to him.

MY PRAYERS HAD BEEN ANSWERED!

My rescuer searched me and found my gun and hunting knife. I was amazed that one of my attackers hadn't wrenched the knife from its scabbard and ended my suffering. The policeman disarmed me, leaving the gun in its waterproof cover. He found several .45-caliber bird-shot cartridges in my pants pocket. These bullets were given to us at the last minute as part of our survival gear. They were intended for shooting birds in case we became stranded at sea in a dinghy.

Japanese clothes do not have watch pockets. He didn't find my 1890 silver dollar good luck piece. The crowd had already relieved me of my watch, silver crash-bracelet, and identification dog-tags.

The policeman produced a length of rope and tied it around my neck. He directed me to walk toward the road adjoining the rice paddy where I had landed. The screaming peasants formed a corridor along our path. A few of the more agitated attackers couldn't restrain themselves and hit my head with their clubs as we passed by. Women super-pinchers got in more of these strange and painful acts. I was in such a state of deep shock that these last mob actions were not even felt. I felt no pain from my flak wounds or from the many injuries that I suffered at the hands of the murderous mob.

Though cautious, the officer was very much in control of the situation. One man against a mob. This reminded me of a famous Texas Ranger saying, "One Riot, One Ranger." We moved across the muddy rice paddy. Walking was an effort. I was dizzy, probably from loss of blood and the shock of my situation.

As we neared the road, I became aware that the tune "**Accentuate the Positive, Eliminate the Negative**" was still pounding through my brain. The tune seemed to be boiling around and around and around inside my head. This strange mental condition must have been reflecting my body's reaction to my dangerous predicament. It tended to blank out the dangerous situation that my body and mind were faced with. I seemed to be in another world, another time.

As we stumbled onto the narrow, dirt road, I saw headlights approaching. An ancient red fire truck, which looked like an early Ford, pulled up beside us and stopped. A heated argument took place between the firemen on the truck and my captor about priorities. He pulled his rank. We climbed on the back of the truck beside a couple of fire fighters. The truck turned around and bumped its way down the rough farm road. The fire crew probably had been on the way to extinguish our crashed and flaming B-29.

The mob followed us all the way to the road. As we drove off, they waved their weapons and roared weird banzai shouts.

Everything was blacked out along our route. B-29s on the mining mission were still passing overhead. I heard their engines. My fellow airmen were so close and yet so far away. I couldn't help but wish that I was up there with them. I prayed for the safety and success of these crews. I asked God to be with them. He had certainly been with me.

We could hardly breathe on account of the fire truck's foul-smelling exhaust fumes. Due to wartime shortages, most Japanese vehicles used alcohol or ran on vapors generated by wood-burning contraptions. The engine would hardly run. Every time we slowed down, the engine wheezed and stopped. There would be a lot of yelling as the driver struggled to get the truck moving again. If this was representative of Japanese fire fighting efficiency, I understood why our fire-bomb missions were so successful.

The truck moved along the rough road and rattled through several small Japanese settlements where people were standing in the streets as we sped through. Our nearby raid must have alerted the whole area of northern Kyushu. Vigorous banzai shouts from excited crowds greeted us at each little township. The ride to our destination took about thirty minutes. The lunging, bumping truck made my wounds begin to hurt. As feeling returned to my body so did the pain.

That song was still pounding through my brain! My mind raced from one thought to another. I had time to speculate. What would an American mob have done if a Japanese airman parachuted in their midst right after Pearl Harbor? What would I have done if people near and dear to me had been killed by the enemy?

Japanese soldiers raped and killed thousands of Chinese civilians at Nanking. I wondered if Japanese peasants really knew what the war was all about, or if they knew that Japan had fired the first shot. Probably not. They were probably told only what the Emperor and the military wanted them to know.

It was still dark when we arrived at our destination. The fire truck jerked to a stop. The policeman helped me off the truck's rear platform. The truck turned around and limped away as the policeman and I entered an ancient looking building.

It was now about two o'clock in the morning of 28 March 1945. I was alive. I was a lone prisoner of the Japanese in a small town somewhere near the Shimonoseki Straits.

☆ ☆ ☆ ☆ ☆

The Japanese military wanted prisoners for interrogation. They needed vital information about this first mining mission to the Japanese Home Islands. There must have been a high priority given to capture crews from this particular mission.

☆ ☆ ☆ ☆ ☆

Chapter 6

Kokura Imprisonment

28 March 1945

As near as I could figure, my capture had occurred near the Japanese city of Kokura in northern Kyushu Island. I was in the small township of Ueki, about five miles from our airplane's crash site.

The balky fire truck which picked me up after my capture hauled me to this small village and stopped in front of what appeared to be the municipal building. A sign over the entrance was painted in Japanese characters. The building's front door was open. I could see dim lights inside. Standing in front of the building were a lot of uniformed people and important looking civilians. They stared at me as I stepped off the truck. I asked my policeman escort where we were. He didn't understand English and didn't answer my question. He shook his head and motioned me inside. Inside the building, I was shoved into an office. The rope around my neck was removed and my hands were handcuffed in front. The crowd from out front had assembled in the room. All eyes were centered on me. I started experiencing the fixed, steady, unblinking stare that is common to the Japanese race. They can hold a stare for unbelievable spans of time.

An unpleasant odor came from within the structure. Japanese people were very concerned with personal cleanliness and hygiene. The smells that I detected didn't fit that pattern. In the dimly lit room, I examined these small, strange looking people gathered around me. Their short stature was obvious. My policeman captor and I stood as giants in their midst. Some wore gauze face masks. This was common practice in Japan and still is today. Maybe the masks help filter out bad odors and some contagion. The masks didn't protect them from colds. Most of those in the room had bad cases of sniffles.

After a lot of conversation between the policeman and the civilian who appeared to be in charge, I was directed to sit on a large plush sofa. The civilian seemed to be the "big chief." I guessed that he was the town mayor. Others in the room seemed to be watching him for direction. I noticed that the policeman piled all my gear on a desk across the room where it was being examined by some of the crowd. The mayor took my gun and carefully inspected it. There were a lot of *"Ohs"* and *"Ahs."* The curious crowd continued to stare at me. I must have been a sorry sight. My clothes were shredded and soaked with blood. I tried to get comfortable on the sofa. My backside hurt. In fact, I hurt all over. The mayor barked some orders and we got down to business. His countenance altered completely. The look on his face changed to a threatening glare. It was so sudden that I jumped.

The mayor motioned to one seedy looking civilian who stepped forward and, to my surprise, spoke halting English. He asked if I was an American flyer. I nodded "yes." Next he asked me how I felt. I told him, "Not too good." He asked if I was wounded. I answered that I'd been hit by flak and that a mob had further injured me. My head and face must have been a pretty sorry sight. I had been badly burned in the airplane and most of the mob's blows had been aimed at my head. I glanced down at my shirt. It was soaked with my blood, as were my pants. He said he could see that I'd been burned and beaten and apologized for the mob's brutality. He turned and said something to my policeman savior, who beamed. He pointed to my captured flight gear. Stacked on the desk were my flak jacket and helmet, tattered Mae West, hunting knife, badly shredded one-man dinghy, .45-caliber pistol, and survival vest. Someone must have collected most of my gear from the mob.

I knew that the policeman hadn't been able to get it. He was too busy saving me. I was glad that the mob hadn't been allowed to keep the booty. I didn't see my identification "dog tags," watch, or silver crash-bracelet.

I didn't see any military uniforms in the crowded room. I hoped the military would show up and take me into custody. I expected the military to follow humane rules governing the capture of prisoners.

My interrogator seemed to have run out of questions. He and the mayor were having quite a discussion about something. I hadn't been sitting on the couch very long when a man and a woman cautiously entered the room. These late arrivals were carrying first aid supplies. I assumed that they were civilian medics. One was a studious looking elderly man, and apparently, the other was his assistant. They came over and timidly faced me. They inspected my head and body and made sympathetic sounds as they discussed the extent of my visible wounds. They pulled up my pant legs and found many flak wounds in both my legs. They insisted that I remain seated on the sofa. I couldn't stand up to show them injuries to my backside, where most of my pain seemed to be centered. They thoroughly cleansed my wounds and applied medical salve after which they liberally applied silk bandages.

While the medics worked, the senior official asked a few questions which were translated by the English-speaking civilian. He wanted to know where I came from. I told him Tinian in the Marianas Islands. He didn't seem to know where this was. He asked a couple of simple, non-military questions which I tried to answer. It was good to hear English being spoken by his interpreter. So far, I hadn't been mistreated in any way in Ueki City, and I was receiving medical treatment for my wounds. The medics finished their work, bowed, and left the room.

All of a sudden, the official stiffened and began excitedly pointing to the sofa where I was sitting. He barked sharp commands to his people. I was jerked to my feet. I looked at the sofa where he was pointing. The area where I had been sitting was soaked with blood — my blood. The town chief was not happy about his soiled sofa! This discovery quickly ended my interrogation.

I was hustled to a small back room which had straw on the floor and a dim drop light. I was directed by hand motions to lie down on the straw. I did this with great difficulty due to my hand-cuffs and wounds. I was left in the room. Another black-clothed policeman with bayonetted rifle stood guard over me. He seemed more scared of me than I was of him. I tried to sleep, but my wounds hurt too much and the tight handcuffs on my wrists didn't help. My mind was whirling with the many events of my misfortune crowding my brain. That crazy music had stopped pumping into my head. I found it impossible to sleep.

Pain in my buttocks was becoming unbearable. I began moaning and pointing to my backside. The guard seemed to understand my problem. He ran to the door and shouted something down the hall. Several people came into the room and jerked me to my feet. I was dragged back to the senior official's office. I noticed that the blood stains on the sofa had been neatly cleaned away. Straw mats were placed on the sofa before I was allowed to sit.

The same elderly man and woman medics returned with their medical supplies. The guards turned me over and pulled down my pants to expose the damaged area. There were more "*Ohs*" and "*Ahs*" and pointing. The observers crowded around and made hand motions about several places on my backside. I must have been hit pretty bad judging from the excited conversations taking place. The medic made signs which indicated that the flak must have hit from below and traveled up through each of my buttocks. Deep wounds, caused by the flak exploding under my plane seat, were on each side of my buttocks. Fortunately, none were in my crotch area. The small piece of armor plate under the center of my seat saved my manhood and probably my life!

The medics opened up their medical supplies and went back to work. The nurse cleaned the wounds and applied a great deal of medicine. The wounds were wrapped with copious amount of silk bandages. The guards sat me upright and pulled my pants up over the mass of bandages. The nurse pulled my shirt open and before I realized it, she plunged a hypodermic needle into my chest. The syringe was filled with a purple fluid which she emptied into *me*. Whatever it was didn't hurt and no doubt helped. These Japanese medics were doing their job and were apparently very good at it. I was fortunate to receive this medical treatment, as I was to find out the hard way.

I thanked them as best I could and was taken back to my straw resting spot on the floor of the back room. I tried to relax and get some rest but I still couldn't sleep. I was too wrought up and in too much pain. The guard never took his eyes off me. He was very vigilant.

I must have been in this building nearly an hour when I heard a big commotion up front. There was much shouting and stomping of boots. The guard jumped up and backed as far away from me as he could and stood in the shadows with his back to the wall.

Suddenly, several heavily-armed, fierce looking soldiers in full battle gear burst into the room. They wore metal helmets, khaki uniforms, and distinctive armbands. Their rifles had bayonets. They were a mean looking bunch. They grabbed me and jerked me to my feet. Though I made no hostile move or resisted them in anyway, they hit me several times with their rifle butts. It was apparent that rifle butt blows were to impress the locals.

This was my introduction to the brutal and feared Japanese Kempei Tai who were to make my life a living hell. They were military police who specialized in brutality. They arrested, tortured, interrogated, and murdered enemy and Japanese alike. They were a law unto themselves. It was obvious that they particularly hated Americans. Kempei Tai, sometimes known as "thought police," were the Japanese equivalent of Hitler's SS. I learned the hard way that they were more expert at torture than Hitler's Gestapo. They were dreaded by all Japanese, both military and civilian. I was to be a prisoner of these sadistic killers until V-J Day.

My new guards placed a blindfold over my eyes and replaced the policeman's handcuffs with their own. My hands were handcuffed behind me. I wasn't allowed to walk but was roughly dragged down the hall and out the front door. They were apparently putting on a show of force to intimidate town officials and villagers.

My blindfold was not fastened tightly. I could see from underneath it. I observed an open-bed truck parked in front of the building. More soldiers were sitting on the truck. A blindfolded and handcuffed figure wearing a flight suit was seated in their midst. I couldn't help being surprised and curious. Who could this captive be? I was thrown onto the truck's bed and suffered several rifle butt blows, mostly directed at my head and wounded rear. Bestial Kempei Tai handling was to become the norm during my stay in Japan.

I tried to figure out who the other captive might be. About this time, he asked something of a guard. I recognized Al Andrews' voice! His voice sounded strong. I hoped that he was uninjured. I wondered how he survived. I tried to greet him and received several rifle butt blows for my effort. Al apparently knew better than to answer me. Kempei prisoners were *never* allowed to talk to each other.

The truck's engine finally started after much starter grinding and growling by the troops. There were about ten soldiers guarding us. They all seemed to have colds. Most wore gauze surgical masks. They sneezed and sniffled all the time. They appeared to be an unhealthy lot.

Fuel was in short supply in the Empire — thanks to sinkings of Japanese tankers by our submarines. B-29 bombing of refineries and fuel depots had also done great damage. The truck's balky engine was running on some sort of charcoal-generated gas. The truck stalled every time we slowed down. Engine exhaust fumes were terrible. We rolled and bounced through the night toward some unknown destination. It must have been about five in the morning by now. It was still dark.

As I sat on the truck bed, I tried to maneuver so as to relieve pressure on my backside wounds, which were really hurting. Any movement gained me more blows from the ever-ready rifle butts of the vigilant Kempei Tai guards. My body was shaking from shock and the cool night. All I could do was hope that we would arrive soon at our destination.

There were many stops — mostly at crossroads. Each stop meant the engine had to be laboriously restarted. The Kempei guards shouted encouragement to the driver. We finally stopped in front of some kind of military building. I guessed that it was a Kempei outpost. Even though blindfolded, I could make out a small stone building with many uniformed soldiers standing out in front. They all wore the distinctive Kempei Tai band on their left sleeve. These new soldiers had the same rough, mean appearance and demeanor as our present company.

Al and I were bodily dragged from the truck and forced into the building. I was left in the front room. Al was taken into an adjacent room at the rear of the building. Encouraged by a couple of vicious rifle blows, I was made to sit in a chair placed in the middle of the room. My blindfold and handcuffs were removed. A Kempei asked me a couple of questions in halting English while a white silk tag was filled out by another soldier using an inked brush. The tag was filled with Japanese characters and must have given my vital statistics. It was sewn onto my bloody shirt.

While all this was going on, I tried to adjust my sitting position so that the hard chair did not add to my pain. Sitting hurt my wounds. Each time I moved, I was rewarded with blows to my head.

I glanced around. The room had the spartan look of a typical military office. It was probably a Kempei Tai field headquarters. It was furnished with just a few chairs and a desk. Directly in front of me, I noticed a charcoal brazier full of glowing coals. My heart gave a jump when I saw several red-hot steel pokers buried in the coals. What were these pokers for? There was nothing around to poke but me. It wasn't that cold in the room — in fact, the windows were open. I was shivering but not from the cold.

Two soldiers seated themselves directly across from me while another vicious, evil looking character sat down on my right. A neatly uniformed soldier, probably the commander of this military outpost, appeared to be in charge. Beside him sat a younger soldier who began speaking to me in halting English. He translated questions asked by his commander. There was a lot of conversation between the two of them, then the interrogation started with, "Now that you are a captive of the Imperial Japanese Empire, you must honestly answer all questions or you will be severely punished." My questioners appeared hostile enough, but it was the brutal looking one beside the brazier that worried me. Other Kempei soldiers in the room stared at me as if I were a prized steer about to be slaughtered.

The English-speaking Kempei asked questions and repeated my answers in Japanese to his commander seated beside him, who noted my answers on a clip-board. The questions surprised me. They were not technical and did not seek sensitive war information. We had been briefed that we could tell the Japanese anything they wanted to know. We were encouraged to exaggerate about the overwhelming power we possessed for defeating Japan. We'd been briefed on how many airplanes, ships, troops, weapons that were available to blast the Japanese into oblivion. Unbelievable numbers! As I was questioned, it didn't appear healthy to brag to these Kempei troops. I didn't believe they wanted to hear how great we were. I didn't want to upset anyone, especially that goon working with the red-hot pokers. Everytime I glanced his way, he glared at me like he'd like to cut my heart out.

By now, I was shaking uncontrollably from pain and shock. The interpreter noticed it and asked if there was anything he could do for me. I could think of several things but knew that none would be acceptable to my captors. I told him that I needed nothing.

The Kempei on my right continued to grin maliciously at me. I noted that he was busily engaged in making some strange and worrisome looking bamboo skewers, about six inches long. These were sharpened to a point at one end. He was splitting the other end and inserting small paper pieces. What were these? Why was he doing this? It was obvious that whatever he was doing was not meant for my entertainment or well being. He continued to cast surly glances my way and occasionally rearranged the red hot pokers in the coals. He seemed to be enjoying my discomfort.

The questioning continued. I gave my name, rank, and serial number, which was all that we were required to divulge per Geneva Convention Rules of War governing prisoners of war, which Japan agreed to, but which their government never ratified. The interrogator asked about our crew's missions and targets. The commander suddenly left the room. He returned shortly and said that Andrews denied being on the Nagoya mission which I had given as one of our targets. He appeared very unhappy and growled some words, which when interpreted, told me that if I lied, it would be *"very, very bad!"* The interpreter emphasized that either Andrews or I was lying. One of us would be severely punished. He meaningfully glanced at the soldier working on the splinters as he said this. My mind raced to come up with an explanation. I replied that Andrews had been sick when we flew the Nagoya mission. We had flown with another co-pilot. The questioner went to the other room and came back smiling and said that everything was all right. Al was cleared. We were out of trouble!

As I answered questions, I was mindful of the soldier with the hot pokers and skewers. I'm sure that this must be part of the Kempei interrogation procedure. They intended that I be intimidated. What he was doing dawned on me. The bamboo splinters would be inserted under my fingernails and burned to encourage me to answer their questions. As the questioning proceeded, the splinter soldier became more surly. It must have been a disappointment to him that I was able to answer the simple questions without his encouragement.

My survival vest and dinghy interested the Kempeis. The contents, such as shark repellent, ocean dye-marker, and drinking-water container puzzled them. They appeared to think that these containers contained exotic or intoxicating substance. The charcoal brazier was moved closer to me. This frightened me until I realized that it was meant to warm me. I seemed to be shaking more as the interrogation proceeded. My interrogator barked some guttural orders. Suddenly, Andrews' flight jacket was brought and placed over my shoulders. I tried to refuse this, but was told that I had no choice but to wear it. March was a cool month in Japan. The jacket felt good. The only covering on my upper body was the thin, bloody shirt. My body continued to shake, in spite of the extra warmth.

My interrogator and a soldier from Andrews' room occasionally met to compare notes. My interpreter told me that my cooperation had been good. He asked if I wanted to go home. When I told him, "Yes," he announced smugly that the war was over for me. I'd have to wait until after the war ended to go home. His statement gave me hope that I might survive Japanese captivity. Until now, I didn't know what my fate might be. Kempeis in the room were grinning like baboons and seemed to be congratulating each other. They must have thought their interrogation a great success. It appeared to me that they had never interrogated an American prisoner before and had been ready to use torture to extract answers.

Andrews was brought into the room. He was not wearing his blindfold. We looked at each other and tried to signal our pleasure in seeing each other. We knew that we'd better not speak. He appeared in good shape with no wounds. I was pleased to see that his flight jacket had been replaced by a heavy Japanese army overcoat. Our blindfolds were put back on and we were taken outside.

It must have been around six in the morning by now. Newly arrived Kempei soldiers led us to a truck. Rifle blows and animal-like shouts encouraged us to climb aboard. This truck started up better than the previous one, but after a few minutes, the engine died and could not be restarted. I wondered if Japanese airplanes operated as poorly as their trucks. We were finally transferred to a another truck. We received more kicks, blows, and animal-like guttural shouts by the guards. My handcuffs were too tight. While trying to keep weight off my wounds by pushing with my hands, the handcuffs cut into and lacerated my wrists. Throughout our incarceration, when we were outside our prison cells, we were always blindfolded and handcuffed.

We bounced down another rough Japanese road for many miles. I could see a little around the sides of my blindfold. We passed through a large city, probably Kokura. I heard a great deal of motor traffic. The stench of these vehicles was indescribable. No wonder so many guards wore gauze face masks. The awful odor came from exhaust fumes caused by fuel substitutes. It was obvious that Japan suffered from a critical fuel shortage.

It was beginning to get light when the truck drove through a well-guarded entrance into what appeared to be a major military base. The truck stopped before an office building with a Rising Sun flag flying out front. I guessed that this was base headquarters.

Andrews and I were roughly unloaded and thrown onto a wooden bench facing a sidewalk in front of the building. Our blindfolds were removed but the handcuffs stayed in place. A fully armed Kempei guard stood on each side of us. We sat there for what seemed hours. We were on display like animals in a zoo. I know now how zoo animals feel when humans stare at them. No one has ever received a stare like a Japanese stare. It is inhuman. A continuous throng of Japanese civilians and military troops passed in front of us. They appeared arrogant, savage, and vicious. It was obvious. These were not civilized people. They were animals. *We* were the humans.

We were quite a curiosity. There was much chatter and amusement at our predicament. Spectators spat in our faces. They hit and kicked us. They obviously enjoyed this. Most of our torment was administered by women. They may have been "comfort girls" since this was a military base.

During our ordeal, a neatly uniformed Japanese officer approached. He wore a sword which almost dragged the ground because he was so short. He huffily and importantly announced that we were prisoners of the Emperor and subject to strict rules handed down by the military authorities. As prisoners, we had no rights, since we had bombed and killed innocent women and children. He barked orders in a guttural voice to our guards. His voice sounded like a wild animal. Guards shouted *"Hai,"* which apparently meant they understood. The officer slapped each of us and walked into the building. A constant stream of onlookers moved by us.

After several hours of this degrading treatment, a contingent of Kempei guards marched toward us. Something was about to happen. The leader looked us over, yelled something, and pointed at me. I was yanked to my feet and dragged into the building. Andrews was left to entertain the crowd.

Once inside the building, I was faced by the same bantam officer who had lectured us outside. He told me that I was to be interrogated by a special board of important high-ranking Japanese military officers from the Imperial Army and Navy. These officers wanted answers about our mission. They wanted them fast. He cautioned me to provide honest and accurate answers or my life would be in jeopardy. He stressed that my life was being spared in order to provide answers. My life depended on cooperation.

I was marched into a large, well-appointed conference room. A long, polished table was located in the center of the room. Sitting around the table facing me was a group of handsomely uniformed officers. They were obviously high-ranking officers. Some were in army uniforms. Some were dressed in black naval-type uniforms. Some wore white uniforms. It appeared that all branches of the Japanese military were present. These were senior military officers. Their haughty appearance radiated command capability. They looked at me in distain. I knew that I was a sorry sight.

My two interrogations so far were insignificant to this gathering. I was exhausted and in pain. I needed sleep. I knew that I had better shape up and come alive for this bunch or the consequences would be dire.

I was led to a position at the head of the conference table. The officers' eyes examined me. My appearance must have been miserable. My tattered, blood-stained clothes and battered head contrasted with the well-groomed officers staring at me. Military guards stood stiffly on either side of me. Atmosphere in the room was brittle. There was total silence for a moment or two as I looked out over the gathering. I had never seen such an important group of military officers. I noted that these were not little grinning, bucktoothed Japanese depicted in American cartoons. They were impressive, intelligent looking, war-fighting commanders. These were senior Japanese officers who would probably help command Japanese defenses when our invasion of Kyushu started.

Eyes centered on me. An officer asked the first question in perfect English.

"What kind of mission were you flying when you were shot down last night?"

The directness of this question surprised me. I hesitated while I tried to gather my thoughts. *Do I, or do I not, give the true answer?* I remembered our intelligence officer's briefing: "You tell them anything they want to know. Tell them how strong we are." I also remembered the Japanese officer's warning: "Provide instant, honest, and accurate answers or your life would be in great jeopardy." I decided to give the true answer. There was intense silence in the room as I formulated my answer. I looked the questioning officer in the eye and answered:

"We mined the Shimonoseki Straits."

After translations, the reaction to my answer was instantaneous. The whole room began to boil in an excited babble of conversations. Officers at the table appeared shocked. They gestured and engaged in serious discussions. Fierce looks were directed my way from time to time. When the conversation level subsided, more questions were asked. Most were in Japanese language and had to be translated.

Another officer asked me how many mines we dropped and what size? How many airplanes were involved? Where in the Shimonoseki Straits were the mines located? A large map of the Shimonoseki Straits area was immediately placed on the wall behind me. I was ordered to point to where the mines were dropped. I stated that I was a flight engineer and had no knowledge of where the mines were dropped. I pointed vaguely at the Kokura area and the channel between Honshu and Kyushu. I'd heard about the stoic, unemotional show of the Oriental face. These officers did not fit that description.

While I stood there, animal-like commands were barked out. I was slammed around by the two guards flanking me. I was in such a state of shock from my wounds and beatings that these new blows didn't seem to register. This beating was meant to encourage me to provide exact answers about mine location. I stuck to my professed ignorance about mine location.

The 20th Air Force's first mining mission had hit a sensitive strategic area. I understood why concentrated flak brought down our plane. The Japanese could not afford to have their Shimonoseki Straits mined! It was obvious that Japanese military strategy was seriously affected by a blocked waterway. We'd struck a great blow at the enemy.

A high priority must have been established to capture a living prisoner from this mission. Prisoners were needed in order to learn where the mines were dropped. It was vital information they must have. Those of us captured that night probably owe our lives to that need.

The book, *Valor At Okinawa*, by Lawrence Cortese, reports that, after B-29s mined the Shimonoseki Straits, the Japanese Second Fleet was forced to sortie on their way to fight at Okinawa via the Bungo Strait. This alternate exit from the Inland Sea made them more vulnerable to American fleet units on station east of the Japanese homeland.

This book discussed a meeting held by the Japanese Combined Fleet hierarchy which met on Kyushu Island in March 1945 to discuss intelligence received about a major American military operation against Okinawa. Defensive action was to be established. Present at the meeting were:

> Admiral Soemu Toyoda, CINC of the Combined Fleet
> Admiral Ryunosake Kusaka, Chief of Staff
> Admiral Matome Ugaki, Fifth Air Fleet Commander
> Rear Admiral Toshiyuki Yokoi, Chief of Staff
> Captain Takashi Miyazake, 741st Air Group Commander
> Captain Kosaku Ariga, Battleship *Yamato* Commander
> Executive Staff members.

I firmly believe that this was the group which I faced on the morning of 28 March 1945.

Not one of the other twelve prisoners, shot down that night, faced this array of top brass. Why was I selected?

After my interrogation was completed, I was blindfolded and taken from the room. I could see a little around my blindfold as I was marched several hundred yards to a long, narrow, one-story wooden building. The building had many doors along its length and looked somewhat like one of our motels. The wooden walls were unpainted. When we reached the end-room, I was shoved through the door. The door was left open and a guard, with bayoneted rifle, took his place outside the room. The wall opposite the door had a window through which I observed a typical military post.

My blindfold was removed but the handcuffs were left on, fortunately in front, which gave me better mobility. I glanced at my bloody, lacerated wrists where rough handling and tight handcuffs had torn my skin. I slipped the handcuffs as far up my wrists as possible to expose the raw wounds to the sunlight streaming through the window. I hoped that the sun would dry the wound and help formation of protective scabs to prevent infection. The sun's warmth made the wrist wounds feel better.

I took stock of my location. I was in a small, unfurnished room, with the rough wooden table in the center. The table had a frame around the top which contained straw. This two-by-five-foot table was to be my bed. It was too short for my body. The roof support beams were exposed, revealing a structure with unfinished poles tied together with simple bent-metal rods. Its construction was wood-working art. Walls were of natural wood with no nails showing. None of the wood was painted. During my Japanese stay, I saw no paint used on wooden surfaces.

There was no place to sit down. I tried to climb onto the table but couldn't because of the height of the table and my handcuffs. I motioned to the guard that I needed assistance. He growled, but came into the room and helped me mount this peculiar bed which was sized for a Japanese body — not mine. I was given a brand new Japanese army blanket. It was wool, very thick, and of excellent quality. The feeling of warmth, for the first time in many hours, gave me a feeling of comfort.

Shortly, a crowd of spectators gathered in front of the door which had been left open. I could see the Kempei guard with his bayoneted rifle standing beside the opening. The crowd's eyes were fixed on me with that strange Japanese hypnotic stare. It was a hostile group. Some of the spectators became braver and were allowed to edge into my cell. The Kempei guard did not stop them. Several of the animal-like brutes spat into my face and slapped me. Females were particularly vindictive. Many gave me the super-pinch using both hands. Pain was excruciating, but I had no choice except to endure the torture and indignity.

Toward evening the crowd gradually dispersed. I tried to get comfortable on the small table. There was no way. The best I could do was to put my head on the wooden frame and let my legs hang over the end.

I wondered what would happen next. What about food? Water? I wasn't thirsty or hungry. My mind was pretty mixed-up. My wounds were throbbing. But I was alive!

That evening there was a commotion outside and a small, shabby civilian was pushed into the room. He carried tools, lumber, and hardware. The door was slammed shut by the guard. The poor workman was left alone with me. He was terrified. Every time I moaned or moved, he jumped. I guess that he thought I might attack him. He went to work while keeping a close watch in my direction.

He had a peculiar small hand saw. The handhold was a straight wooden extension of the blade and was held like a knife. He sawed a small hole in the door and constructed a peep hole with a small hinged panel. He then installed a massive hasp and lock on the outside of the door, and a conical shade for the drop light so that its light was concentrated directly on my bed. He installed wooden bars over the room's only window. My room began to look more like a prison cell.

I forgot my troubles as I watched and admired the work of this master craftsman. He was an expert carpenter. When he finished working on my room, he went next door where Andrews was held and modified that room. He quickly transformed the office rooms into jail cells. Escape would be more difficult — not that I had any thought of trying to flee. Where would I go?

After the carpenter left, my cell door was slammed shut and locked. I was alone at last. It was good to be free from the crazy, fixed stares and abuse of the hostile crowd. My solitude did not last long. A poorly dressed, peon-looking Japanese came into my cell. He helped me sit up. He brought a saucer containing a small rice ball and two slices of what looked like pickles. He was a food soldier. He made motions for me to eat. "*Onigre,*" he said.

By now I was hungry. I picked up the rice ball, which was so small that I could close my fist around it, and took a bite. I needed water to help me get it down and made signs for something to drink. He left and returned shortly with a small aluminum bowl of water. *"Misuit,"* he said. I tried the pickles. They tasted awful. They were inedible. *"Dykon,"* he said. I ate the rice but left the dykon, which was a pickled radish-type root. A couple of days later when I was starving, I wished that I had eaten the pickles. I could hear Andrews telling the food soldier that he wasn't hungry. I'll bet Al remembered later about that food he refused.

This was my first meal in Japan. The last meal I'd eaten was the flight-lunch while flying toward the Japanese target. It consisted of the usual peanut butter sandwich and tropical chocolate bar for dessert. The food soldier could speak a little English. He returned to my cell and asked how I liked the meal. I told him it was pretty good and asked if he could teach me some basic Japanese words. He told me, rather huffily, that prisoners do not need to know Japanese words. The Japanese Army would look after me. I should mind my own business.

It was a cold March night. I asked for and was brought another thick Japanese army blanket. I was amazed at the blanket's excellent quality and my good fortune to receive it. It was the equivalent of two of our American Army blankets. I thanked the guard with one of the few Japanese words that I knew, *"Arigato."* He grinned profusely with a mouth overstuffed with teeth and acted as if I had given him a big tip. This guard did not wear the Kempei Tai arm band.

I felt the "call of nature." I got off my table-like bed and hobbled over to the door and called to the guard. He opened the peep hole. He did not understand that I was asking to go to the bathroom. I made body motions to illustrate what I wanted. He grinned and said *"Benjo."* He unlocked the door, tied a rope around my neck, and led me to an adjacent building which had a conventional western-style commode. The guard held onto the rope around my neck. I noted there was no toilet paper available and asked the guard for some. He grinned, reached in his pocket, and gave me several sheets of what looked like rice paper. He said, *"Benjo comee,"* as he handed the paper to me. Each soldier carried his own *benjo comee.* None existed in toilet facilities.

When I returned to my cell, this guard, who was nicer than others I came in contact with, helped me back onto my hay bed. I was beginning to learn basic Japanese words — *"benjo"* was toilet — *"benjo comee"* was toilet paper — *"onigre"* was rice ball — *"misuit"* was water — *"dykon"* meant those awful pickles.

2d. Lt. John A. Brown's B-29 Combat Crew. First Row L/R — James E. Griffith/LH Gunner; Charles A. Anderson/CFFC Gunner; Richard E. Dunlavey/RH Gunner; Leroy F. Rose/Radio. Second Row L/R — Albert A. Franceson/Radar Operator; Baxter J. Love/Bombardier; John A. Brown/ Airplane Commander; Albert Andrews/Pilot; Harlan E. Fintel/Navigator; Fiske Hanley/Flight Engineer; Richard Hall/T. Gunner.

504th Bomb Group B-29 damaged during fire-bomb mission over Tokyo by bombs dropped by another B-29.

Author on 4 February 1944 commissioned 2d. Lt. Engineering Officer at Yale University Air Force Technical School.

Author during Aviation Cadet jungle training.

B-29 Flight Engineer's Station showing the many instruments and controls.

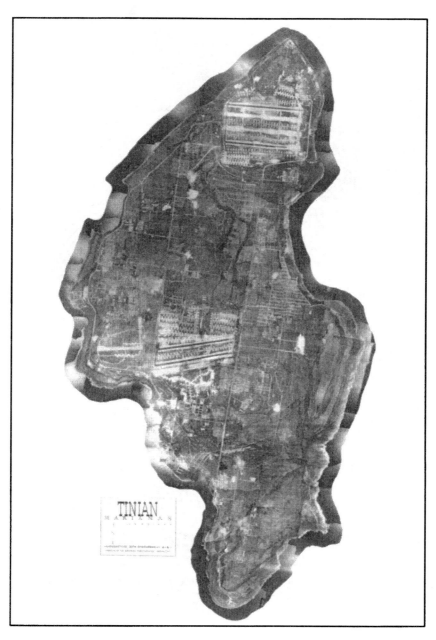

Air photo of Tinian Island showing North Field, the largest airfield in the world at that time.

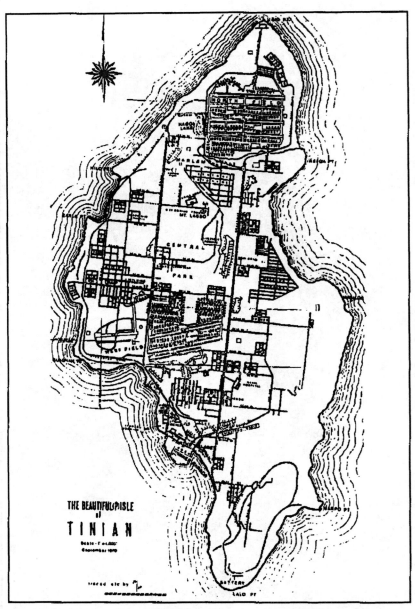

Map of Tinian. 504th Bomb Group camp area is at upper left, which looks like a bite taken out of the island.

The filing time shown in the date line on telegrams and day letters is STANDARD TIME at point of origin. Time of receipt is STANDARD TIME at point of destination

FWA6ODC13 WM50   1945 APR 17 AM 9 59

W=WMUD 19 43 GOVT=WUX WASHINGTON DC 17 1036A

CLAUDE W HANLEY=   ... FORD TEXAS

2715 UNIVERSITY DRIVE FTW=

THE SECRETARY OF WAR DESIRES ME TO EXPRESS HIS DEEP REGRET
THAT YOUR SON 2/LT HANLEY FISKE HAS BEEN MISSING IN ACTION
IN PACIFIC OCEAN AREA SINCE 27 MAR 45 IF FURTHER DETAILS OR
OTHER INFORMATION ARE RECEIVED YOU WILL BE PROMPTLY NOTIFIED
=J A ULIO THE ADJUTANT GENERAL=

27 45

THE COMPANY WILL APPRECIATE SUGGESTIONS FROM ITS PATRONS CONCERNING ITS SERVICE

Telegram — 17 April 1945 — War Department "Missing-in-action."

504th Bomb Group Chaplain Earl Raitt at his typewriter preparing messages for worried American families.

27 April 1945

Mr. C.W. Hanley
University Drive
Ft. Worth, Texas

My dear Mr. Hanley:

As Chaplain of the 504th Bomb Group, to which your son, Fiske, was assigned, I am writing to give you my word of consolation for your son who has been reported by the War Department as missing in action. Please extend to other loved ones of the family my sincere word of hope and comfort.

I would have written sooner but military regulations require that I wait for 30 days before writing.

Lt. Hanley has been reported by the War Department as missing in action since the mission of March 27th over Shimonoseki Straits. We do not have complete information in regard to the loss of his plane. Two planes were seen going down over the target. One was very probably the plane in which your son was flying. No one saw the plane crash and no one knows whether the men were able to bail out.

Whether or not the crew were able to bail out and are now prisoners of war we cannot say. The situation may not seem too encouraging. But until we have definite evidence otherwise, we have a right to hope that they may be saved.

May God grant you and son's loved ones His Comfort and His strength to face the uncertainty, the anxiety, and the heartache which must be yours in the face of this kind of an experience.

War is terrible business. May God grant that it is soon over. And may He grant us the wisdom and the strength to build a better world and create a permanent peace so that the sacrifices which are being made shall not be made in vain.

If I can be of any help to you in any possible way, please feel free to write me.

May God bless you.

Earl Raitt
EARL RAITT
Group Chaplain

Letter from Chaplain Raitt to author's parents.

IN REPLY REFER TO:

AG 201 Hanley, Fiske
PC-N POA037

19 April 1945

Mr. Claude W. Hanley
2715 University Drive
Fort Worth, Texas

This letter is to confirm my recent telegram in which you were regretfully informed that your son, Second Lieutenant Fiske Hanley, 0868805, has been reported missing in action in the Pacific Ocean Area since 27 March 1945.

I realize the distress caused by failure to receive more information or details; therefore, I wish to assure you that in the event additional information is received at any time, it will be transmitted to you without delay. If no information is received in the meantime, I will communicate with you again three months from the date of this letter. It is the policy of the Commanding General of the Army Air Forces, upon receipt of the "Missing Air Crew Report," to convey to you any details that might be contained in that report.

Inquiries relative to allowances, effects and allotments should be addressed to the agencies indicated in the inclosed Bulletin of Information.

Permit me to extend to you my heartfelt sympathy during this period of uncertainty.

Sincerely yours,

J. A. ULIO
Major General
The Adjutant General

1 Inclosure
Bulletin of Information

Letter from War Department describing loss.

HEADQUARTERS, TWENTIETH AIR FORCE
OFFICE OF THE COMMANDING GENERAL
WASHINGTON 25, D. C.

AAF-201 (13462)   Hanley, Fiske
0868805

MAY 12 1945 ✓

Mr. Claude W. Hanley
2715 University Drive
Fort Worth, Texas

Dear Mr. Hanley:

The Adjutant General notified you that your son, Second Lieutenant Fiske Hanley, has been reported missing in action since 27 March 1945.

Additional information has been received indicating that Lieutenant Hanley was a flight engineer on a B-29 (Superfortress) bomber which departed from Tinian, Marianas Islands, on a mine laying mission to Shimono-seki Straits on 27 March 1945. Details of the mission, and the cause and circumstances surrounding the disappearance of this bomber are unknown at the present time, inasmuch as your son's plane was not seen after it departed from its base about 4:35 p.m. It is regretted that there is no other information available in this headquarters relative to the whereabouts of Lieutenant Hanley.

Believing you may wish to communicate with the families of the others who were in the plane with your son, I am inclosing a list of these men and the names and addresses of their next of kin.

A continuing search by land, sea, and air is being made to discover the whereabouts of our missing personnel, and agencies of our government and allies frequently send information which aid us in giving further details to you.

Very sincerely,

LAURIS NORSTAD
Brigadier General, U. S. A.
Chief of Staff

1 Incl

Letter from 20th Air Force Chief of Staff describing loss.

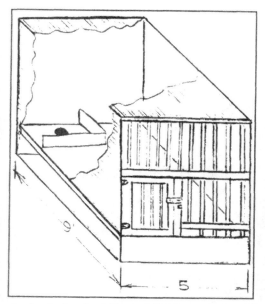

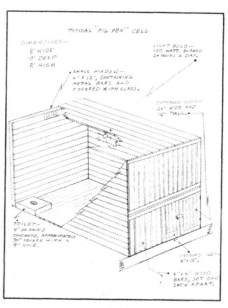

Author's sketch of Kempei Tai Dungeon Cell. About eight prisoners squeezed into each of these cells.

Typical "Horse Stall" (sometimes called a "Pig Pen") Cell. Drawn by Marcus Worde. About 18 to 20 prisoners crowded into each of these cells.

1st. Lt. Ernest A. Pickett, shot down near Yawata, Japan, on 20 August 1944 — Wounded and badly beaten — Restrained by two Kempei Tai Soldiers with their distinctive armbands — He was beheaded.

Japanese searchlight.

B-29 bomber caught in deadly searchlights surrounded by flak bursts.

Front view of Kempei Tai Headquarters.

Rear view of Kempei Tai Headquarters showing "Horse Stall" cell building.

August 1995 view of Kempei Tai Headquarters site now occupied by a high-rise Japanese government office building. Wartime, concrete barracks for Kempei Tai soldiers are shown in foreground.

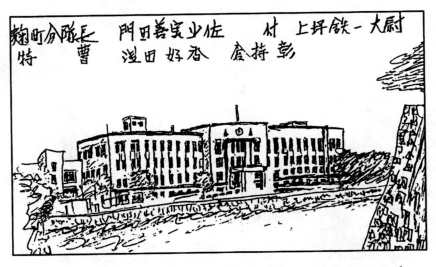

Sketch of Kempei Tai Headquarters obtained by author's U.S. Embassy driver during 1991 visit to prison site.

Colonel Keijiro Otani, Kempei Tai Headquarters Commander who ordered, "Execute all American prisoners on 14 August 1945."

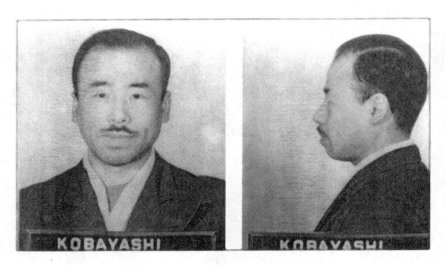

Yasuo (Shorty) Kobayashi, chief civilian torturer and executioner of "Special Prisoners" at Kempei Tai Headquarters.

Ensign Kazuo Sakamaki, first Japanese POW — Captured at Pearl Harbor after wrecking his midget submarine.

General Korechika Anami, Japanese war minister, who visited author's dungeon and ordered "Execute all allied POWs the instant Japan is invaded."

Emperor Hirohito and Empress Nagako — aware and responsible for horrors inflicted on B-29 "Special Prisoners."

At dusk the food soldier returned with another small rice ball and more of the inedible *dykon* pickles. I tried to give the pickles to the guard but he didn't want them either. The drop light was turned on and stayed on all night long. The shaded light didn't put out much light. The guards did not cover my barred window with blackout curtains.

The peephole was opened periodically to inspect me. Guards were changed every two hours with many guttural commands and "*Hais.*" I heard Andrews talking to the guard. The sound of his voice made me feel a lot better. I was not alone in my POW predicament.

I tried to sleep but couldn't get comfortable on my small, hard bed. My faith in God comforted me through the long, difficult night. I prayed and prayed and prayed. I offered prayers of gratitude for having been spared. I prayed for my family. I prayed for Andrew's wife, Roberta, who was expecting their second baby. I prayed for our crew but felt that they had not survived. I didn't know whether those in the aft cabin were able to bailout. I asked that God look after Anderson, Brown, Donlavey, Fintel, Francescon, Griffith, Love, and Rose. My prayers gave me the comfort and strength to face a bleak future. I finally fell asleep. My tragic day was over.

The next morning as the sun was rising, I was awakened by the sorriest sounding bugle call I ever heard. Through my window's bars I observed troops deployed in an adjacent field doing exercises which were both physical and verbal. I listened to some of the most inhuman sounds I'd ever heard. It sounded as if a bunch of gorillas were warming up for an orgy.

A formation of Japanese women in black and white uniforms marched by. They appeared tough, homely, and well-fed. Thousands of Japanese women were recruited in the last few months of the war and trained to fight to the death when the invasion of their homeland began. They were to be armed with bamboo spears and other homemade weapons. Japanese civilians and military were ordered by their emperor to die fighting for every square foot of their homeland. My friend, Reverdie Ater in Hawaii, had told me about *Operation Olympic,* the American invasion of Kyushu planned for 1 November 1945. I was a captive on Kyushu.

After breakfast of a rice ball and water, I had time to better assess my situation. I found no flak wounds in my upper body. My whole body was lacerated and bruised by the mob attack and by soldier gun-butt blows. My head and hands were badly burned from passing through the airplane's flames. My hair was completely burned off and what remained was a blob of hardened blood. The mass of silk bandages put on the night before were completely soaked with blood. They needed changing. My ears and skin were badly burned. Bamboo pole jabs and rifle butt blows resulted in a badly swollen face. Fortunately, I'd lost no teeth and I still had my eyesight. *I was alive!*

My worst wounds were in my backside. I am certain that if I had not placed that small piece of armor plate in my seat, I would have sustained fatal wounds. My tattered and torn shirt told me another story. Combat crews were supposed to fly missions wearing flight coveralls. I didn't like to wear coveralls and usually wore a khaki shirt and pants.

I was not a "spit-and-polish" military type. I had a missing button on the left sleeve of my shirt before the mission, but hadn't replaced the button. The cuff of this sleeve was shredded. I was lucky not to have lost my left hand. The cuff hung down as I performed my duties at the flight engineer's station. The cuff now looked like it had been hit by a shotgun blast. If the flak burst had been a couple of inches higher, my wrist would have been separated from my arm. It was obvious that I'd been hit by at least two flak bursts. One blew up right under my seat and the other hit the airplane's side next to my arm. Fortunately for me, neither burst was from large caliber artillery. They were explosive rounds — probably 25-millimeter cannon shells. A larger round would have wiped me out.

After assessing my physical condition, I decided to ask to be properly treated as a prisoner of war. We had been briefed that if captured, we should insist on the rights guaranteed by the Geneva Rules. I gathered what little bravado I could muster, knocked on the door, and asked the Kempei guard for bathing arrangements and soap. The guard looked at me like he thought I was crazy. I was persistent and finally he shouted for help.

A neatly uniformed officer with a Samurai sword at his hip and an official looking diagonal sash across his upper body arrived. He could speak some English. He was probably the Officer of the Day. I repeated my request for sanitary supplies. He looked at me disdainfully and said, "American prisoners are due nothing. You are not covered under the Geneva Rules. You are lucky to be alive." He told me to shut up and informed me that conditions in this camp were going to get worse, much worse, and that I'd better keep quiet and cause no trouble. He told me that we were sub-humans and would be treated like animals.

How right he was! I was to find out the hard way just what he meant.

I pointed to the bandages that were soaked from the bleeding wounds and I told him that my wounds were hurting quite badly. I insisted that I needed medical attention. He carefully looked me over and seemed to agree that I did need medical help. He left without promising anything.

In a couple of hours, a handsomely uniformed officer came into my cell. He looked as if he came out of a display window. His Samurai sword handle had a chamois cover. His uniform was meticulously tailored. He was an army doctor. He was accompanied by a neatly uniformed nurse carrying a brightly colored knapsack strapped to her back. This was her medical bag. I was impressed by this Japanese medical team! They were intelligent, good looking people.

I was directed to strip to the bare flesh. The nurse removed the old dressings, one at a time. The doctor spoke perfect English. Each of my many wounds were treated individually and carefully. They worked on my head first. They snipped off burned hair, completely washed the dried blood away, and treated the wounds and burns. My head was almost totally bandaged. They inspected my upper torso and found no damage other than bruises and lacerations. They noted that my shirt was so stiff from hardened blood that it stood by itself on the floor. They were not pleased with what they saw from my waist down. They examined my buttock area. The doctor told me that my wounds back there were severe and apparently were a challenge to medicate and bandage. They used surgical instruments to remove some of the shrapnel pieces. They must have used pain-deadening injections which helped the operation. They sprinkled some kind of medicinal powder into my wounds and applied iodine to the lacerations. They treated and bandaged the buttock wounds with yards of silk gauze. My wounds were bandaged in a very professional manner. My body was covered with gauze from the waist down. They seemed pleased with the results of their mercy mission.

As they were finishing my medical treatment, a bell sounded outside the building. The doctor told me that they had to leave for a moment. All Japanese in my cell quickly went outside and turned to face in the same direction. They all bowed together. I wondered what was happening. The medical officer and nurse returned and finished my treatment. As they worked, I asked the doctor what the bowing ceremony was all about. The doctor told me that what I'd seen was a ritual ceremony performed every day in which the Emperor received the respect of his subjects. All Japanese performed this ceremony. The doctor gave me a serious look and warned that the Emperor was a sacred person to Japanese people.

"It is a death offense for a barbarian to mention the Emperor's name. All non-Japanese are barbarians."

I was grateful for his advice and glad to have learned about this "capital offense" the easy way. I could have inadvertently mentioned the Emperor's name and not even known why I was being executed. I heeded the doctor's advice religiously and warned other prisoners.

This was the last medical treatment that I would receive during my months of long imprisonment.

I thanked the doctor and nurse. I noted that the doctor did not wear the Kempei Tai armband. They must have been from the base's Japanese army and not aware of the Kempei Tai orders of *no medical care for American flyers.*

Rice balls were supplied for all three meals on my second day of captivity. Use of the bathroom was denied me. A wooden box was brought into my cell. By motions, the guard directed me to use it for my body functions. Not good, but adequate!

The guards watched me through the peep hole. I was inspected by many inquisitive visitors. It was apparent that Andrews and I must be the first prisoners held at this army base. We were curiosities.

Later that same afternoon, a Japanese officer, accompanied by an armed guard, came into my cell. I was blindfolded and marched to another room in the same building. When my blindfold was removed, I was standing in front of a table behind which sat three Japanese Army officers. They were neatly uniformed and intelligent looking. None of them wore the distinctive Kempei Tai armband. I was made to sit on a chair directly in front of the officers.

All the officers spoke perfect English. One officer recorded while the other two questioned me. I was told that if I truthfully answered the questions, I wouldn't be punished. They began by asking me simple questions about my personal life, name, rank, serial number, etc. The questioning continued into details about our mission to the Shimonoseki Straits. These investigators asked general questions and did not seem to be as interested in the mining mission as were my high-ranking interrogators.

A wicked looking piece of jagged shrapnel lay on the table in front of me. I asked about it and was told that the Japanese doctor dug it out of my body. I requested to be allowed to examine it. I found it to be a chunk of steel about the size of a marble. I was glad to be rid of it!

My dog tags were also on the table. The chief interrogator played with these throughout my interview. I thanked the inquisitors for the medical attention given me. The military at this base apparently did not know about the Imperial General Headquarter's directive that banned medical treatment to B-29 crewmen.

The session seemed harmless enough. I was given water to drink and was even offered a cigarette, which I declined. I asked about the fate of our crew. They had no information on survivors other than Andrews and me. They said that our B-29 crashed and an investigation was still under way. After the interview ended, I was marched back to my cell.

After returning to my cell, the door opened and two uniformed non-Kempei officers entered. One spoke English. The other officer gingerly carried a small green ball about two inches in diameter with a short steel cable attached. They demanded to know what this object was. I asked where they'd gotten it and was told that it had been found near our crashed B-29. Looking at the green ball, I instantly knew that it was the activation knob from an oxygen bailout bottle. Before answering their question, I asked about the fate of the rest of our crew. I received vague answers with no assurance that any of them had survived.

Again they demanded to know about the green ball. I reached out on pretense of inspecting it, and that threw them in a panic. The bearer of the object drew back with a horrified look as if he thought

I was trying to trigger a bomb. I told them that without closer inspection I couldn't identify the object. I was not allowed to touch it. They left the cell shaking their heads. I wonder if they ever learned what this harmless item was.

Darkness came. Before trying to sleep, I offered my prayers to the Almighty and asked that my fellow crewmen be saved or looked after on their final flight. I lay back on my hard, undersized bed and began a troubled sleep.

Around midnight, I was aroused by loud shouts and the sound of stomping boots. The cell door burst open and a uniformed Japanese officer entered. He had a Samurai sword swinging from his hip and a gaudy sash over his upper torso. He did not look friendly. Two armed Kempei guards with their armbands came into my cell with the officer. He barked guttural orders and the guards jerked me from the bed and dragged me from the cell.

My handcuffs, which had never been removed, were still in place. I was not blindfolded. I observed about 20 fully armed and helmeted Kempei soldiers in neat formation in front of my cell. All had rifles with fixed bayonets. I was positioned in their midst and guttural orders were barked out. By now, nothing surprised me. I wondered what this was all about.

We marched about four or five hundred yards and stopped at the edge of what looked like a parade ground. I was placed facing a freshly dug hole and left standing alone. The officer positioned himself off to my right about ten paces behind me. The soldiers were formed into a firing line behind me. This didn't look good! By slightly and slowly moving my head from side to side, I could see that the soldiers were about 30 feet behind with their rifles leveled at me.

The officer drew his Samurai sword, raised it in the air, and shouted a command. I stood stiff and motionless, waiting . . . waiting . . . waiting . . .

Nothing happened for what seemed to me a very long while. Another command was barked out. I heard the sound of bolts sliding bullets into firing chambers, followed by complete silence for what seemed like hours. I moved my eyes downward and looked at the deep hole in front of me. I was standing with my back to a Japanese execution squad lined up behind me. Their loaded rifles were aimed straight at me. They were waiting for an order from their officer to fire!

This was a no-win situation. If I moved or tried to run, the "fire" order surely would be given. If I stood where I was, would I be shot? I decided that if they were going to shoot me, it would have to be in the back and in cold blood. I stood motionless. The officer stood motionless. The firing squad stood motionless. Not a sound was heard. Silence, complete black silence!

After what seemed like an eternity, I heard the Samurai sword sliding back into its scabbard and guttural orders barked out. I expected gunshots but instead, two Kempeis grabbed me and dragged me backwards, away from the edge of that hole. I was placed in the center of the Kempei formation and marched back to my cell. A guard was left at the door and the execution squad marched off. There was no explanation by the officer or the guard. What did all this mean?

Why had they done this? Why me? What about Andrews? They didn't do this to him. Did they think that I had not told them something that I knew and would now crack and confess? Was this just a fun evening's entertainment for a drunken, sadistic Japanese officer? I lay there and shook and shook and shook. I'd survived another crisis. I finally dozed off . . . or maybe I passed out.

It was still dark when another commotion in front of the cell block awakened me. I heard Japanese soldiers shouting. There was a lot of scuffling, door banging, thuds of rifle butts hitting human bone and flesh, and cries of pain. I heard American voices. None of which belonged to Andrews. I moved over to my door and asked my guard what was going on. He answered, *"Bee Nee Ju Ku Americans,"* which meant "B-29 Americans." These were newly arrived American prisoners being placed in our cell block. A complete B-29 crew had arrived. We had eleven more prisoners to keep us company.

There were now thirteen American prisoners in this row of improvised cells, not quite half of the crew members from the three B-29s shot down during our mission. Andrews and I were the only survivors from our plane. There were no survivors from one plane. Eleven survived from the third plane. The newly arrived prisoners were:

2d. Lt. William C. Grounds
2d. Lt. Jack Hobbie,
2d. Lt. W J. C. Leslie,
2d. Lt. Ollin W. Williams,
M. Sgt. Neal R. Cooper,
Sgt. Arvid A. McPherson,
Sgt. Maynor B. Hanks,
Sgt. Julian W. Steel,
Sgt. Harold P. Peterson,
Sgt. Clarence L. Pressgrove,
Sgt.Warren R. Thompson.

This crew was from the Sixth Bomb Group on Tinian which had almost made it to the Japanese coast before their plane crashed. They bailed out, were captured, and finally brought to this army base which was near Kokura.

Day number three was uneventful. The sorriest bugle calls I've ever heard started the Japanese army day. Apparently, the bugler's sounds made sense to the troops. It sounded like the bugler must have been a gorilla taught to blow bugle calls. I watched the drills and exercises of Japanese army troops outside my barred window. These were weird activities executed with great discipline and unearthly sounds.

I received rice balls for breakfast, lunch, and dinner. The food soldier brought a bowl of water with lunch. I tasted it and found it hot. Not realizing that hot water is a delicacy in Japan, I thought a joke was being played on me and refused to drink it. I goofed! The food soldier straightened me out pretty quickly on the special treat. In the future, when hot water was offered, I always accepted. I had a new word to add to my Japanese vocabulary: "*oh yu*" means hot water.

My feeling of shock was beginning to subside. My wounds began to feel better or maybe I was just getting used to the pain. My bleeding wrists developed natural protective scabs and did not appear to be infected.

I was beginning to become adapted to my new life. When night fell I used my empty survival vest, which had been given back to me, for a pillow on the hard wooden bed edge and fell into a fitful sleep. The Kempei Tai did not believe in a full night's sleep.

About midnight I was awakened by guttural commands,

shouts, and truck noises. My door was flung open and through the opening I could see a bunch of Kempei guards milling around in a dreary, rainy night. My first thought was that this was another firing squad. A guard came in and hit me with his gun-butt, meaning that I should stand up. Another guard blindfolded me and tied a rope around my neck. I was dragged over to a truck already occupied by many manacled and blindfolded American captives. There was one guard per prisoner. Some of the prisoners tried to talk to each other and rifle butt blows were their reward. I misunderstood an order and tried to get to my feet and received a rifle butt blow to my stomach. I got the message. We were to receive plenty of punishment that night.

The truck rumbled off and exited through the army base gate. It rattled down the road for about an hour. We finally arrived at another military installation where the truck stopped at a guard post then drove to another prison building. We were unloaded one at a time. When my turn came, I was pulled from the truck and gunbutted into the building.

This prison had the appearance and putrid smell of long use. It was not a temporary jail like the one we had just left. Prisoner processing appeared practiced and professional. These Kempeis had been in the jail business a long time.

The tag sewn over my left shirt pocket was replaced with another silk identification tag with more Japanese characters written on it. Next, I was asked a few questions then pushed, shoved and dragged down an aisle between two rows of barred cells. My guards stopped in front of a small door set low to the floor. They removed my blindfold and neck rope but left the handcuffs in place. I wondered if these cuffs would *ever* be removed. I'd worn them for many days now. The small door was opened. My neck was pushed forward and down so that I was in a low, stooped position when I was pushed through the small opening. I ended up on my back staring into pitch black nothingness.

I lay there afraid to move for fear that I would find that I was in a coffin with no way to sit or stand up. After a few minutes I moved one foot to explore around me — I did not touch the side of a "coffin." Good, there was space around me. I sat up. My head didn't bump anything. So far, so good. I stood up and breathed a sigh of relief. I could stand up. This was not a coffin.

By then my eyes were becoming adjusted to the dark and I could make out some features of the cell. The cell was about nine by nine feet in size. There was a very bad animal odor, like a lion cage in a zoo. The concrete floor had a hole in one corner. I found that the hole was the source of the bad odor. It was over a latrine bucket. The door side of the cell had floor to ceiling wooden bars with a small pass through opening at the bottom. There was a small window located near the ceiling.

I heard guards bringing in more prisoners and throwing them into other cells. I knew I was not alone. We tried talking to each other through the bars but immediately found that this was not a good idea. Bayoneted rifle barrels were thrust through bars and guttural threats and "No talkee" commands shouted at us. I placed myself in the center of the cell so as to be as far away as possible from bayonet stabs through the bars. After searching the cell for blankets and finding none, I curled up in a fetal position, trying to keep warm on the cold, concrete floor.

The cell was cold in the late March night. I'd never been so cold in my whole life. I shivered as I lay on the bare concrete floor. I tried to imagine that I was wrapped in those warm army blankets left behind in my last prison. My imagination was not good enough to help. It was a miserable night.

The next morning, sunlight streamed through the small window located near the cell's ceiling. I inspected my cell. I saw strange markings on the walls which didn't make sense to me. Previous prisoners were, no doubt, Japanese. The window was covered with wire mesh fastened to the frame with sturdy nails. The wooden walls were smooth with no fasteners showing. The wooden bars looked very sturdy. The room looked pretty escape-proof. Even if I could manage to escape, then what? I immediately dismissed the idea of an escape attempt.

Later, a small, shabbily clothed soldier brought my breakfast rice ball. It was a bit larger than those we'd been receiving. I thanked the soldier and surprisingly he replied in fair English. "You are welcome." He was polite and friendly. He appeared scared that the Kempei guards would hear us and cautioned me to talk quietly. He was proud of his English and said, "Japanese airplanes big and strong. Shoot down American airplanes." I agreed with him that their airplanes were big and strong. This pleased him. He continued, "American soldiers will lose war." I told him that the war was about over and that the Americans were winning. He said he was sad about this but glad to hear that the war would soon be over.

He said, "I am Christian." This surprised me and I replied, "I am a Christian and the good Lord saved me from death." I asked where he had learned English. He said that all Japanese high school students take two years of English language. His Christian friends often spoke English and sometimes their sermons were in English. He said, "Me low class Japanese, but me very happy."

After our short conversation, he continued with his prison chore of feeding all the prisoners. I didn't hear him make any conversation with other American prisoners. For some reason, he and I struck up a friendship that would last as long as I was in that prison. I had found at least one Japanese who was not out to do me bodily harm.

My new friend did do some good for my prison mates. They had problems. They wore flight coveralls. I didn't. With manacled wrists, I could pull my pants down and perform nature's call easily. They couldn't. Their flight coveralls zipped down the front and were seamless in back. There was no way they could have a bowel movement. They tried to tear a hole in the back of their suits without success. They were in great pain and becoming desperate. They were shouting to me to ask if I could get my new friend to intercede with the Kempei guards in their behalf; to remove the handcuffs so they could use the hole in the corner of their cells. The Kempeis paid no attention to their anguished pleas. When my friend showed up with the next meal, I told him about our problem and asked for his help in communicating with the guards. After he understood the problem, he began laughing. He thought it very funny but agreed to explain the problem to the guards. He succeeded. The Kempeis took off the handcuffs for the short time. For friends in need, he was a friend indeed. But he couldn't talk them into freeing us of these painful handcuffs, or even loosening them. Mine were awfully tight.

I pondered just how I was going to loosen the cuffs since my requests to the Kempei guards had not worked. They obviously did not understand my problem and probably didn't care. Pleading with my new Japanese food friend didn't pay off either. He was as scared of the Kempeis as I was. He had zero influence and must have been the lowest peon in the Japanese Army chain of command. My handcuffs were really hurting. I inspected the cuffs and tried to figure out how I could pick the lock and loosen them. It didn't appear too difficult if I could find something to use as a makeshift key. There was nothing on my person that would work. My metal uniform insignia had been taken away. Trying to solve this problem kept my mind busy and off my predicament.

I finally thought I had found a way to solve my tight handcuff problem. The meticulous, but not thorough, Japanese searchers had never found the 1890 silver dollar hidden in my watch pocket. When night came, and the guards were not watching. I would pry one of the nails holding the mesh screen over the window using the dollar coin. I would bend the nail into a sort of a key shape and work it into the handcuff key-hole and turn the lock mechanism. A great plan, but it didn't work! I worked all night on this problem. When daylight came, I was still stuck with those tight handcuffs.

Day number four passed slowly. Solitary confinement was beginning to get to me. I began to hallucinate about whether I'd done the right thing to bail out of the B-29. Was it really our airplane that I saw crash or some other B-29? Maybe our airplane had not burned and crashed and the other eight on our crew had flown back to Tinian leaving Andrews and me behind in Japan. To keep my mind away from such bad thoughts, I began reciting the Lord's Prayer, the 23d Psalm, and Bible verses I had learned in Sunday School. My faith meant everything at a time like this. It kept me sane and gave me hope.

I tried working mathematical problems in my head. My mind ranged through my college work. I reviewed my courses in great detail. I reviewed my life — What I'd done right, what I'd done wrong, and what I would do over a better way.

I thought about food constantly. I was always hungry, even though my little Japanese friend was doing all he could to help with his three rice balls a day.

At the end of our prison day, the guards shouted "*Shoto,*" meaning it was sleep time. This apparently occurred about nine at night. At around five in the morning, we were awakened to "*Sho.*" If we were slow sitting or standing up, the guards become agitated and shouted guttural threats and poked their bayoneted rifles through the bars. I closely observed the many Kempei guards who came and went. They all wore wrist watches. I compared this with American soldiers who didn't all wear watches. The soldiers had red collar tabs which displayed their rank. The lowest private had one yellow stripe on a red background. The next rank up had a star on the stripe and the higher the rank the more stars until another yellow stripe was added and so on up the rank scale. Most of our guards were one and two star privates. They were low ranking troops. There was definitely a caste system among the Japanese Army ranks. The upper ranks yelled at the lower ranks and it passed all the way down the chain of command.

The Sunday following our shootdown was 1 April 1945. It was the fifth day of my captivity. I didn't realize what the significance of this day was until my small friend delivered *onigre* rice balls and whispered to me, "Today is Christian Day!" I asked what he meant by this statement. He said this was the day that Christ rose from the grave. *It was Easter!*

He leaned close to the bars and told me he was going to bring me a surprise for lunch. I wondered what he could possibly do for me. At lunch time, he brought the usual *onigres* for the other American prisoners. For me, he brought an aluminum bowl of the most delicious stew I had ever eaten. It had many types of vegetables. Japanese civilians had not seen beef for months. My treat had large chunks of tasty beef floating in the gourmet preparation. I couldn't believe my good fortune. He put his finger to his lips and said. "Secret, no tell guards." This was the first, the only, and the last good meal I had in Japan.

The last time I saw my little Japanese friend he told me that he liked me very much and that he hoped that my captivity in Japan would be over soon and that I would survive the war. I thanked him for his understanding and help. He said the word I should use is "*arigato*" which is "thank you" in Japanese.

I wish I knew where this Good Samaritan is today. I'd like to repay him in some way. He was a true Christian! There were bound to be some good people in Japan during the war. He was the only one I saw. All we saw were uncivilized goons and sadists!

The sixth and seventh days of my imprisonment passed very slowly. I stood up much of the day to relieve pressure on my buttocks. I had trouble standing due to the wound in my left ankle. It still had a large piece of flak in it. I hobbled around the cell to exercise my body. My bandages were becoming filthy. I was afraid that my wounds would become infected. I asked for medical treatment and was told that Americans who killed innocent women and children neither deserved nor received medical treatment.

My hair, pants, shirt, and underwear were caked with dried blood. I found that by wrinkling the cloth, the caked blood scaled off. My clothes looked a lot better after I spent hours giving them this treatment.

Across the road, outside my window, I could see a second floor military office with people at work. I heard telephones ringing and they answered with, *"Mushee, mushee."* From the amount of telephone traffic, this must have been a major Japanese military center. Occasionally, during the lunch hour, classical music could be heard coming from the office. I looked forward to the middle of the day and the beautiful music.

Telephone and electric lines ran outside my window. I watched birds perched on the wires and heard their chirping. I watched them fly freely away. The thought of such freedom really got to me.

Several times during the day I heard noises of airplanes flying overhead. Most sounded like single-engine types. The Japanese must have been getting ready for our upcoming invasion. We were never interrogated while imprisoned at this location.

Very early on the morning of the eighth day of captivity, we were awakened earlier than usual by many Kempei guards. One at a time they were opening cell doors and shouting for American prisoners to leave their cells. There was one guard per prisoner. We were blindfolded, ropes put around our necks, and led outside to waiting trucks. We were loaded onto the trucks with less than the usual brutality. The trucks were crowded with thirteen American prisoners and thirteen guards plus their commander. Our Kempei guards appeared super-groomed. They appeared to be dressed for an important occasion. They even seemed to be in a good mood.

Dawn broke as our truck drove through the city, which must have been Kokura. The trucks pulled to a stop in front of a large railway station. I heard sounds of trains and also heard sounds of boat whistles and foghorns. This bothered me. I hoped that we wouldn't be loaded on a boat and be subjected to the deadly mines that we'd laid or be sent to China. Our navy was subjecting the country to frequent raids all along the coastal areas. Boats and trains were very vulnerable to air attack.

There was a mob of people scattered up and down the street outside the station entrance. The crowd backed away from the dreaded Kempeis. They had no trouble clearing a way for us into the railway station. We were led through the station to the tracks. A long train with many fully loaded passenger cars was waiting to move out.

The Kempei commander shouted an order. About six Kempeis left our group with their rifles at the ready. They approached the passenger car directly in front of us and split into two groups. Half went into each end of the overloaded car.

What happened next is unbelievable!

The car that our Kempei chief selected was packed so full of passengers that they jammed the aisles and hung out the windows. The two Kempei groups entered the car wielding their bayonets and threatening the passengers. The passengers were panic-stricken. They literally flew out of the car in every direction, some through windows, others crawling over fellow passengers to exit by the doors.

When the last passenger cleared the now empty car, guards motioned for our small group to enter the train. We found the large passenger car completely empty. In place of 200 or so passengers, our group of 13 prisoners and 14 Kempeis took over the entire car. There were plenty of seats. The Kempei Tais are a potent force and a law unto themselves.

Two people sat in each section — a prisoner and his guard. The Kempei train commander apparently was a friend of my guard. He sat in our seat section. He was a senior non-commissioned officer.

Shortly after we settled into the car, the train lurched and roughly started moving. I've traveled on a lot of American trains, but have never experienced such a rough start. The train engineer must have attended the same school as the Japanese buglers.

We were off to somewhere on a train. Where were we going? Would our situation improve or worsen? I tried to figure out if we were going south or north. I hoped north! The invasion of the Japanese mainland would begin in the south.

Chapter 7

The Train Ride

An agitated crowd of Japanese civilians surrounded our rail car. They had been the passengers until a few minutes before. They were now looking into the windows, shouting, and shaking their fists at 13 Americans and 14 Kempei Tai guards who now occupied their train car. Our guards grinned and appeared unperturbed by the commotion outside. Window shades were closed to shut out the threatening scene outside.

Prisoners had been in solitary confinement since capture. Although we were together on the train car, we could not talk to each other. Each prisoner and his guard occupied seat sections along the car's length. Guards held a tight rein on neck ropes of their prisoners. We remained blindfolded and handcuffed.

The early April weather was cold. The train was not heated. Kempei soldiers were comfortably clothed in wool winter uniforms. A few prisoners had cloth flying jackets. Most were clothed in thin flight coveralls. Guards were aware that the prisoners were shaking from the cold. I was puzzled that we had not been beaten during our trip to the train. This was curious behavior for Kempei

Tai troops. Sadistic behavior was their trademark. I had observed this in their efficient removal of civilians from our train.

It was still dark as the train pulled out of the station. With the blinds closed, there was no way of knowing which direction we were moving. We were leaving a large Japanese city which I figured was Kokura. We were somewhere on the extreme northern shore of Kyushu. Since Kokura was a large city located beside the Shimonoseki Straits, it must have shipping docks. Fog horns and boat whistles indicated that the city's train station was close to a waterway.

If the train moved onto a ferry or crossed a long bridge, I figured that we would be heading across the waterway. We would be heading north. If the train stayed on land, we would be traveling south.

I hoped that we would head away from the planned invasion of Kyushu. Being near that battle could be fatal.

The train did not load onto a ferry. It did not cross a long bridge. My heart sank. We must be headed south.

After leaving the station, guards raised the blinds. My loosely tied blindfold allowed observation of my surroundings fairly well. The sun was rising on the train's right side. We were headed *north*.

How did this happen? There must have been a tunnel under the Shimonoseki Straits. The train jerked and bounced its way along the rough road bed. The train's engine was steam-driven. It emitted a constant stream of smoky cinders which blew past the closed windows. I could smell coal smoke and the ever-present, putrid odor of human fertilizer.

Out of the righthand window I could see a coastline with large waves indicating an ocean. If we were heading north as my observations seemed to show, I was still puzzled how we crossed the Shimonoseki Straits.

The train made many stops at small villages where passengers and freight were discharged and picked up. Passengers were small, shabbily dressed people. They appeared to be Japanese peasants similar to the ones who almost murdered me. None looked to be middle or upper class citizens. Maybe, due to ravages of war, all classes looked alike.

Our guards were exceptionally well-dressed and appeared to be in an unusually good mood. They enjoyed the scenery and shouted back and forth to each other as we traveled. They were a happy bunch and were enjoying their outing. Our train environment was much better than cell life. None of the prisoners were abused during the entire trip. As I think back about this trip, I am greatly surprised by this humane treatment. Brutal Kempei guards enjoyed seeing human misery.

I tried to talk to my guard and the commander during the trip. Neither appeared to understand English. They did not want to talk to me. Their aloofness may have been a Kempei Tai directive. I asked several times where we were going. I received no answers.

After a few hours, I made motions to my guard and mumbled the word, *"benjo."* I needed to visit the train's toilet. He grinned at my Japanese language fluency and led me to the rear of the car where a conventional train restroom was located. He held onto my restraining rope through the open door. Never during the entire train ride was I farther than a rope's length from my guard. I was an animal on a leash and felt like one.

During my passage down the train's aisle to the toilet, I observed my fellow prisoners. Each, with his guard, had facing seats. They appeared dejected and dirty. I could see that their morale, like mine, was rock bottom. We'd been captives for over a week. We'd suffered severe beatings and existed on little food. I counted twelve prisoners. They were all strangers, except Andrews. His face was bruised and puffy, probably caused by Kempei rifle butt blows, otherwise he appeared in pretty good shape. He wore the long Japanese army coat given him during our first night of captivity.

During a stop around noon, a guard detachment left the train and procured small lunches which were neatly packaged and artistically arranged in a small wooden, compartmented tray. I was surprised and pleased that the prisoners were to be fed something besides a rice ball. My guard gave me a set of bamboo chopsticks to use. Both he and the train commander had a good laugh as I tried to use these sticks with my handcuffed hands. My Kempei companions wolfed down their food as if they were starved. Their eating manners were atrocious. They made a lot of noise as they gulped down their food. Lunch consisted of rice, fish, edible pickles (not *dykon*), and a dessert sweet. I ate my gourmet meal slowly and savored every small bite. Everything in the small wooden tray was tasty. It was my second most delicious meal in Japan. *No meal* would ever top that Easter stew given me by my little Japanese Christian food soldier.

The scenery we passed by was beautiful. Japan is a picturesque country. Even under the stress of captivity, I couldn't help but enjoy the lovely countryside. Though my view was limited by my blindfold, I still enjoyed what I could see. The land through which we traveled was mostly agricultural. Small farms could be seen on both sides of the train. Japanese used every square inch of land for farming. The plantings extended almost to the train tracks. New leaves were beginning to show on trees. I could see mountains on our inland side. We often skirted the sea shore on the train's other side.

Our train traveled throughout the first day in bright daylight. I was concerned about movement during daylight hours. American naval units prowled offshore and continually raided up and down the Japanese mainland. Navy fighters could easily spot our train. They were skilled at destroying Japanese trains. My brother flew a P-51 fighter in the European theater. Hunting and shooting up Nazi trains was a fine-tuned practice over there. It was called "train bustin'."

Our train offered a perfect target for a bomb or strafing attack. I wondered why the train didn't seek shelter during the day in one of the many tunnels we passed through along the rugged and mountainous coast. Why did the train travel during daylight? Why not travel only during the night?

Where were our navy's attacking aircraft that constantly ravaged the Japanese countryside? Heavy fighting was in progress just 350 miles south of Kyushu. The invasion of Okinawa was in full swing. Marine and army troops landed there on Easter Sunday, 1 April 1945. Japanese kamikaze planes were taking a terrible toll of our ships around Okinawa. US Navy battle fleets were prowling southern Kyushu coasts trying to knock out kamikaze airfields where these deadly weapons were based. Our train was far to the north of this activity. I should not have been concerned.

Darkness finally came after our second day of slowly traveling northward. The train never picked up speed. There were many stops, mostly at small villages. The train ride continued all night as the train chugged and jerked along. Prisoners and guards slept very little during the night.

I hoped that we were *not* being taken to China. I preferred to be on Honshu Island to be liberated shortly after the Kyushu invasion. I figured that the Japanese would surrender shortly after that invasion.

I didn't know about the Japanese Imperial General Headquarters' order to execute all prisoners the moment an invasion started!

During our third day of travel, we were given small rice balls at mealtimes. My guard shared his canteen of water with me. He also let me drink his leftover tea. He did not share his mealtime ration of muffins, fish, beans, and candy. He made so much noise during his meals that it made me hungrier just listening to him. He slurped his food while eating like a hungry animal. This must have been a Japanese national characteristic. Slurping sounds must have indicated the food's excellence and the eater's enjoyment.

Usually, guards lowered the blinds while we were stopped in a station. Occasionally they forgot. When the shades were left open, I observed the crowds acting as if they wanted to board the train and attack us. With only 14 guards, I worried that they could overpower the guards and do us harm. We were protected by their great fear of the Kempei Tai Military Police.

I tried to understand the rage of these people. I was sure that the terrible B-29 fire raids had in some way affected almost everyone in the Empire. The raids killed and wounded hundreds of thousands of people and destroyed millions of homes. Japanese civilians must have been very unhappy about continual bombings. These little peasants must have had no idea what this war was all about, much less which side fired the first shot, or why their homeland was being attacked.

The train passed through several large coastal towns and major train marshaling yards. All appeared to have suffered heavy damage. Cities were mostly destroyed. Homes were burned to the ground. Factory buildings were charred hulks. Our travel continued through the third day and on into the night.

Finally, we traveled through an enormous burned-out city and pulled into a giant train station which was similar in size to New York's Grand Central Station.

Our guards started talking excitedly about an hour before this stop. This trip must have been a big deal for them. The train commander was obviously pleased that we had arrived at our destination and that there had been no trouble during the trip.

Our long ride through a hostile country had been uneventful.

We hadn't been attacked by our own forces. This was good and bad — good that we survived the trip, bad that our forces had allowed a Japanese train to safely move several hundred miles in broad daylight. We observed no knocked out bridges. If Japan was to be brought to the surrender table, more damage must be inflicted.

Kempeis waited until the entire train was cleared of passengers before unloading us. People in the main lobby were belligerent and threatening. Kempeis surrounded us and conducted us through a very crowded main concourse. I wanted no more attention from the bitter Japanese citizens.

We were herded into a large room which adjoined the lobby. The room had been completely cleared of people. We were made to stand at attention for what must have been more than two hours. Finally, two trucks pulled up to a side entrance and we were loaded onto the trucks without any blows from the guards.

For some reason, our Kempei guards were behaving humanely. They barked rough and guttural commands but there were no rifle butt blows. Why the change?

We traveled through the large city. Where were we? What city was this? It was a very big city that had received great bomb damage. Even though it was night, I observed total desolation. Burned-out buildings and acres of ashes were evident as we drove down rubble-strewn streets. The city had been burned to the ground. It was a terrible sight. Thousands of people must have burned to death. The scene was awful!

Could this be Tokyo? If this city was Tokyo, I had been here before. I participated during the 9 March fire raid which destroyed one-third of Tokyo. We'd been told that almost 100,000 people were killed. I wondered what surviving citizens would do to me if they knew I had taken part in that raid on their capital.

Our train journey had taken three days and two nights. We must have traveled at least 500 to 600 miles. We passed under the Shimonoseki Straits and traveled north along Honshu's east coast. We'd seen some rugged country.

Our destination had to be Tokyo, the seat of Japanese government. It was the home of Emperor Hirohito. It was here that the infamous Japanese raid on Pearl Harbor was ordered. I had arrived in the center of the *Number One* target of all the Pacific Theater Allied forces.

Chapter 8

Tokyo Reception

During our tenth day of captivity, which was 6 April 1945, 13 survivors of the Shimonoseki Straits mission arrived in Tokyo. We had been brought all the way from southern Japan by rail. Why were we brought to Tokyo, a distance of over 500 miles? There must be a good reason for this. Our two trucks left the train station and rumbled through the destroyed city. Around my loose blindfold I saw terrible destruction on every side. I was partly responsible for this destruction. My 504th Bomb Group bombed Tokyo. My crew flew on three bombing missions to this city. Were we brought here to allow the local people to exact revenge?

After leaving the train station, the two trucks bounced over rough downtown Tokyo streets. The Kempei guards were unusually jolly and seemed unaware of the desolation. It was still night when the trucks stopped in front of a darkened building that looked like a small hotel. Half the guards from each truck gathered in front of the building, huddled for a minute, and then directed the other guards to remain with the trucks. The dismounted group then entered the structure. I wondered what this was all about. The night air was pretty cold. Our guards were sniffling and coughing. Prisoners were shivering, worried, and tired.

After we waited about an hour, smiling, giggling, and half-drunk Kempeis staggered out from the building. They excitedly greeted their comrades who had been guarding us. A lot of jabbering and back-slapping took place. Something great must have happened inside the building. Whatever it was appeared good for Kempei morale as well as our well being. We prisoners were almost ignored as we sat on the truck beds, manacled and blindfolded.

Happy guards took over guarding the prisoners. The second shift of guards entered the building. We waited another long and cold hour. The guards with us were in high spirits! Their visit to the building must have been something. The second shift group finally emerged. They were tipsy, making obscene gestures, and excitedly talking amongst themselves. It appeared as if they'd won a major battle. What was this all about?

It did not take me long to figure out what had just happened. Japanese soldiers were furnished prostitutes as part of their fringe benefits. The small building must have been one of the army comfort-houses staffed with women, kidnapped by the Japanese, to serve their military. Our guards had been entertained in a whorehouse, perhaps a fringe benefit for escorting us to Tokyo. This event may have been the cause for their happy mood and lenient treatment of prisoners during our journey to Tokyo.

Now that prisoners and guards were united again, the trucks wheezed their way another half-mile or so through deserted Tokyo streets. About four in the morning our truck drove by a modern five-story office building. The building fronted on a major Tokyo street across from the Emperor's Palace moat. The building didn't appear to have suffered any bomb damage. The truck pulled to the rear of the building and stopped in a courtyard. Prisoners were unloaded with much hilarity by our happy guards. We were made to stand at attention.

We had arrived at Kempei Tai Headquarters. New Kempei guards surrounded our group. Our former guards were dismissed and melted away. Even they seemed afraid of the new rough looking Kempei guards. Our Kempei train commander began negotiations with an agitated, shouting Kempei Tai officer who emerged from the building accompanied by a short, cruel looking civilian who wore a black suit and black-framed eyeglasses. The civilian spoke excellent English, had grown up in California, and attended Ohio University.

The civilian screamed at us, "Stand at attention like Japanese soldiers." He rocked back on his heels and harangued us about Japan's war successes and told us that we had arrived at the headquarters of the Imperial Japanese Army's Kempei Tai Secret Police. We would be made to pay for our criminal atrocities against Japanese civilians. We were kept standing at rigid attention for over two hours while negotiations and paper signing took place between the booted civilian and our train commander. This pompous, self-important, haughty little bastard's name was Yasuo Kobayashi. He was about five feet tall. We nicknamed him "Shorty."

Shorty was in charge of American prisoners and their interrogations at Kempei Tai Headquarters. He was our "master," as we would find out the hard way. He would be in complete charge of our lives. We were to become well acquainted with this cruel, vicious, sadistic, inhuman, murderous little bastard. Shorty was the embodiment of Japanese cruelty and atrocities. He was directly responsible for all our suffering. He decided who was to live, who was to be tortured, and who was to die. He caused many prisoner deaths and enjoyed the continuous agony suffered by the rest of us. He thrived on our misery. I could not then, nor can I now, imagine why anyone so vile should be allowed to live on this earth.

The Tokyo night air was cold. Standing at rigid attention made my wounds hurt all over. I hadn't slept well in days. I was thirsty and hungry. I was shivering from the cold. I felt miserable. Shorty stood in front of our group and shouted that we were animals and would be treated like animals. We were war criminals and deserved to die. Japanese soldiers did not surrender. We were cowards.

The Kempei train commander finished his paperwork with the arrogant Tokyo officer, took his troops, and left in the truck. There didn't seem to be any love lost between Tokyo Kempei troops and those who brought us.

We were led into the building, as Shorty called our names. He delighted in abusing each prisoner before a guard dragged us off. I was one of the first taken into the headquarters. When my turn came, two names were called out, "Hanks and Hanley." Maynor Hanks was from Sweetwater, Texas. Our names were often confused during our stay with the Kempei Tai. Once inside the building, Hanks and I were separated and led to separate rooms.

I was dragged to a small room in the basement of the building. My blindfold was removed and I was seated in a chair in front of a desk. Seated across the desk was a sharp looking young soldier. He became known to us as "Junior" during our interrogations because he looked so young. He spoke excellent English. He told me that he had gone to school in Los Angeles before the war. He directed my guard to remove the identification tag sewn on my shirt in Kokura. He took the tag and transferred data from it onto a new tag which was sewn over my bloody shirt's right pocket.

My chair was hard and painful. I tried to get comfortable by squirming around. Junior noticed my problem and asked about my wounds. He told me that I would receive no medical attention at this headquarters. It was against orders. One of the mean looking guards gave me a menacing look and drew his finger across his throat. Junior asked me if I knew what the guard meant. I feigned ignorance. He told me to disregard the guard.

During my welcome session with Junior I learned what a "*kendo*" club was. Shorty stuck his head in the door, barked some orders to Kempei guards standing on either side of me, then closed the door and left. A guard used a bamboo bat to deliver several blows across the back of my head and shoulders. This was my introduction to the Japanese fencing sport of *kendo*. His torture tool was a *kendo* bat. Its blows were vicious and painful.

Junior asked me the usual questions about my personal life. By now, I had become familiar with these standard Kempei questions. He carefully noted my answers and became more interested in my wounds.

Shorty came back into the room, looked me over carefully, and said, "You are an accused war criminal subject to a war crime trial and execution. Because you killed innocent women and children, you are designated a *Special Prisoner* by Imperial Japanese Military Headquarters. *Special Prisoners* are not prisoners of war. They are not covered by Geneva POW Rules. *Special Prisoners* are covered by Kempei Tai rules and receive special treatment and punishment which is worse than regular POWs receive. *Special Prisoners* receive no medical treatment. You may die of your wounds. You will be imprisoned in the dungeon of Kempei Tai Headquarters until you die or a court-martial sentences you to be executed. Do you understand?"

He proudly announced, "This building is where two American criminals of Jimmy Doolittle's B-25 raiders were executed. They were killed right here in this basement." I sat there stunned. It was almost too much to take in all in one dose. My fatigue and my pain shielded me from the complete realization of what he was telling me. I didn't understand this *Special Prisoner* war criminal designation, but would come to thoroughly learn its dire meaning.

Shorty left and Junior continued his interrogation. He was interested in the 398th Bomb Squadron logo on Andrews' flight jacket that I was wearing. He remarked that he had never seen an emblem like this one before. He asked me if I could guess his age. He appeared quite young so I guessed that he was about 18 years old. He said most Americans misguessed his age. He told me that his age was 24. He asked if I knew what his Japanese army rank might be. He had tabs on his collar with one stripe and one star. I guessed that he was a sergeant. He said that I was wrong. He was a private first class.

I asked if there were other Americans in this prison. He answered that there had been a few American B-29 crewmen captives, but they were transferred to a prison camp. Prisoners brought in tonight were the only Americans presently held here.

Disregarding what both Shorty and Junior had already told me, I asked for medical care for my injuries since my bandages were bloody and dirty. He repeated that I could expect none at all. Kempei rules did not allow it. I asked about blankets for keeping warm. He said we would have plenty of blankets. He even offered me some tea in a small cup and warned about possible aftereffects, because Japanese tea sometimes gave prisoners severe diarrhea. I declined the tea offer. Getting a case of diarrhea was a death sentence. Prisoners with detected diarrhea received no food and were allowed to starve to death. Junior confirmed that I was in Tokyo. I asked about the prison's location. He told me that Kempei Headquarters was located close to the Emperor's Palace. It was in the center of Tokyo.

Shorty re-entered the room and barked an order. A guard hit my shoulders and head with a bamboo club. The other guard hit me repeatedly with his rifle butt, directing most of the blows at my head. I wondered what I'd done to deserve this treatment. I learned the hard way that *kendo* beatings were routine during Japanese interrogations. *Kendo* blows were painful but not lethal. Kempeis didn't need a reason for beating prisoners. They did it for enjoyment. Shorty shouted at me "Americans are inferior people. You are barbarians and are sub-humans. You are animals. You killed innocent women and children. You are not a prisoner of war. You are a Special Prisoner and will be held, tried, and executed for your war crimes . . . if you live that long." He was in such a rage that he was shaking. He continued, "You are badly wounded and will not survive. You will receive no medical treatment here. Your death is assured." It was a great satisfaction to me that, one day at a time, I was to prove him wrong. He stood and watched as I was beaten, smiled, and stomped out of the room. He was the animal, not me. He was a mad dog!

Junior continued his questioning. When he found out that I'd flown a mission over Tokyo on 26 February, he told me that the Japanese couldn't understand how we bombed Tokyo that day because a snowstorm was raging at the time. He told me that bombs dropped through the storm and hit Tokyo. I told him that we had excellent bombardiers. He didn't ask about radar and I didn't tell him that this was the bombing raid when Brown had accidentally led the bombing formation. I let him be amazed at our bombing prowess.

The fact that he confirmed that our formation hit the target that day pleased me!

He asked about my family and said that after the war he'd like to visit the United States and get better acquainted with me. Maybe he could date my sister. I told him. "Sure, sure, just come on over," and thought to myself, *And bring Shorty along. I would love to get the two of you on my turf and reciprocate the treatment.*

Shorty re-entered the room with a paper in Japanese script and directed me to sign the document. He said, "If you don't sign the paper, you won't live through the night." I asked what the document said and was told that it contained my confession of war crimes. It stated that we were ordered by our government to bomb innocent women and children. I refused to sign the paper. Shorty ordered the guards to continue beating me. They hammered at me with bat and rifle butt. Shorty gave me several kicks. My wounds and head were bleeding profusely. Even though it appeared that I wouldn't survive the beating, I refused to sign the document. I didn't sign it, and I *did* live through the night.

Shorty was wrong again. I knew that Japan would be invaded in not too many more months. Somehow, I had to survive until then. I *would* survive and I *would* be liberated.

Shorty ordered that I be dragged into a basement guard room where I was thoroughly searched. They did not find my 1890 silver dollar hidden in my watch pocket.

Before I was dragged from the guard room, my handcuffs were removed for the first time in eleven days. The cuffs had practically grown onto my wrists. Fortunately, my wrist lacerations had scabbed over and seemed to be healing. One of the guards took a wrist restraint device and wrapped it around my wrists. The restraint consisted of a two-foot length of silk cord with wooden handles on each end. My hands were moved behind my back and this device was wrapped around my wrists and the handles were twisted together. It was a very effective restraint device. (Recently I read in *The New York Times* about a discovery that our police authorities had made. It was an effective device for quickly restraining unruly prisoners. The article went on to describe the exact restraint that the Kempeis used. It took our own police over forty years to come up with this efficient Japanese security device.)

Due to the beating session, I was unable to stand or walk. I was dragged from the guard room like a sack of garbage. I passed Hanks and his guard in the hall. The look of horror on his face when he saw my bloody and battered condition told me much about my appearance.

I was dragged to a foul-smelling dungeon cell. I was shoved into the cell. My shoes were removed and placed on the concrete floor outside the cell. Guards jabbed me with their bayonets when I attempted to lie down. They propped me against the wall. The cell door slammed shut and I heard a key turn in the lock. This was the dungeon where I would spend most of my imprisonment while at Kempei Tai Headquarters.

Chapter 9

Kempei Tai Imprisonment

APRIL 1945

It was very early on 6 April 1945. I was a captive in a small, foul smelling dungeon cell in Tokyo. After my head cleared from the beating I had received the night before and my eyes became adjusted to the cell's dim light, I examined my surroundings. I saw, sitting on the wooden floor against the opposite wall, a Japanese soldier. All of his insignia had been removed from his uniform. Junior had told me that, due to prison crowding, I would be sharing my cell with a Japanese prisoner. Who was he? What was his crime? He was looking at me with hate-filled eyes, obviously resenting my intrusion.

The Kempei dungeon held six small, wooden cells — two rows of three cells separated by an aisle. The aisle was divided lengthwise by a heavy curtain to prevent prisoners observing inmates in facing cells. A narrow walkway ran completely around the cell block so that the guards had access to the backs of the cells.

Each cell was about five feet by nine feet. Three of the walls were wooden with no fasteners showing. The carpentry was excellent. The fourth wall, facing the center aisle, had stout, wooden bars, a small door, and an open slot at floor level where food could be passed through. The cell door had a heavy lock which reminded me of locks I'd seen in movies about medieval dungeons.

The cell's wooden floor was about two feet above the concrete basement floor. A low wooden fence surrounded the latrine hole located in the cell's back corner. Human waste was saved and used as fertilizer. Toilet buckets, called *benjos*, were located under each hole between the concrete and wooden floors. These buckets were emptied daily by an American prisoner.

One or two well-worn, filthy, pest-ridden blankets lay on the floor. A small, dim, drop light illuminated each cell 24 hours a day. The basement became totally dark when power failures occurred during frequent air raids.

Kempei guards armed with bayoneted rifles constantly patrolled the dungeon area. One of their jobs was to assure that prisoners did not talk to each other. Immediate and dire consequences resulted to prisoners discovered breaking this firm Kempei rule.

This day I sat barefoot across from my cellmate. My socks had been confiscated along with my belt and military insignia. Anything which could be used to commit suicide had been taken away. All I had left were my bloody shorts, shirt, pants, flight jacket, and empty survival vest. And . . . my 1890 silver dollar good luck coin. It became a symbol of my hope for survival.

Many questions ran through my mind. What was a Special Prisoner? Why had I been brought to Tokyo, which was a long way from the Shimonoseki Strait area where I'd been shot down? Who were the Kempei Tais? Why were they my captors? What kind of place was this? Why had I been threatened with execution? Why was I sharing a cell with a Japanese? Why had I been beaten during the reception interrogation for no reason, other than that I had fought for my country after it had been attacked?

Shortly after arriving in the cell, a shabbily dressed soldier threw two tangerine-size rice balls onto the cell's dirty floor. My cellmate grabbed the larger of the two; I picked up the other. We wolfed down this small breakfast.

Even though conversation was prohibited, when the guard was out of earshot, I tried to talk with my cellmate. He glared at me. He wanted nothing to do with me. He ignored me. I pointed to my collar and then to his collar to try to find out his rank. The quality of his uniform indicated that he must be or had been a high level officer. All his symbols of rank were missing

About mid-morning the Japanese prisoner was removed from the cell. Even though the guards treated him with a certain respect, it was obvious that he was in deep trouble. He must have been in big trouble to be a ward of the Kempeis. When he was returned, about mid-afternoon, he appeared very worried and very dejected.

While alone in the cell, I received another small rice ball for the noon meal. I consumed the small ration in about two bites and was as hungry after I had finished as I was before I ate. I hadn't had a drink of water in two days. After several requests for water, I received a small cup of water dipped from a dirty bucket. All prisoners received their water from the same cup and bucket.

When the rice balls were thrown on the floor for our evening meal, the Japanese soldier jumped to his feet and, with fists clinched, dared me to reach for one before he had made his choice. He snatched the larger one and glared at me while he ate. We stood there sizing each other up as we devoured the small rations.

About two hours later the guards shouted, "*Shoto.*" The soldier motioned to me that it was time to bed down on the hard floor. We divided the dirty and well-used army blankets between us. I placed the threadbare cover over me and lay down on one side of the five-foot-wide cell. I pulled the blanket over my head and tried to get more comfortable in the confined quarters. The blanket was thin and the cell was cold and damp. I was shivering. The thought of spending a night in the same cell with this unfriendly enemy soldier was an uncomfortable one.

The guard peered through the bars at our supine bodies and started shouting and pointing his bayoneted rifle at me through the bars. I didn't know what he was yelling about. My cellmate made motions that I was not to cover my head with the blanket. I found that this strictly enforced Kempei rule was apparently aimed at preventing suicide attempts.

I slept fitfully through my first night at Kempei Tai Headquarters. My wounds hurt whenever I moved or turned. Even the slight pressure of the thin blanket hurt. The hard wooden floor really hurt. I was afraid of my cellmate and I worried about what he might do to me while I slept. My worries were unwarranted. I made it through the night and was awakened at about five in the morning by the guard shouting *"Sho."*

I dragged myself into a sitting position and folded my blanket and sat on it. The guard began shouting and jabbing his bayonet into the cell. He didn't want me sitting on the blanket. My cellmate motioned to me that I was to put the blanket on top of his and stack it in the cell's corner. A few jabs of the guard's bayonet convinced me that I should comply with his order. Sealed off from outside light, we couldn't tell whether it was day or night in the dungeon. I did not see daylight during my entire Kempei Tai Headquarters captivity.

I learned to count my days between *"Sho"* (wake up) and *"Shoto"* (bed down).

Three rice balls a day and sometimes a cup of water made up our complete daily food ration. The menu never varied, except for the size of the rice balls. The size of the balls in the spring started out about the size of tangerines and became golf ball sized toward the end of the summer.

Another constant for each day's activity was my transfer to an interrogator's office for my daily beating. The questions were always the same and usually meaningless: questions about my family, my education, training, thoughts about the progress of the war. Between each question and answer, the guards would beat on me as if I had refused to reveal some very important bit of military information. They never struck me with their fists or hands. They hit us with the *kendo* sport bat and the butt end of their rifles and kicked with their heavy boots. Since my head and legs were bandaged, they aimed for these areas when they had me on the floor. A knee or a kick to the groin "made their day."

If Shorty missed their performance he would have them repeat it for his entertainment when he came in to scream his usual lines, "You are a war criminal, a Special Prisoner. You get no POW treatment. You get no medical treatment. You killed women and children. You won't live to be tried because your wounds are gangrenous. You are going to die." He took my refusal to die as a personal affront.

The nights were miserable. There was no comfortable or even bearable way to lie on my injured hips, backside, or legs. I never knew when the door would be opened and the guards would come in and hit me with their rifle butts. Usually Shorty was with them, perhaps just passing through the cell block, and he would march in, kick me awake with his heavy boots, and order a beating. He left the military prisoner alone. In fact, he seemed to be just a bit in awe of him.

When *shoto* was shouted in the mornings I quickly stumbled to my feet and folded my blanket and carefully placed it against the wall with my cellmate's. Any delay would result in a bayonet poke. We received our first rice balls for the day, then I was taken from the cell for another interrogation and beating. It varied very little from day to day.

Every time I was interrogated, I asked for medical treatment and was always given the same answer. Junior always apologized and said, "It isn't allowed." Shorty screamed and ranted about how I did not deserve medical treatment. I had killed women and children, and on and on and on. Another theme of his was, "Japanese soldiers are never captured; they die fighting. Americans are cowards. Cowards do not deserve medical aid. You deserve to die."

On my fifth day at Kempai Headquarters my cell door was noisily unlocked and my name called out. My name was hard to recognize because of the "L" syllable. Two guards entered. While one handcuffed my hands behind me, and placed a blindfold over my eyes, the other guard aimed his rifle at me. I was roughly dragged out of the cell and directed to put on my shoes. The laces had been removed.

I could barely walk because of the large, open, bloody cut in my left ankle. The guard had to drag me along as he muttered threats. Another guard walked behind us and pushed me along with his bayoneted rifle. At the end of the passage between the cells, we entered an orderly or guard room where I was processed out of the dungeon area by the guard commander who made a chopmark, the equivalent of a signature, on an order.

I had great trouble climbing the steps to the next floor where they took me to an interrogation room. My blindfold was removed but the handcuffs remained in place. The guards positioned themselves on each side of me and by hitting me on the head with a rifle, they forcibly sat me on a hard wooden chair. I faced a Japanese officer, one I had not seen before.

The Japanese officer, speaking excellent English, began asking questions about my family, home, and ideas about the war. His avoidance of military subjects puzzled me. Every now and then, he'd growl an order to the guards who dealt me blows with rifle butts and the bamboo *kendo* bat. I had answered his questions and done nothing to deserve this brutality. By now I knew that this brutality was standard interrogation procedure for all prisoners. If the interrogator suspected a lie, then the prisoner was beaten senseless.

I answered all questions as best I could, there were no questions asked that were of any importance to the war, but this did not make the beatings ease up.

After about three hours of this torturous treatment, I was led back through the orderly room where I was thoroughly searched. The guards missed my good luck coin again.

I was not returned to my former cell but was led to a *different* cell in the dungeon where I was roughly pushed against the wall. As soon as the guards left and locked the cell, I crumbled in a heap on the floor. When I looked up I saw a man sitting on the opposite side of the cell watching me. Unlike my other cellmate, there was no hatred in his eyes. He was Japanese and appeared to be in his 60s. He was dressed in a clean and neatly pressed western style suit and was barefooted like me. He was as surprised to see me as I was to see him.

When the guard was out of hearing, he spoke to me, very softly, and in English. I was greatly surprised at his fluency. He asked if I was all right. His concern was genuine.

His name was Sugai. He was a graduate of the University of Chicago and was an Episcopalian Christian. Before his arrest, he had taught Romance Languages at the University of Tokyo. I asked why he was a prisoner. He said that the Kempeis were permitted to arrest anyone on mere suspicion of anti-government or anti-war thoughts. He did not know exactly what he was charged with but thought that he would be released in a few weeks.

We were fed small rice balls at each mealtime. The professor didn't wolf his food like my previous cellmate. He ate very slowly, making his small ration last almost an hour. He told me that this would make the meal more satisfying and seem more filling and help pass the long, dreary hours. He taught me to savor each grain of rice.

When the guard shouted *shoto*, Professor Sugai showed me how to prepare a more efficient bed out of the two filthy blankets on my side of the cell. Before we lay down on the hard floor, the professor looked at me and said that he was going to say a prayer and asked if I would join him. Together, we silently offered our prayers to God, each in our own way. I cannot adequately describe the secure feeling that faith offers.

The professor and I slept through the long night. I was not worried about being in the same cell with him. His presence gave me a feeling of security in that small cage. I felt the most peace I had felt since Tinian and slept less fitfully.

The guard shouted *"sho"* the next morning. We stumbled up, folded our blankets, stacked them in the corner, and waited for our rice balls. As we sat there, the professor and I quietly conversed when the guard was out of sight. Professor Sugai asked if he could examine my wounds. He peered under the dirty bandages and uttered many *"Ohs"* and *"Ahs."* I asked him what he meant by his sighs. He didn't reply, just apologized for his government's lack of concern for my condition.

He went to the bars, called to the guard, and began arguing with him. The guard called for his superior, then the three of them talked, shouted, and pointed my way. Obviously, I was the topic of conversation. The Japanese word that I kept hearing was *"tinkee,"* which I later learned meant "badly wounded."

Finally, Professor Sugai told me that he had not obtained medical help for me; he said he had tried but failed. I thanked him for his effort. The Kempeis would not provide medical treatment, but he had convinced them that due to my foul smelling wounds, I could use one of the blankets over my lower body during the daytime so as to cover the offensive odor of my dirty and blood-saturated bandages. The foul smell apparently troubled Professor Sugai.

I don't think he made any personal points with the guards while going to bat for me. He secured some sort of special operating orders regarding me. After his intervention, I could lie down during the day and could use a blanket to confine the offensive odors coming from my wounds. To my knowledge, no other prisoners were ever given this privilege, even though many of them died in their cells from their injuries.

Shorty Kobayashi came into our cell the next morning and looked me over. After kicking me a couple of times, he shouted that I was a war criminal, an American coward, and I should not have been taken prisoner. He repeated his favorite harangue: "Japanese soldiers die in battle. They do not surrender. You are a disgrace to your country." He lifted the blanket and looked over my lower body with his nose crinkled, then rapidly threw the cover down. He shouted, "You have gangrene and will die. You deserve to die. You have killed innocent women and children." He ignored my Japanese cellmate.

I was lucky to be in the same cell with Professor Sugai early in my imprisonment. After the war I tried to locate him, with no success.

He made my prison life more endurable by his heated discussion with the guards. After I was allowed to sit during the day, I worked to find the least painful position. I finally found that I couldn't sit with my back against the wall but had to semi-lie down with only my head braced against the wall, which lessened the pressure on my buttocks. I spent the entire remainder of my daytime Kempei imprisonment in this wretched position.

Each new guard that came on duty gave me a bad time when they saw me lying against the wall, covered with the blanket. The professor would point to me and yell back, *"Tinkee, tinkee."* The guard would call for his superior and after a heated discussion, they would both glare at me, then leave me alone.

In a few days Shorty stopped by to give me his usual kick and *kendo* beating. Before he left the cell, he looked triumphantly at me and announced, *"Japan has won the war!"* He said that my president, the criminal Roosevelt, died on 13 April, and now that he was gone the new president, Harry Truman, would sue for peace. He kicked me again, turned on his heels, and strutted out the door.

I was stunned by this news. I knew that President Roosevelt's health was not good. For him to die at this stage of the war seemed a disaster. Shorty was a liar and would do and say anything to torture us and shouldn't be believed — but this time my gut feeling was that he was telling the truth about Roosevelt's death.

The next day I wasn't taken out for interrogation. Professor Sugai and I spent an uneventful day together whispering about the war's events. Professor Sugai was amazingly well-informed on the recent Japanese battle reverses. He questioned me as to what I thought the Americans would do in Japan once we won the war. His questions were such that I wondered if he could be a Japanese plant seeking information from me. His influence to establish my "*tinkee*" status was powerful.

I was taken out of the cell the next day for another interrogation — the usual non-military questions. It appeared that these Kempei "Thought Police" were more interested in personal thoughts and family background than military subjects. The American public's thoughts on the war's progress seemed to highlight his questions. I was glad that our Tinian intelligence briefings allowed us to answer questions beyond the old limit of "Name, rank, and serial number."

I received the usual brutal rifle blows and hits from the bamboo *kendo* club. Guards and interrogators thrived on anguished cries of pain. We were always handcuffed and couldn't fight back and we had to grit our teeth and bear the pain.

As I did at every interrogation, I asked for medical aid and received more blows for my trouble.

During each of my many interrogations, I always asked when I would be sent to a POW prison camp. If I was given any answer at all, it was the memorized and quoted line, " due to prison overcrowding, a shipment will be made in the near future." The Special Prisoners thought about this possibility almost daily and looked forward to being transferred somewhere so we could see the sun, wash up, wear clean clothes, shave, talk with each other, receive Red Cross packages, and write home. A prison with these few necessities of life seemed like Utopia to us in our animal-like environment.

After this interrogation, I was taken back to the cell I shared with Professor Sugai.

That day another Japanese civilian was thrust into the cell with us. He spoke excellent English and said that he was from Brooklyn. He was a dentist by profession. He appeared friendly enough. He and the professor talked together in Japanese, and occasionally looked over at me. When they finished their discussion, the new arrival politely asked if he could inspect my injuries. He was appalled at the dirty bandages and asked if he could remove them and get a better look. Being very wary of the guards, he removed and replaced the bandages, one at a time. He examined each wound and told me that fortunately none appeared to be infected. He thought that the foul odors were from my bloody bandages and dirty, bloody clothes.

I told him about the medics in Kokura. He said that the injection administered by the civilian medics and the powdered medicine applied by the military surgeon seemed to be doing some good. He gave me hope by saying that he thought the wounds appeared to be healing; that blows from the sadistic guards had not done additional damage. I felt a lot better after hearing his diagnosis and thanked him for his concern.

I asked the dentist what his offense was and found out that like the professor, he was a political prisoner guilty of no particular crime. He did not know what he had been arrested for, but thought that he would be released soon. He thought that the Kempeis arrested people off the streets, particularly if they spoke English, in order to impress the population. A Kempei arrest was much like a death threat to an ordinary citizen and to see citizens arrested kept them frightened and in line.

I noticed that my two cellmates spent most of their time picking at their clothing. I asked what they were doing and was told that they were killing the vermin that had infiltrated their clothing. I had felt many bites but had not been able to see anything that could be causing them. I inspected my dirty uniform and found that my clothes were heavily infested with fleas and lice. The bites were those of blood sucking fleas who jumped around and were extremely difficult to catch and kill. The lice crawled around and apparently lived on sloughed off skin particles. Lice were easy to kill, but hard to find, because they hid in the clothing seams. Hunting and killing these creatures became a recreation of sorts. We sat around like a group of monkeys inspecting our clothes, picking at the seams, and grabbing at jumping fleas.

Before our night's sleep, my cellmates and I discussed conditions in Japan. I learned that the civilian life was harsh during this, the fourth year of war with the United States. They told me that there was little food and other necessities of life. The military took almost everything. The air raids, which were increasing in frequency and intensity, were taking a tremendous toll in civilian lives and homes. Both cellmates were very much against the war and hoped for peace as soon as possible. This attitude was probably the cause of their imprisonment.

That night, as the professor and I were saying our prayers, our new cellmate told us that he was a Buddhist, but he respected the

Christian religion. We shared our meager blanket supply and found room on the small floor for the three of us to bed down.

During my several days in the dungeon cell block, I heard American prisoners in other cells asking the guards for water and emitting cries of pain from their wounds or when being beaten. Through a splice in the curtain, I'd gotten a brief look into the opposite cell and observed a red-headed American prisoner there. He was Maynor Hanks, shot down on the same raid as I, and who had entered the building with me when our names were called together.

The following day I was taken to a third floor office where an English-speaking senior Kempei Tai officer asked the questions. This time there was a change in procedure. After ordering that my handcuffs and blindfold be removed, he dismissed the guards. He had me sit in a chair and even asked me if I was comfortable.

I was suspicious of this officer from the beginning. He was different. It took me three interviews with him to figure out why.

He began with the usual lecture: I was an accused war criminal and was subject to trial and execution. He worked around to our bombing innocent women and children. I corrected him that we had bombed military and industrial targets. While describing the terrible damage caused by our fire-bombing, he worked himself into a rage. He was shaking and in quite a frenzy as he told me about our war crimes. I was glad that there were no guards present that he could order to hit me. I was sure that with his angry attitude, he would have joined the guards in the beating. After a while he regained his composure.

He asked me if I'd ever heard of a "War Court." I shook my head "no." He said that after my interrogations were completed, a decision would be made about when my "War Court" trial would take place. I would be transferred to another prison to await my fate, which would be execution, if found guilty.

He warned me that I would have to sign a document admitting my crimes, and that I'd better watch my step or I'd never survive until my trial.

I asked if any B-29 flyers had been tried yet. He told me that since the B-29 operations against the Japanese homeland had started, no trials had taken place. Evidence was being collected for the first trials. He told me that a "War Court" had tried some of the captured Doolittle flyers and three of them had been executed right here in Kempei Tai Headquarters.

He asked about my injuries and how I had received them. I told him that I had repeatedly asked for medical treatment but had received none nor had my wounds been cleaned and dressed since leaving Kokura over two weeks before. Again, I asked him for help. He seemed surprised that there had been no medical care provided here at his headquarters and told me that he would see that they were attended to on my way back to my cell.

Lunch time came, and he enjoyed a full, beautiful Japanese lunch. I was given another small rice ball. He told me that he'd like to share his lunch with me but that it was against orders. American war criminals, by order of Imperial Japanese Headquarters, could receive only half of standard POW rations.

He never once asked a question about the B-29 or any technical question. I was returned to my cell and got no medical attention en route.

The next day I was again taken to see that same officer. He dismissed the guards and we spent five hours going over the same questions about family and my thoughts on the war. This time, he never got mad nor raised his voice. In fact, he became friendly and told me that he had traveled extensively in the United States before the war. He liked our country and really missed eating our good ice cream. His peaches and cream approach made me wary.

The big drive behind his lengthy questioning was the American public's attitude toward the war.

I told him that I didn't know what the American public thought about the war. I was in the military and didn't have any contact with civilians. He said that I no doubt read United States newspapers and should have a fair idea of American thinking of war events. I lied and said that I did not have ready access to newspapers on my military bases and that I really was not interested in such news. I lied that all I ever read was the comic page.

He pointed to the newspaper on his desk and said that, as a Japanese officer, he read the news every day and understood where the Japanese stood on the war. He stated that the Japanese cause was just and that they would win the war. He stood up, preened himself, and boasted that as a Japanese officer he received the newspaper every day and read every word. He held up the little one page newspaper for me to see. I tried to appear impressed at his knowledge of current events.

His questioning led around to his suspicion that the Americans were planning an invasion of the Japanese home islands. He wanted to know how and when the invasion was to be accomplished. I told him that as a lowly second lieutenant I was not privy to this kind of information. He said that, since I was an officer like he was, I should be able to figure out what the American strategy would be.

I knew: *where and when* Operation Olympic *and* Operation Coronet, *the invasions of the Japanese homeland, were to take place.*

I shouldn't have known this! I wished that I didn't. I wished that my well-meaning friend in Hawaii had not shared this invasion information with me when I visited with him on my way to Tinian.

My interrogator became very insistent that I discuss the possibility of an invasion with him. He ordered me to tell him how I thought Japan should be invaded. I launched into a theory that I have laughed about many times since. The very thought of a lowly second lieutenant sitting there expounding on how Japan should be invaded is laughable. I said that if I were in charge, since our troops were already in the Philippines, I would cross over to the Chinese mainland and move northward up the coast until opposite the west coast of Japan. I would invade the home islands from the west side where the defenses were probably not as well set up as on the east coast. I said that, as the good officer was aware, most of their defenses faced the east. We would avoid these if we attacked from the west. He listened with great interest and wrote copious notes as I talked. As the end of my interrogation approached, I noted that he was happy with my invasion strategy.

He asked if I wanted the war to end soon. "Of course," was my reply. "I am looking forward to the Japanese surrender." This was the wrong thing to say and ended our "friendly chat."

"*We* surrender?!" he shouted. "We'll never do that!"

He predicted that the war would last a long time, that the American people would tire of the losses and expenses, and would sign a peace treaty favorable to Japan. He said that I would have to wait a very long time, until the war's end, to go home. This statement sounded better to me than his earlier threats of trial and execution.

He then surprised me with a new tack. He asked if I knew who was getting rich back home as a result of the war. He stated that the only people gaining from this war were the Jews who kept the war going for their personal gains. He then brought up the subject of the blacks in the United States. He said that the Japanese considered them an inferior race. They were not fighters. Why was he belaboring me about our American blacks and Jews?

I didn't mention the Emperor's name, having been warned that this was sure death for prisoners. Never once, in all my interrogations, was the Emperor's name mentioned.

Again, I watched as he ate his delicious lunch while I was served my rice ball. Again, I tried to get him to give orders for immediate medical care for my wounds. He expressed surprise that his order of yesterday was not followed. He again promised to issue the necessary orders. He promised that I would be taken to their medical dispensary immediately after this questioning session.

I was returned to my cell and there was no medical treatment. The next morning I was again taken before the same senior officer. He dismissed the guards and "invited" me to sit down. He appeared overly friendly. Why? I was subjected to another full day of questions. The same questions as before, the same answers as before. Then he branched off to a discussion centered around American feelings about the war and Japan's will to win a settlement for an honorable peace or fight to the last Japanese life when the Americans invaded. He said that Japanese culture dictated that death was better than a disgraceful peace. I didn't understand what he was telling me and was puzzled that we were having this "buddy-buddy" discussion.

I really came to attention at his next statement. He told me that my relatives would not know that I'd survived and would never be notified as long as I was a Special Prisoner. "But," he said, "your status could be changed." He went on to say, very confidentially, and in a low, soft voice, that many prisoners volunteered to broadcast messages to America. . . .

Now I knew what he was after. It suddenly dawned on me why he had seemed different from the other interrogators; why I had been suspicious of him from the beginning. He was sifting out American prisoners for their Propaganda Prison. He was looking for the soft underbellies of traitors.

These snakes were first tested and found acceptable before being sent to the "model" prison where they received preferential treatment, tobacco, books, Bibles, a healthy diet, clean clothes. They lived better than regular POWs — and served the Japanese government as American turncoats. We had been briefed that under no circumstances could we, if captured, participate in such propaganda activities. We were not to become "Lord Haw Haw," "Tokyo Rose," or "Axis Sally." I would have forfeited my life before participating in such a propaganda program. I was shocked that I had been suspected to be an American who would.

My poker face must have let me down. I must have shown, in some manner, that I was suddenly on to him — that I understood what he was up to. I had been sitting there in a stupor . . . tired, hungry, weak from loss of weight and beatings, and in excruciating pain from sitting on a hard chair for five hours. But I heard this last sentence loud and clear. My head jerked back and I stared at him. He continued, "Would you be interested in letting your family know you are alive and being treated well in a better prison than this one, in a camp where you would have medical treatment and good food?"

We sat across from each other, eyes locked. To accept his offer would have been traitorous. I knew that if I flat refused I would be of no more use to them and would be executed. I hoped that if I appeared "on the fence," I might bluff my way, at least for a time.

I said, "Yes. I would like for my parents to know that I am alive. Yes, I want very much to be transferred to a regular POW camp."

He knew that I knew *exactly* what he was offering and would not be of value to the Japanese propaganda program. His whole countenance changed. He frowned. He closed his interrogation log. The matter ended that instant.

Our session had lasted well into the evening. I had watched him eat two of his fine meals. His last proposition came, as planned, very late, when I was very weary. He had hoped that I would be caught off my guard and agree to anything. It hadn't worked that way; he had no further use of me. He stood up, turned his back on me, and called the guards.

As the guards were putting on my blindfold and handcuffs, the officer was working himself into a rage over something he was ordering them to do. They pushed me out of his office and escorted me up several flights of stairs to an antiseptic-smelling room.

My blindfold and handcuffs were not removed. I could tell from the conversations taking place that several people were present, including women. I could see that most of the occupants wore white shoes. I believed that I was in a medical facility of some kind, hopefully a dispensary.

I was lifted and placed face down on a table with clean, white sheets. My pants were removed and my bandages unwrapped. Each of my wounds was examined. I could feel a probe being painfully inserted into each of the many flak penetrations. As this examination was taking place, I could hear a lot of giggling and excited whispers. This painful process was not funny to me — why was it so funny to them?

The medics did not bandage any of my wounds. I asked about this and was answered with more giggles. Every place they had treated felt like it was on fire. What had the Japanese medics done to me?

Not one word of English was spoken during this treatment session. I tried to thank the medics for looking after me. More laughter.

After the medical treatment, I was roughly shoved off the examination table and fell to the floor. The guard jerked me to my feet and marched me back down stairs to the basement cell area. I was not returned to the cell I had left that morning. My new cell was on the other side of the curtain.

It was late and *sho* had been called. Two occupants were bedded down on the cell floor. I was glad to see that one was a fellow American. He was the red-headed prisoner I'd noticed earlier. His name was Maynor B. Hanks. We had been shot down during the same mission. He was a member of Bill Grounds' crew.

Hanks appeared as happy to see me as I was to be with him, and in whispers we discussed our plight. Hanks was from Sweetwater, Texas. He was 19 years old and a gunner on his crew. Hanks appeared to be in pretty good shape, in spite of our starvation rations.

The entire crew on Grounds' plane had survived. None of them had been wounded during their shoot down, bailout, and capture.

They had two engines on fire, had bailed out, regrouped and had evaded capture for two days, which was the reason for their late arrival at my Kokura prison. We had all been on the same train from Kokura to Tokyo.

The other prisoner was a mean looking Japanese civilian. He

resented being penned up with us and showed it in his surly attitude. Our cellmate did not like our quiet conversation and called to the guard who had been out of earshot. The guard thrust his bayonet through the cell's bars and growled some guttural threats. We glared at our snitching cellmate, and he slunk further over in his corner of the cell. This Japanese prisoner was removed sometime during the night.

I missed my dentist friend and Professor Sugai — especially Sugai, who had prayed with me each night. But it was a great comfort to be with a fellow B-29 crew member.

The next day we experienced a terrific air raid conducted by our navy's aircraft. Bombs hit close enough to our building that we could hear rocks and shrapnel hitting the outside of the structure. We could hear the nearby anti-aircraft flak guns. We could hear airplane engines; they must have been flying pretty low. The navy planes strafed and bombed the area for what seemed over an hour.

Hanks and I were pleased that Tokyo was under attack. We were glad our navy men were giving the enemy a good show. Unfortunately, a few of our planes were shot down. The PA system reported 15 down.

The Japanese guard appeared unconcerned, almost as if he was unaware of the attack. His only reaction to the air raid was to wear his steel helmet, which was normally strapped on his back. He would have made a good poker player. His face was a fixed mask with no emotion showing.

The effects of the questionable medical attention I'd received two days earlier was beginning to show. All my wounds became infected. They were running sores and soaked my clothes and blanket with pus. I now knew what the giggling, laughter, and whispers in the dispensary was all about.

The Japanese medics had intentionally probed my wounds with infected swabs. They intentionally infected them! The bastards!

My hatred of the Japanese cranked up another notch. Why had they done this? They wanted me to die. I hadn't revealed any military secrets. I hadn't volunteered for their propaganda program. They had no more use for me.

Shorty came to my cell shortly after our discovery. He knew all about my medical problem. He berated me and shouted, "You are going to die. You shouldn't have insisted on medical treatment. Why did you ask for medical treatment when I told you that Special Prisoners could have none? You are paying for your stupidity. Our medical doctors fixed you. You deserve what you got. You will die." He kicked me a few times for emphasis and left.

Even though my last interrogator had questioned me without the usual beatings, I had noticed that Shorty had been especially attentive during that time. I am sure that Shorty and this interrogator were dancing the "good guy, bad guy" routine. Shorty would, without fail, show up shortly after I was returned to my cell. I was required to stand when he entered with the guard. First, the guard would knock me down with his gun, then Shorty would begin his kicking. He was a small, little specimen of a man, but his kicks with his heavy boots were mighty. Oh, how I hated him!

By now the month of April was almost at an end. The day after I was rejected as a traitor, I was marched in before an enlisted military interrogator. The questions were the usual about my personal life, accompanied by the usual beatings. Shorty stuck his head in several times to be sure the treatment was adequate. This was an especially brutal interrogation.

Afterwards, I was taken to a building located in the rear of Kempei's main brick building. This was to my "home" for the next ten days until I was returned to the dungeon.

This building was a long, wooden structure enclosed within a high, wooden fence. Pre-war, it had been a stable with six stalls, used to house the Kempeis' ceremonial horses. A wooden barracks for the Kempei guards was located in this rear area compound of the headquarters complex.

Horse stall prisoners were well-aware of their life-threatening vulnerability to incendiary bombing attacks in their completely wooden building.

The prisoners called this structure "the horse stalls," sometimes referred to as "the pig pen cells." The cells housed about 20 American prisoners and an unknown number of Japanese prisoners. The horse stalls had been modified into a row of six eight-by-tenfoot wooden cells. The floor, ceiling, and three walls of each cell were of smooth, unpainted wood with no fasteners showing. A cell's fourth side had wooden bars running from floor to ceiling, a small entrance door, and a floor-level food pass through. A latrine hole was located in a back corner of each cell. A dim light bulb dangled from the ceiling of each cell.

All windows in the cell building were covered with blackout curtains, making for poor ventilation. No light penetrated the building. Filth and biting insects abounded; lice, bedbugs, and fleas were rampant. These varmints were busy 24 hours a day. We spent most of our days going through our clothing killing the fleas and lice.

The Kempei's pig and chicken enterprise added to prison misery. Terrible smells caused by the foul latrines and the farm animals compounded the torment. Larger pigs scraped the cell floors as they scrambled around underneath. During feeding time (farm animals' feeding time—not ours), we envied the creatures. They received better food and more of it than did the starving prisoners.

In my new cell in the horse stalls I was housed with four American prisoners. They were:

Otto J. Marek from Chicago
Ferdinand Spacel from Chicago
Douglas Bannon from Portland, Oregon
John W. Meagher from Ligonier, Pennsylvania.

They were all from the same crew, based on Saipan, and had been shot down on 3 April 1945 in the Tokyo area. They were all gunners from the rear of the airplane and figured that the people in the front cabin had been killed.

Even though we were in a closed building, it was very cold during the late April Tokyo weather. Being cold *and* starving was a miserable state. Fortunately, there were blankets in the cell. We divided them among us at night and I was allowed to cover my body with one blanket during the day due to my *"tinkee"* status. Guard instruction to allow this departure from prison rules apparently carried over to this cell block.

We could hear low groans from an adjacent cell. We found out from the *benjo* soldier, during his rounds, that the cries of pain came from a badly burned American. His name was John S. Houghton. He had third-degree burns over most of his body. He had been brought into his cell on 2 April. As punishment for war crimes against the Japanese, Houghton received no medical treatment.

The latrine buckets were drained daily by an American prisoner. His name was Maurice W. San Souci. Accompanied by a Kempei guard who, in order to stand apart from the stench, kept a rather loose rein on him, San Souci, the *benjo* soldier, performed his duty each morning, in the dungeon as well as the horse stalls, and spent a lot of time at each cell while puttering with the waste container. He could be easily heard through the waste hole in the floor of our cells. His rounds served as a prison information network. He listened to the muted words coming from each cell as to new occupants' names, conditions in the cell, and latest war news. He shared this information with each cell as he made his rounds. His guard apparently thought he was talking to himself. We looked forward to his daily visit and were able to keep up with the latest war developments and got fairly good information on other American prisoners. For this unpleasant chore San Souci received two rice balls each meal instead of the one. He always shared his bounty with his cellmates.

Shorty's daily visits were not confined to the dungeon. He came daily to the horse stables. He shouted at the horribly burned prisoner in the nearby cell. His cellmates pleaded with Shorty for help. Their pleas were ignored. The badly burned prisoner cried and groaned continuously 24 hours a day. He was removed from his cell several times for interrogation, even though he could not walk.

Finally, he lapsed into delirium—screaming, raving, completely out of his mind. When this was reported to Shorty, he came into Houghton's cell and kicked his prostrate body, then left and returned shortly with a medical officer who gave Houghton an injection. The next morning Houghton was dead. His body was removed from the cell and left lying on the dirt floor where we could see it from our cell and it was not removed until the next day.

When my fellow prisoners asked for help for my wounds, Shorty launched into angered temper tantrums. He kicked each of my cellmates. He would lift my blanket and turn up his nose at the stench coming from my wounds. He continually predicted that I'd never survive. He took it as a personal offense that I continued to live. *How dare I!*

During each of my many interrogations, I asked when I would be sent to a POW prison camp. Any camp had to be better than the

Kempei Tai prison. The answer was always the same: "Due to prison overcrowding a shipment would be made in the near future."

We had been briefed to request from the Japanese the same treatment we thought Japanese prisoners in the United States were given. Any request we made was denied.

It was now 23 April. A new cellmate was shoved into our small cell. He was Anthony F. Scalero from Chicago. He had been shot down and had parachuted into the mountains. He had roamed around for several days before being captured by friendly civilians. They had treated him well and fed him well until the Kempeis came for him. He was in pretty good shape in spite of his Kempei beatings.

We now had six people in the eight-by-ten cell. We thought this was crowded but eventually as many as 20 prisoners would fill each of these filthy and vermin-infested horse stalls.

Tony took an immediate interest in my wounds. He told me I had to lie on my stomach and allow the wounds to scab over. Tony had received a small flak wound on his arm. He'd wrapped the wound with a medical compress bandage from the first aid kit in his survival vest. He removed this bandage from his arm and studied it for a moment. It was composed of a cotton fiber center section about three inches square enclosed in gauze with tie on straps of gauze about a foot in length. He looked at my open, running wounds and pulled some of the cotton fibers from the compress and spread them carefully across each of my open sores. These fiber reinforcements caused the bloody pus in the open wound to harden into a protective scab.

He insisted that I keep the bandage and hide it in my clothing. As long as I had it, I worried that Kempei searchers would find it. I knew that Shorty would not permit me to keep such a luxury.

Scalero's donated compress held enough fibers to last out my imprisonment. My smaller wounds, even though badly infected, slowly healed over. Scalero was appalled at the condition of my bloody, filthy, tattered undershorts. He had me remove them and he pushed them out of the cell through our food opening. As soon as my wounds had scabbed over, he removed his relatively clean underpants and insisted that I wear them as a sort of bandage.

Scalero's friendly attitude impressed the food *(onigre)* soldier. Because of his admiration of Scalero, our cell began to receive slightly larger rice balls. Scalero would engage the food soldier in friendly conversation during his deliveries and sometimes an extra rice ball came our way. We never complained if there was an extra one, but if we were one short we raised a ruckus.

There were many mortally wounded American prisoners in adjacent cells. My injuries were minor compared to the wounds of these poor fellows. Their groans and screams of suffering were terrible to hear and were heard day and night. I still have nightmares about this part of my experience. It is burned into my memory. The Kempei guards enjoyed their extreme suffering.

Shorty shouted at the dying prisoners that they were being "punished for killing innocent women and children"—and on and on and on. He bellowed that all Japanese hospitals were full of the innocent people we had injured during our war crime activities. "Anyhow," he screeched, "there is no dispensary and no medical supplies in the building." I knew that this was a lie. There *was* a military dispensary on the top floor. I had been there.

We knew that the miserable and dying flyers tried mightily to stifle their terrible cries of pain. Often when one cried out, it was reason enough to beat all the prisoners in his cell.

The most severely wounded American was two cells over. His name was Roland Nelson. From our prison grapevine, we learned that he was "burned to a crisp." The mortally wounded prisoner was a P-51 pilot who had been on fire when he bailed out of his burning plane. He had arrived at Kempei Tai Headquarters on 25 April. He had received no medical treatment and had been tortured and beaten by the Kempeis.

His cellmates said that he was dying and that he couldn't eat. They begged and pleaded with Shorty to show some mercy. Shorty paid no heed. Nelson finally lapsed into delirium from his pain. I had never heard, and hope never to hear again, such blood-curdling screams like the poor fellow emitted. I prayed and prayed that he would get some relief from his unbearable suffering.

Nelson died in his cell on 27 April 1945. The poor suffering soul's body was removed from his cell and dragged onto the dirt floor in front of the cells like a dead animal. His corpse lay there for most of a day before it was finally dragged off like a sack of garbage. Shorty and the guards laughed and joked as Nelson's body was dragged from the cell block.

Our hatred of the Japanese, particularly the Kempei Tais, and *especially* Shorty, escalated.

One of the blankets Nelson had been wrapped in was thrown into our cell when we asked for extra cover. It was soaked in blood and pus. When the guards refuse to replace it with another blanket, we pushed it out of the cell through the food slot. This caused trouble with the guards, but they finally took it away.

Another prisoner, William Henry Osborne, in the cell where Houghton had been murdered, was also suffering from third-degree burns over most of his body. He could not feed himself and was fed by a fellow prisoner named John Walker Evans. Osborne was removed from the cell, dying, and was never heard from again.

A B-29 prisoner based in Saipan, Kenneth Peterson, had just been brought in and put in a cell adjacent to ours. He was suffering from gangrene from frost bite in all toes on one foot. Two of his crew mates were in the same cell with him and did the best they could for him, but his condition worsened. During Shorty's daily visits, they pleaded for help with his badly deteriorating toes. Shorty berated them and said that Peterson had only himself to blame since Peterson had evaded capture for several days. Shorty did not like this because it made the Japanese look bad. His cellmates asked for medicine and were refused. He said that Peterson was young and healthy and that his body could bear the loss of his toes. I don't understand how Shorty could enter the cell and look at the poor fellow and refuse aid. But then, he was Shorty. He was happy with Peterson's plight.

Peterson's cellmates asked for medicine and were refused. They begged for bandages and were refused. One of his cellmates was Maurice W. San Souci, the *benjo* soldier, who was able to get some extra pieces of cement sacks given us for toilet paper.

They tried to bandage his disintegrating toes with these dirty sacks. When the toes began to fall off, Peterson's cellmates begged for a knife so they could amputate his gangrenous toes and were refused and beaten for their request. During all this, Peterson was dragged out of the cell for interrogations and had to stumble along on his bloody, hurt, foot as the guards berated him for being slow.

On 30 April I was taken from my cell to be interviewed once again by Junior. I was always relieved when I saw that Junior would be my questioner. Though I received beatings when he interviewed, they were not as severe as those I received from other interviewers. Once I asked Junior why I was being questioned so many times. He appeared puzzled by my question and finally answered that his superiors believed that flight engineers knew more about world affairs and technology than other crew members.

I asked him again about our chances of being transferred from the Kempei Headquarters to a POW camp. He told me that the Kempei Tai Special Prisoner prison was becoming overcrowded. A shipment to another facility was being arranged and would take place in the near future. He promised to request that I be included in the shipment.

He described the new camp as "out in the country." He said there were American doctors at the camp and the food would be much better. This sounded like a break. I couldn't wait to be "dragged" back to the horse stalls and share my good news with my cellmates.

When I told my buddies the good news, they were overjoyed. It was strange that we could be so happy to be sent to a Japanese prison camp, but another camp, any other camp could only be an improvement to this one. If our present situation continued, we would die before the American invasion and rescue.

When we prayed together that night we included a plea for Peterson to be in the transfer group. As we prayed we could hear his moans of pain.

After the loss of his toes, the gangrene moved up his leg. We figured that Peterson's days were numbered, which they were, but not from these wounds. On 10 May Peterson was removed from his cell, supposedly to be moved to a prison camp where American medical doctors could give him medical attention. Instead, he was massacred along with the other prisoners who were transferred that day from Kempei Tai Headquarters.

My cell population now numbered seven. Douglas Bannon from Portland, Oregon, joined us. He was a central fire control gunner and was the only man to survive the destruction of his B-29.

By now, Tokyo was being bombed about once a week and always at night. The PA system announced the approach of the raiders even before Tokyo's air raid sirens went off to warn of the threat. We knew the type and quantity of the approaching bombers.

During the entire bombing alert period, which usually lasted two or three hours from original alert until the all-clear signal was given, the American prisoners were made to stand at rigid attention while extending their arms in the air. This stand-up punishment was a painful ordeal for starving and weak prisoners.

Emaciated prisoners passed out from this subtle torture. Guards entered their cells and beat them with rifle butts and kicks to assure that they weren't playing 'possum.

We discussed food almost all the time. Each of us talked about our favorite food and what we'd eat first when liberated. We told what we'd eaten, where, what was our favorite, how good it was, and how it was prepared. Each prisoner told about his food preferences. We savored every meal description from each of our cellmates.

It was strange that of all the subjects we discussed, we never got around to the fairer sex. The human body and mind looked after first things first and according to man's needs: food, clothing, and shelter tends to be all-important when they are not available. We had clothing, of sorts, and shelter, such as it was. We needed *food*.

Three times a day the shabby food soldier appeared. He didn't wear the distinctive Kempei arm band. He was a low caste soldier. He counted the prisoners in our cell and tossed exactly that many gooey vermin-ridden rice balls onto the dirty floor. The rice balls were small and cold. The balls stuck to the floor. Instead of snatching the meager food like hungry animals, we began developing a way to assure equality in sharing the food time ration. We made a sport out of eating time. It gave us something to do. The seven Americans decided that since the balls varied in size, we would rotate selection of our floored meal. The rice balls were first placed in a line on the floor. We rotated first, second, and so on choice priority. The prisoner with first choice carefully examined the sorry looking rice balls. After much deliberation, he selected what he thought was the largest ball. This ceremony took quite a long time. We had nothing else to do. The time spent meant that some of the miserable day passed by. We sat back and slowly chewed each grain of rice.

Shortly after food distribution, the shabby soldier came back around with a dirty bucket of water and one cup. Each prisoner was allowed to drink one cup of water. If that did not suffice, it was too bad; that was all allowed each prisoner. If the attendant didn't fill his cup, the prisoner went thirsty until the next water ration came after the next meal. We were always thirsty, as well as hungry. Starvation and lack of water were other subtle Japanese tortures.

Most of us were walking skeletons. We would eat anything. Our rice contained protein in the form of worms and bugs and they tasted mighty good. If a rat could have been caught in our cell, we would have torn it apart and shared the raw pieces.

I had weighed 175 pounds when I was shot down. My guess was that now I weighed less than 120.

MAY 1945

The month of May started off with the loud and guttural shouting of *"sho"* by the Kempei guards. This meant that the prisoners were to arise for another day of dismal existence while being beaten and starved.

Every day or so the food soldier brought around a broom made out of a straggly bush. Even a witch would discard this sorry excuse for a broom. It was laughable! We were supposed to move this bush around the filthy cell for what passed as a clean sweep. All this did was stir the filth around. This activity did nothing to cleanse the nasty cell floor, but it became entertainment for us. The prisoners took their time with this task. We did not do this because none of us wanted the job, but because we all welcomed something to do. We got a little exercise out of this useless task. It became a contest to see who did the best job.

After breakfast we awaited the visit of the *benjo* soldier, fellow B-29 crewman, Maurice San Souci. Somehow he had been selected by the Japanese for this onerous task. He whispered the latest prison scuttlebutt as he slowly emptied our honey pot. He knew more about our prison than anyone. We were so segregated that we never knew for sure who was here or how many Americans the prison held. I didn't know where Andrews was and San Souci could not find out for me. I did learn that Hanks had come to the horse stalls, and was in pretty bad shape from diarrhea, malnutrition, and mistreatment.

During most of the month of May our navy's carriers and 20th Air Force B-29s were busy hitting kamikaze bases in Kyushu. Japanese kamikazes based on Japan's southern island were dealing death and destruction to the 1,450 naval ships gathered around Okinawa. Our navy lost 4,907 sailors and had 36 ships sunk. Our aircraft assigned top priority to stopping these suicide pilots who gave their lives for their Emperor.

On 5 May we had an air alert when the 58th Bomb Wing hit the Tokyo area. The 58th were flying for the first time out of Tinian after transferring from their China-India bases.

On 7 May I was dragged off for yet another beating and interrogation with Junior. During my last session with him he had promised that I would be sent with the next shipment to a regular POW camp. I asked him when this would likely happen. He said that my name and that of Hanks had caused a mix-up in the records. As soon as the records were corrected I would be in the next transfer.

I asked about the location and description of the regular POW camp where we would be sent. He said, "It is a very nice place and you will be happy there." But he had a peculiar look on his face as he said this and didn't look at me while he was talking. I wondered what the look meant and suspected that he might be lying.

Very early during the morning of 9 May about 30 Kempei guards entered the cell area. They were chattering and excited. Shorty was with them. He began to read out names of many American prisoners. When a name was called, guards jerked the prisoner out of his cell, made him put on his shoes, blindfolded him, handcuffed him, and led him out of the dungeon area. I figured that with the many names being called out this must be the prison transfer. Junior had promised that I would be included in the next shipment. I waited patiently for my name to be called.

My cellmates Otto J. Marek, Anthony P. Scalero, and Douglas Bannon were removed from the cell when their names were called. The prisoners selected were delighted to be chosen. I envied them.

Finally, all the designated prisoners and their guards were gone from the dungeon area. Three prisoners were left behind in our cell — Meagher, Spacel, and I.

Hanks and I had been left out. *Why?* Junior had assured me that Hanks and I would be part of the transfer. My morale hit rock bottom. I didn't know where Hanks was, but I knew that his name had not been called. The next few days were of ultimate misery for me. I was interrogated twice with the usual brutality and the same questions. I asked why I was not taken along with the other prisoners to the regular POW camp. The interrogators ignored my question.

When I finally drew Junior for interrogation, I asked why Hanks and I were left behind. He said that the prison authorities had not been able to straighten out Hanks' and my prison records. As a result, we were left behind. I asked when the next shipment would take place. His answer was vague.

I missed my fellow prisoners who had become such good and close friends — particularly Tony Scalero, who added much to our morale and looked after my wounds.

Historical records vary, but 62 to 65 Special Prisoners were taken out of Kempei Headquarters that fateful night of 9 May 1945. They were taken to the Tokyo Military Prison. This was the "nice prison camp." If there was a prison more horrible than the Kempei Tai, it was the Tokyo Military Prison. On 23 May the Tokyo Military Prison burned down during a B-29 raid.

All Japanese prisoners were safely evacuated from the prison. The American flyers imprisoned there were left locked in their burning wooden cells. Those who were able to break out were slaughtered with swords and bayonets. They were chopped to pieces by the guards and by the prison director. The others burned to death in their locked cells.

It is interesting to note that all members of Grounds' crew who were taken captive in Kokura survived captivity. With the exception of Hanks, Grounds' crew members were held at satellite Kempei jails scattered around the Tokyo area. Andrews was held in one of these. Hanks and I were the only members of those two crews to be imprisoned at Kempei Headquarters. Why weren't we transferred on 9th May 1945?

During the night of 23 May 1945, Tokyo experienced a tremendous B-29 incendiary raid. More than 500 B-29s hit the city. This was the biggest incendiary raid of the war up to that time. Several hours before the first bomb dropped, the PA system warned of approaching *Bee Nee Ju Ku* (B-29) aircraft. Later, the air raid sirens sounded a long blast, meaning that the attack was imminent. When a series of short blasts sounded, the low level bombers began to be heard overhead. They flew over the city starting about midnight and came in a steady stream for two hours.

Flak batteries near our building went crazy with their deadly salvos. I identified with the poor B-29 crews flying overhead taking all that punishment. I could picture in my mind the cones of search-light beams centered on a victim aircraft. All flak guns in the area would target the illuminated plane. Its chances of survival were nil at the low altitude flown.

I heard the steady clump of 500-pound bombs going off near-by and knew that the incendiaries were also hitting their targets and setting awful fires. A large crowd gathered outside our prison. I could hear the excited sounds of strange voices discussing the raid. Why weren't these people in an air raid shelter? Every now and then I heard much cheering and clapping. This crowd reaction must have meant that flak guns had hit and shot down a B-29.

Seventeen B-29s were lost that night. Almost 200 crew members were in those airplanes. How many would survive capture and be brought to our prison? Not many . . . Possibly 20 crewmen or so survived capture and were brought to Kempei Headquarters.

Strong winds were blowing that night. Fires started by this raid burned close to our prison. I could hear the wind howling outside our wooden horse stall cell block. We were vulnerable to the fire-storm raging outside. Awful and noxious fumes seeped into our cell block. Nauseous odors came from burning buildings, burning flesh, and strange smells of cordite anti-aircraft gun explosives. Sounds of the raid were terrible in the dark cell. Our small light bulb went out. The three of us in the cell wondered if our time had come. My two cellmates had been standing at attention for hours during the raid. Fortunately, neither of them fainted during the torture of being poked with bayonets.

Due to Professor Sugai's earlier intercession on my behalf, I was excused from this senseless exercise. During the raid the guards stood poker-faced and seemingly unconcerned that a major part of their city was being incinerated. After the raid was over, prison life went on as usual.

We welcomed the raids, as they meant that the war was being vigorously pursued by our comrades. Since our fate was in great doubt, we had little to lose.

Burn the damn city to the ground!

On 24 May I was interrogated by a high-level Japanese officer who wanted to know more about bombing tactics used by B-29s. I was puzzled that I was undergoing all these brutal interrogations. My cellmates were not questioned and beaten so frequently. Why me? The officer told me that in their military and society, engineers were required to have a broad knowledge of related operations, and he thought that it was the same for our military. I told him that he was mistaken. Flight engineers knew only how to operate the mechanical and electrical systems on the airplane. We only knew how to keep the B-29s engines running and had nothing to do with bombing strategy or tactics. I was called a liar and received as vicious a beating as I had incurred to that point. He was interested in data about our B-24 bomber. I told him that I had no knowledge about this airplane. Again, I was beaten for not telling him what he thought I knew.

I asked why so few prisoners were captured on the last raid. He said that Japanese soldiers were ordered to capture all parachuting Americans alive and to bring them to the Kempei Tai Headquarters. Not many flyers came into the hands of the Kempei because the civilian hate for the B-29 murderers was increasing; when they got their hands on a survivor, he died. Japanese police or soldiers just couldn't get to them quickly enough.

The night of 25 May brought another PA system air raid alert. Soon the long blast of air raid warning sirens could be heard. First, we heard the drone of airplane engines in the distance, then the sound of distant flak guns. We listened as the planes came closer, working their way toward our prison area. I was surprised that this raid was coming only two days after the awful raid of 23 May. I could still smell smoke from the previous raid. Bomb blasts had been continuous, since two nights before, from the delayed action bombs. General LeMay, the General Patton of the air force, was really targeting Tokyo. We had destroyed a third of its urban area back in March. By now, the city must be just about wiped out.

Four hundred sixty-four B-29 bombers hit the city that night. The city of Tokyo was removed from the strategic bombing target list after this raid. It no longer existed as a military target. It had been wiped out. Financial, commercial, government, factory, and home war production areas were totally destroyed. I was surprised that Kempei Headquarters still stood. The fires raged right up to our prison walls.

Our B-29s were ordered not to bomb the Emperor's Palace. They didn't. Flames were so out of control in the city that sparks jumped the moat near our prison and set the wooden sections of the palace on fire. The Emperor and his family cowered in the plush Imperial Bomb Shelter while the wooden section of his palace burned to the ground. How could he continue to deny that he was being defeated? How could he let the Japanese people continue to suffer?

Our mission planners added high explosive bombs to the prime load of incendiary bombs to discourage fire fighters from doing their duty. Some of the general purpose (explosive) bombs were time delay types set to provide random explosions during and after the raid. Some went off during the raid and some went off hours and days afterward.

The Japanese gunners exacted a high toll. Twenty-six B-29s were shot down. A few surviving crewmen were brought into the horse stall cells soon after the raid. It was obvious that they had been badly beaten by civilians and Kempeis. Many were suffering from flak wounds.

I underwent another brutal interrogation the day following this Tokyo raid. I could hear them beating on Maynor Hanks in the next room. After our interrogations were over, Hanks and I were taken back to the horse stall area and put together in a cell. Starvation had been hard on Hanks. He had several bouts with dysentery which left him emaciated and weak. I felt sorry for him. There was only the two of us in a cell and the prison's electricity source was still knocked out, so we did not have the light on all night.

Shortly after the wake-up shouts of *"sho,"* Hanks and I were moved from the horse stall area to a dungeon cell. As we sat there wondering why we had been moved, there was commotion and shouting outside our cell and another American was roughly pushed through the door. His name was Nick Gazibara from Export, Pennsylvania.

Nick had been shot down on the last raid. He had been badly beaten but had no flak wounds. He was worried that he had not been allowed to bring his shoes with him. Of course, we were always barefoot while in our cells. Hanks and I told him not to worry—he wasn't going anywhere for a while.

As the day passed we heard other American prisoners being

brought into the cell area. I figured that they were from the airplanes shot down on the recent air raids. As they were dragged down the aisle outside my cell, I could see that they had been worked over pretty good. They were in bad shape.

During the day four more captured B-29 crew members were pushed into our small cell. We had thought that we were crowded before, but now we knew what crowded could be. We now had seven Americans in the small five-by-nine cage. We were tightly packed in like sardines in a can. We could tell that all six dungeon cells were loaded to capacity with the airmen captured from the last two air raids.

The latest arrivals were:

> Bill Grounds
> Jack Hobbie
> Neal Cooper
> Warren Ransler

They were different from the earlier arrivals. They wore clean clothes and were clean shaven, including their heads. The guards were so busy with the overload of prisoners that they did not try to keep us from whispering to each other. The new group was able to tell us their strange story.

The small satellite Kempei prison where they had been kept caught on fire during the second fire raid. When their wooden prison building had been hit and set on fire the guards fled the prison, leaving them locked in their cells. When the fire burned through the wall of their cell they were able to break out of the burning building by putting blankets over their heads and butting through the burning cell bars.

Twenty Americans flyers gathered together, with the fires raging around them, and tried to figure out how to survive in the holocaust. They were still imprisoned in a compound. They decided that their best chance of survival was to help the fire fighting crews.

They joined the Japanese fire fighters and formed bucket brigades to pour water on burning structures. The Japanese noticed that the Americans were helping and appreciated their efforts, but once the fire was under control Kempei guards surrounded them. They were marched down the burned out streets toward our prison. Their Kempei guards protected them from the angry, jeering crowds who tried to get at them.

During their march a passing Japanese colonel shouted an order to the Kempeis to halt the group. He carefully inspected each prisoner. It was obvious that he was unhappy about something and the Americans figured that their end had come. Instead the colonel turned his rage on the guards. He was displeased and they knew it. He berated the guards for the prisoners' slovenly, unsoldierlike appearance. He was not a Kempei officer and probably didn't know the special rules for these Americans. The colonel barked some guttural orders to the Kempei guard in charge and stalked off.

The guards took the prisoners to a nearby army command post where they were allowed to bathe. Their beards were shaved off and so was their matted hair which had been singed in the fire. Their ragged clothing was washed.

After the cleanup, they were marched about a mile to Kempei Tai Headquarters. They underwent the Kempei reception questioning. They met Shorty, received their beatings, and were brought to our dungeon cell.

I noticed that the flyer who sat across from me kept looking at me as if there was something that puzzled him. In the cell's five-foot dimension, we were sitting almost eyeball to eyeball. I wondered why he was studying me so closely. He didn't even look at the others.

The next time the guard walked out of earshot, he leaned forward and whispered, "Are you from Texas?" I told him I was from Fort Worth, Texas. He said, "So am I. Did you go to college at NTAC?" I was so shocked that I could only nod a "yes." His next question really amazed me. "Are you Fiske Hanley?"

His was Bill Grounds, and he remembered me from our cadet days at North Texas Agricultural College. I remembered his name, but we had not known each other very well. I certainly didn't recognize him with his smoothly shaved head and face. How in the world could he have recognized me in my starved and filthy condition with my matted beard and hair?

Hanks was ecstatic. Three of the new arrivals were from his B-29 crew. Bill Grounds was his airplane commander. Jack Hobbie was his bombardier. Neal R. Cooper was his flight engineer. Five of us who had been on that fateful Shimonoseki Strait mission were in the same cell.

Warren Ransler was a radar operator from Syracuse, New York. He was from the same crew as Tony Scalero. He was in poor physical condition. He had evaded capture for 23 days during which time he became pretty emaciated. He had eaten all the rations out of his survival vest and then subsisted on dandelions and grass. I didn't hold out much hope for him on our accelerated starvation diet.

He was a strange sort of fellow, full of peculiar ideas, and he liked to argue. He was to bring a lot of misery to our cell.

Our cell population was now seven. We were really crowded. Since seven people cannot sleep side by side in a five-foot space, we had to arrange ourselves across the short dimension of the cell. We all faced in the same direction and when one turned all had to turn. Sleeping on our sides with our skinny hip bones pressing on the hard board floor was painful. The low, wooden wall around the latrine hole in the cell's corner further cramped our sleep space. This problem was solved when Ransler said he preferred to curl around the latrine than sleep in the "line-up."

We were allowed the usual amount of rice doled out to a cell, only now it was divided into seven balls. The rice balls now varie from walnut size to golf ball size. We were all pretty well into an accelerated starvation spiral. We knew it, but didn't talk about it. We had been on one-half regular POW rations . . . now we were on less. We practiced our rotating priority rice ball selection system. The new prisoners were amused and amazed at this sport.

Grounds told me that most of his crew had been taken to a small Kempei precinct prison about two miles from this headquarters. He said that during their march to this prison, they saw total destruction to the city through which they passed. The only things still standing were scorched concrete walls here and there.

Toward the end of May, I was hauled from the crowded cell and taken before Junior. He told me that there were no more shipments planned to regular prison camps. Our war criminal trials were being set up and our fate would be decided pretty soon. Since President Roosevelt had died, Junior's superiors felt that Japan would win the war and all Special Prisoners could be properly punished. He had a sort of sad look when he told me this. I always thought that my beatings during his interrogations were at the whim of the guards and not him.

For the remainder of May we managed to exist — barely. We talked about food, food, and more food. We starved. We starved. We starved. We ached; more than that — we hurt like hell. The beatings never stopped. We were beaten for standing up, we were beaten for sitting down. Ransler constantly went out of his way to irritate the guards, his fellow prisoners, and Shorty, and when Ransler irritated a guard or Shorty, all the cell members were punished.

Our nights were miserable. We couldn't turn over without waking the others. The moans and screams of the suffering, injured prisoners in our cell block never stopped.

We learned through our *benjo* grapevine that the war in Europe ended on 8 May 1945. We fervently hoped that now all Allied efforts could be directed at beating the Empire of Japan. We hoped to survive war actions directed at the enemy's capital city, but our chances appeared pretty slim.

May brought another hazard which we had not counted on. Several times during our captivity we felt mild rumblings in our cells. The cell shook and the drop light overhead swung crazily. *Earthquakes!* The Kempei guards appeared unconcerned, just as they were during air attacks. Maybe this was another way they could happily die for their Emperor. *Crazy people!*

We thought that after the recent two air raids on the Tokyo area, our comrades in the Marianas would have to pause for repairs and rest. Not so! On 29 May 459 B-29s escorted by 101 P-51 fighters hit the nearby port city of Yokohama. With incendiary bombs, they burned over nine square miles of the business district, the waterfront, and military targets.

The city of Tokyo and our prison were placed under an air raid alert during the entire raid on Yokohama. Several prisoners in the cell block passed out from the extreme pain of standing at attention with arms raised for the entire four-hour period. They were prodded awake and back onto their feet by bayonet thrusts and buckets of water thrown through the cell's bars. Ransler, in particular, suffered badly. His health was deteriorating fast and his mental condition even faster.

Seven B-29s and three P-51s were shot down during the Yokohama attack. My 504th Bomb Group was particularly hard hit. Two of our combat crews were shot down. Capt. James W. Cornwell's crew of 12, including his senior observer, Col. James T. Connally from LeMay's headquarters, were all killed in action. Colonel Connally had been our group commander before being promoted to LeMay's staff.

As far as I know, of all the almost 500 B-29s shot down over the Japanese Empire, only two crews survived and were liberated intact. These crews were those of Bill Grounds and Marcus Worde. Capt. Marcus H. Worde's crewmen were brought to Kempei Tai Headquarters, interrogated, beaten, and lodged in the overcrowded horse stall cells. Marcus Worde was so badly beaten during his capture and Kempei interrogation that when dragged into his horse stall cell, he wasn't recognized by his own crew members. His head was swollen to the size of a watermelon. It is a wonder that Mark Worde lived through his first few hours in Japan.

Two of his enlisted crewmen were dressed differently from their comrades. Earlier they had traded their army issue clothing with Navy Seabee friends. "For luck" they wore their navy clothes on missions. Dress code for combat crewmen was somewhat relaxed on Tinian. When these navy-garbed crewmen were captured, the Japanese figured that they were American Navy personnel and took them to the notorious prison camp, Ofuna, run by the Japanese Navy. They spent the rest of the war at Ofuna prison camp. Their treatment was no better than ours at Kempei Headquarters.

JUNE 1945

The Kempei prison was full and overflowing with American prisoners from the three end-of-May fire-bomb missions. Fifty B-29s had been shot down. We had no way of knowing how many prisoners had been captured. According to my Kempei interrogators, all B-29 prisoners, no matter where captured within the Japanese Empire, were to be wards of the Kempei Tai and were to be brought to Tokyo for interrogation, imprisonment, trial, and execution.

Our big concern during June was that there were *no* air raids. We wondered why the war was not being vigorously pursued. We welcomed the sound of B-29s or navy fighters overhead and bombs going off. We heard none during the entire month of June. Where were our war planes? What we didn't know was that Tokyo had been removed from the target list. Militarily, it had been destroyed.

We were so weak that it no longer bothered us that we got no chance to exercise. We received so little to eat and even less to drink that we seldom needed to go to the latrine bucket. Our hands were so grimy and dirty that to clean them, we rubbed our hands together and the scummy accumulation on our skin just rolled off. Our fingernails showed a history of our starvation. It was obvious when our imprisonment had begun just by looking at the change in the appearance of our nails. The thick protective skin on the bottom of our bare feet fell off. Our hair grew; it was filthy, matted and unhealthy looking. We smelled bad. We had the smell of sickly rice odor, unwashed bodies, infected, rotting flesh, and the latrine bucket. Fear has a strong odor. Our Kempei guards wore gauze face masks when they had to get too close to us. I don't know how *they* stood the stench; I don't know how *we* stood the stench.

My wounds were slowly healing, but the odor of the infections was still a problem to me and all around me. Flak fragments worked out of my smaller wounds before they healed over. I kept the small, wicked looking metal pieces secreted in my flight jacket.

Every day one or the other of our cellmates was removed from the cell to undergo torturous interrogations. We worried until they returned. Usually, they came back barely conscious and bleeding from head wounds.

About the middle of June, Hanks and Gazibara were removed from our cell and did not return. We were relieved when we learned that they were "safe" in another cell. Even though we needed the room they vacated, we missed them. The reason the Japanese shifted prisoners around didn't make sense. There was no rhyme or reason for the movements.

We hardly had time to adjust to our added sleeping space when a native was thrust into the cell. He was a youth of about 18 years of age. The Kempeis had arrested him for beating up a couple of Japanese soldiers. He must have done a pretty good job to be brought to the hell-hole prison.

He was friendly. His few words of English were supplemented with sign language. We understood what he was telling us and he could understand us. He told us that he was a Korean. He had been kidnapped by Japanese soldiers in his home country and brought to Japan as a slave laborer. He was a survivor!

He told us that he had been free during the last two incendiary raids on Tokyo. He said that many Japanese had been killed and the fire damage to the city was almost total. He'd heard that all other major Japanese industrial cities had been burned to the ground. This was good news. He told us that he'd been brought to our cell from another dungeon room and that two Japanese prisoners would soon be placed in our crowded cell. This was not good news. He said he did not like those prisoners and did not want to be in the same cell with them. He seemed glad to be in the cell with Americans.

Later that day the Kempeis pushed two Japanese civilians into our cell. We now had eight people in the one-man cage — three natives and five Americans!

The first Japanese was "ushered," politely and gingerly, into the cell. The guards showed unusual respect. This civilian was well-dressed in a tailored black suit, white shirt, and tie. He was middle-aged, wore thick spectacles, and appeared scholarly. His name was, as best I understood, Anidatas. He was a university professor whose crime was communism. He was a high level communist whose father held a senior job in the Japanese army as lieutenant general and governor of the occupied island of Java. I could tell that he was of high rank, even though he was put into our crowded cell.

Anidatas spoke excellent English. He told us that his communist party was strong and active in Japan. They had constant radio communications with American propaganda people on Saipan. He had listened to American broadcasts every day. He was sure that the Japanese homeland would be attacked any day now — by the Russians.

He told us that the Japanese civilians were starving, ill, and injured. Few people had been spared a death in their family. They were tired of war. All the Japanese civilians wanted the war to end. The common soldier wanted the war to end. He said that the Japanese military did not want the war to end — they loved war and dying for the Emperor. Anidatas told us that the Japanese High Command believed that since President Roosevelt had died on 12 April, they could win their war by negotiating an honorable peace with the war-worn Americans headed by an unknown and unproved president, Harry Truman.

His father and mother had visited the United States. He and his father did not get along well. I could understand this. The Japanese military hated communism. In fact, before Pearl Harbor, the army wanted to attack northward and fight the hated Russians. The navy wanted to attack south to gain badly needed resources, such as oil and minerals and valuable land areas. The navy won out!

Anidatas was taken out of the cell each morning and was gone all day. He told us that with his skills, the Kempeis used him for office duties. The guards never beat him and seemed to respect him, which was unusual for the brutes.

I always wondered if he wasn't with us to do a bit of eavesdropping. We were careful when he was in the cell.

The other Japanese entering our cell had been arrested by the Kempei for black market activities. He was crudely dressed and appeared rough and cruel. Anidatas told us to beware of him. He stared at us like he would like to cut our hearts out. He hated Americans. His entire family had been killed in the March fire raid on Tokyo, so who could blame him? He spoke no English and made no effort to communicate with us. In our crowded cell, he stayed as far as he could from our group, which was only a matter of inches.

The three natives took an instant dislike to Ransler. Ransler made no effort to get along with them or us or the guards. He was always arguing about something or other. He annoyed the natives with his hostile voice. Several times his cellmates were made to stand at attention for hours because of his behavior. He was made to kneel Japanese fashion on his knees many times as punishment for his hostility toward the guards. His fragile health caused him to pass out. Guards would enter our cell to pour water on him, spit on him, kick him, and prod his unconscious body with bayonets. Koro, the Korean, on several occasions beat Ransler senseless while the guards looked on with approval. We tried to get Ransler to improve his attitude but to no avail. Ransler had a mental problem which almost led to his death and made trouble for all the prisoners.

The long days of June dragged by. Our physical condition became weaker and weaker. Special Prisoners were dying from starvation, beatings, wounds, and poison injections administered by Kempei doctors. We were all on a collision course with death. We were becoming so weak from starvation that sometimes we passed out just from raising our heads too quickly. Blood flow to our brains must have been so marginal that any rapid movement of our heads affected our consciousness. I no longer tried to keep my mind active by solving problems. I could no longer concentrate. I seemed to exist in a dazed state. Sometimes I would realize that I had had no thought at all in my head for some time.

My memory and recall abilities became impaired. During a June interrogation I was asked which bomber command I belonged to. Without thinking, I mumbled that I was in the 20th Bomber Command. This was wrong. I immediately received several blows from the ever-ready *kendo* bats. My interrogator snarled at me that I'd lied and would be punished. I told him I didn't know what he was talking about. To me, with my feeble mind, the 20th Bomber Command answer had been correct. It wasn't. I was in the 21st Bomber Command.

He reached for a hard-bound red and black book about one inch thick. He thumbed through pages of organization charts and stopped at one. He shoved the book across the table at me and pointed to the 21st Bomber Command organization chart and snarled, "Your 504th Bomb Group was in the 21st Bomber Command."

This impressive book gave the order of battle for the whole 20th Air Force. Where did the Japanese get this book?

I was shocked. The Japanese must know *everything* about us. Their intelligence was far better than ours . . . *far better!*

During a late June interrogation I was questioned by a Kempei intelligence officer who had graduated from Georgia Institute of Technology. He told me that he could tell *I* was a Southerner by my accent. He spoke better English than I did. After I was seated across the interrogation table from him, flanked by two brutish Kempei guards, I glanced at the items displayed on the table. One of them caught my eye. It was located upside down to me on one corner of the table nearest me.

It was the latest stateside issue of Time *magazine!* It was not the thin, overseas version of *Time.* How in the world did the Kempeis obtain and get it to Tokyo in just a few days?

I noticed that my arrogant questioner was watching me, intently awaiting my reaction to this amazing, morale-shattering discovery. He had meant for me to see it. I made no comment on my discovery during the entire interview. I watched the Kempei officer carefully to see if I could detect any disappointment in my ignoring his prized possession. He would have made a great poker player. His face was impassive. He said nothing about the magazine and neither did I. Strangely, I received no beatings at this officer's direction.

I'm sure that both book events were attempts to show me that the Japanese knew more about our latest military and civilian information than I did. This was a warning that I had better answer their questions truthfully. Why not answer truthfully? Their stupid and repetitious interrogations never varied. The same personal life, civilian attitude, and minor military questions asked were pointless.

San Souci, the *benjo* soldier, came by the rear of our cell each day on his collection rounds. He told us that recently shot down navy and P-51 pilots brought news that the war was being vigorously pursued in other parts of Japan. All Kempei cells were filled to overflowing with B-29 crewmen, and still a few came dribbling in daily from somewhere.

As we obtained whispered news from San Souci, our cellmate, Anidatas, listened carefully. He even interjected questions to San Souci about Russian actions in the war. As a communist, he wanted to know anything about Russian affairs that our *benjo* soldier heard on his rounds.

The end of June finally arrived. There had not been one air raid on the city during the entire month. Though we knew that the war was being fought somewhere, we were very frustrated and unhappy that we could not feel a part of it, even if just to listen to our bombs being dropped.

Ransler became more and more a problem. We believed that his mind had left him. He didn't make sense when he talked. He constantly argued with the guards and received continual beatings from them. Koro took nothing off him and they fought. When there was too much commotion in the cell, we were all beaten.

Shorty, our chief tormentor, came into the dungeon area each day and threatened us. He told us that we wouldn't live much longer. He was certainly doing all he could to speed that prediction along. After his visits, Kempei doctors came into the cell area and administered poison injections to the dying prisoners.

The corpses of several Special Prisoners in our cell block who died or were murdered were left to lie on the cold concrete floor just outside our cells. After several hours their bodies were dragged away like dead beasts. We never knew where the bodies were taken.

Post-war research, war crime evidence, and the depositions from the pathetically few B-29 crewmen liberated from Camp Omori at war's end, testify that only a few Special Prisoners made it to Kempei Headquarters, and even fewer left there alive. Kempei commanders murdered most of the B-29 prisoners under their jurisdiction. The Osaka Kempei commander ordered over 50 airmen savagely beheaded shortly after the Emperor's surrender speech.

An Osaka prisoner, a P-51 pilot, Lt. Marcus McDilda, escaped death when he faked knowledge of atomic bombs. Facing the execution squad, he was asked if he knew how the bomb was made. He said he knew ALL about it; actually he had never heard of one before in his life. He was immediately flown by special plane to Tokyo Kempei Headquarters for rigid interrogation. His tall tale, fabricated from what he remembered from his high school science course, enhanced by his vivid imagination, saved his life. He was liberated before the Japanese knew that the bomb he described wouldn't have made a decent 4th of July firecracker. (See Appendix D: Affidavits.)

We were getting stir crazy. We couldn't move without bumping into each other. The natives were really becoming unhappy with us. They wouldn't rotate the choosing of the largest rice ball. They always grabbed the largest and gobbled it like wild animals. The Americans took over an hour to eat their ration. We had learned to chew and savor each grain. This seemed to "fill" us better. The natives complained to the guards about our slow eating habits. They were ignored. Fortunately for us, Shorty never heard their complaint. He would have made us swallow our rice ball in one chunk, just for the pleasure of watching us choke.

The Kempeis allowed families of Japanese prisoners to bring food supplements. Koro never received food packages from outside, but Anidatas and the black marketeer did. They never shared. While they ate their extra food, we scraped stray grains of rice off the filthy floor and were happy for the extra bit of nourishment.

The month of June finally ended. Our morale was at rock bottom — no air raids during the whole month. We knew that we didn't have long to live on rice half-rations.

JULY 1945

The month of July arrived with a tremendous morale booster. Our navy's airplanes attacked Tokyo! There was a very short advance warning of the raid on the PA system which indicated that the navy carriers must have been near the Japanese coast. Japanese spotters in far out islands didn't get the opportunity to send early warnings as they did with B-29 raids.

Air raid sirens blasted within minutes after PA announcements of strange plane numbers. We were not familiar with these new Japanese language designations.

Soon we heard what sounded like many single-engine aircraft attacking and zooming overhead. We could hear the sound of bombs exploding nearby. Strafing machine gun fire hit our building. The Japanese flak batteries went crazy. We heard no crowd noises or cheering. Tokyo citizens who still lived in the devastated city must have taken cover in air raid shelters to avoid the strafing navy fighters attacking during broad daylight. We knew that Japanese gunners were bound to be hitting the low level attacking aircraft. Our aircraft must be hitting military targets left over from the massive B-29 attacks during March, April, and May.

Even though our building was often sprayed with machine gun fire, we were glad to know that our navy was still out there fighting. We had been despondent over the lack of B-29 raids over Tokyo during June. During the entire month of July, there were no major B-29 attacks. We had no way of knowing if they were busy elsewhere.

A few hours after the navy raid, we heard the PA system announcements signaling the approach of single or small flights of B-29s. We surmised that they were flying nuisance and reconnaissance missions, probably photographing the city and nearby areas to determine damage from the navy air raids. They needed the aerial photos to map the territory for our invasion planners. They must have up-to-date information for *Operation Coronet*, the invasion of Honshu's Tokyo Plain planned for early 1946.

I knew that unless conditions improved Special Prisoners would not survive that long. Even if a miracle happened and we were still alive in November, Imperial General Headquarters' orders for our execution, the moment the *Operation Olympic* invasion hit the shores of Kyushu Island, would end our lives. If the date for the Kyushu invasion was still 1 November, we had only two months to live.

I never told the others about my knowledge of the invasion. I kept that secret to myself. In fact, I tried to forget it, but the "knowing" haunted me.

One day the PA reported that English carriers were off the Japanese coast. Their fighters hit the Tokyo area. This meant that our British allies were coming to the aid of the Americans, now that V-E Day had ended the threat to the British Isles.

Anidatas translated most of the PA announcements for us. We became familiar with Japanese language naval aircraft designations. He placed himself next to the *benjo* every morning so that he could query San Souci about what the Russians were doing. He believed that very soon Communist Russia would sweep south over the Manchurian border and defeat their hated enemy, Japan. The war in Europe ended on 8 May 1945. Russia had plenty of time to declare war on Japan and turn their mighty war machine against the Japanese enemy. He was puzzled why the Russians had not already attacked.

Anidatas told us that the Japanese High Command believed that since President Roosevelt had died on 12 April, they could win their war by negotiating an honorable peace with an unknown and unproved president, Harry Truman.

San Souci's source of information came from recently shot down fighter pilots who knew nothing of the Russians. I could see why Anidatas was imprisoned by the Kempeis. He was a dedicated communist. He was greatly against his own government. I wondered what would happen to him after the war.

Toward the end of July, several P-51 pilots were shot down and were captured and jammed into our cell block. The attacking P-51s flew 700 miles from their base on Iwo Jima to attack Tokyo. Previously, their main task had been to escort B-29 missions. Now they were free to pursue fighter attacks on the Japanese Empire. They were free to strafe and bomb selected targets such as Tokyo. We were pleased that they gave so much attention to the Emperor's city.

Defending Japanese fighters were being saved to serve as kamikazes against the upcoming American invasion. Very few were used against B-29 missions at this stage of the war.

One day a lone P-51 came over and was shot down by the near-by flak battery. His strafing run hit the sides of our prison building. His plane crashed with a loud explosion. We heard shattering window glass from the nearby impact. He must have been carrying a 500-pound bomb to have caused such a violent explosion.

One captured P-51 pilot in our cell block was Newby from Wichita, Kansas. Another was Grant from California. One other, whose name we never knew, was badly injured from hitting the tail of his aircraft while bailing out. He was paralyzed on one side and had several bad flak wounds. He was dumped into a nearby crowded cell. His cellmates pleaded with Shorty that he would surely die without medical aid. He received none. He went out of his head from his extreme pain. He cried out recollections of his last moments in his airplane.

His cellmates tried to calm him with no success. A Kempei doctor came around the next morning, gave him an injection, and murdered him. He died within minutes and was dragged out of the cell and dumped like a sack of garbage on the floor outside his cell. His corpse lay there several hours before being dragged off.

Another P-51 pilot was dumped (literally) in the cell opposite ours. He had just undergone a violent, brutal, interrogation at Kempei Headquarters. He was badly injured and suffering from burns over most of his body. His screams of pain pierced the entire cell area. Shorty came and inspected him, then announced, "He machine-gunned innocent women and children. He will pay for his crime. He will die without medical attention." The pathetic pilot complained to Shorty that his Japanese cellmates were stealing his food — and they were. He went out of his head a couple of days later. Before he died he shouted, word for word, the questions asked during his brutal interrogation. He would yell the question, then answer it. He died and his body was dragged off — we could never find out where they took it.

Another P-51 captive by the name of Fox was in good physical shape when taken prisoner. The Kempeis beat him almost to death during his interrogation. He was taken to the horse stalls where he was beaten and kicked by Shorty. He died in his cell in the arms of Worde's pilot, Art O'Hara.

Macabre events such as these fed our intense hatred of the Japanese. Even today I ask myself, "How can we forgive these animal-like people for their inhumane treatment of those defenseless, ill, dying humans?"

To the present, as I write this book, the Japanese people have never apologized for their barbarous conduct.

Things were going from bad to worse in our crowded cell. The three natives in our cell kept to themselves and seemed to blame us for their misfortunes. My American cellmates and I existed like animals. We had deteriorated to that level. We were being consumed alive by fleas and lice. We had sores and red bumps all over our bodies from the bites. We slept fitfully and little because of the extreme crowding. Our mental condition had been reduced to a foggy haze. We didn't joke and laugh anymore. We no longer talked about food. Our hope for survival was gone. My cellmates and I were luckier than most of those in our cell block. No one had died from starvation, murder, or wounds—yet.

In our advanced stage of starvation, we began to develop symptoms of vitamin deficiency diseases such as beri-beri and pellagra. My teeth became so loose in my gums that I could wiggle them. It was a good thing that the rice was soft. I could not have chewed anything harder than the gooey rice ration. I developed painful hemorrhoids from sitting on the damp, hard cell floor on my skinny behind. I had been imprisoned by the brutal Japanese for over four months now. I figured that with luck, I might live, at the most, one more month.

San Souci told us that conditions in the horse stall cells were every bit as bad as in the dungeon, maybe worse. Prisoners were dying and being murdered there. Prisoners were being beaten to death, poisoned, and starved just as they were in our cells. Their six cells had populations of 19 to 20 Americans packed inside the eight-by-ten-foot walls. One prisoner to every two-by-two-square-foot of floor space. If they slept, they did it standing up.

Navy raiders came over every few days. B-29 scout planes were overhead almost every day. They flew at such high altitudes that we couldn't hear them, but the PA system announced their presence over Tokyo.

Some of our *benjo commee* came from torn up newspapers. We scanned every scrap of paper for photos or maps of war actions. Anidatas helped us interpret some of the scraps. According to the

Japanese propaganda, their war was being vigorously pursued and they were winning. Their small maps showed that Japanese-held territory extended far beyond islands that we knew had fallen to our forces. Japanese people were being misled, lied to, and sacrificed for the ambitious military leaders.

We no longer talked—just sat or stood and stared at nothing. I felt nothing. Our hatred of the Japanese military, the Japanese culture, the Japanese inhumanity, cranked up notch after notch. How many more notches could our hatred go? This intense hatred built up in me until sometimes I thought I would choke. About all we could do was pray and hope that God heard us. We prayed and prayed to our Almighty God for help. I worried that God would not hear me through such hate. I tried to overcome it. I really tried. Once I even tried praying for Shorty, but I wasn't sincere. I doubt that I helped him any.

If I thought at all, my thoughts centered on how I would better enjoy life if I survived the war. I thought of the basic civilized things that I missed and craved: food, drinking water, soap, clean clothes, shoes, toothpaste, ice cream, bread, combs, haircuts, a razor, baths, commodes, toilet paper, clean sheets, a good bed, movies, newspapers, radios, watches, calendars, letters, paper, pencils, a toothbrush, cars, sunlight, church, shaves, books, magazines, and medical attention. These things would mean more to me than anyone else because I would never forget being without them. In America I took these things for granted; I would never again. I would enjoy every second, minute, hour, day, month, and year to the ultimate.

I don't remember being interrogated during the entire month of July. Even that diversion was denied us, not that we would have wanted it. The last day of July I remember thinking, *one less month until November and the invasion.*

AUGUST 1945

The month of August began drearily and without any hope for change. It was unlikely that we would be rescued by our own forces. The enemy would murder us before that could happen. The guards and Shorty were not going to have a change of heart. They had no hearts. Our food ration was not going to be increased; all of Tokyo was without food. Our quarters were not going to become habitable; we were living in a corner of hell. Hell never improves.

We no longer worried about danger or beatings or death or cleanliness or mental health. We just existed . . . waiting . . . waiting . . . waiting. For what? American prisoners in the crowded dungeon cells were in such poor physical condition that we were no threat to the guards. It made their job easier. They enjoyed our plight and grinned and pointed at our misery. Shorty made his daily rounds, harassing, kicking, screaming, threatening. Morning came, the day passed in a haze, evening came. The long nights were the worst part of a 24-hour day.

My infected wounds, in spite of the poor diet, were healing. Somehow I had the impression that infected wounds would not heal until the infection was stopped. Fortunately, this was not true. About half my wounds had healed over; my skin had grown over the deep flak penetrations. The need for cotton fiber to reinforce scabs to protect my open sores was reduced. This was good, because the compress bandage that Scalero had given me was about all used up.

I was not interrogated during August. I guess, in my dazed mental condition, interrogating me was not worth their effort.

Anidatas was removed from the cell each day to assist in office functions somewhere in the building. His once neat and clean clothing was now filthy and vermin-riddled. His hair and beard had grown into a matted mess. His appearance would make an American hobo look like a millionaire. I don't know how he could be permitted into a clean office area with his fleas, lice, and offensive odor. He would contaminate anything he touched or was near. Maybe the Kempeis wanted their enemies, the communists, to appear like this as an example to the other citizens.

On 7 or 8 August, Anidatas returned to the cell after his office work and said, "You are in real trouble. The Americans have done something bad — very bad." He had overheard conversations between high level Kempei officers. A Japanese city, Hiroshima, had been destroyed by one tremendously powerful bomb. Thousands of Japanese had been killed, including many Kempei soldiers. They had never before experienced this amount of devastation from just one bomb. He said that the officers in his office were debating possible retaliation against the American prisoners. He wasn't sure what they were planning; but he warned us to be very careful and not cause any trouble.

Three miserable days passed after Anidatas's warning. The short period seemed like three weeks. We noticed that the guards seemed nervous and were watching us closer than ever. At the same time, and for the first time, they seemed afraid of us. That was a switch!

On or about the tenth of August, Anidatas returned to our cell with the news that another large Japanese city, Nagasaki, had been wiped out by a single terror bomb. Nagasaki had been the headquarters of the Japanese Second Army, charged with the defense of Kyushu. The Japanese didn't understand what had happened. They did not know what to think, what to do or what to expect. The Kempeis were furious. Only strict Kempei discipline was keeping them from killing all American prisoners. The whole prison was in a state of alarm. Shorty was agitated and paced up and down the cell block, screeching and threatening.

As I tried to make sense of this new turn of events I remembered that the 393rd Bomb Squadron had been separated from our original 504th Bomb Group and sent to their new and secret base at Wendover, Utah. Their unit was given elite status. Letters back to members of our group had mentioned that their mission was to shorten the war; they didn't know how or why. They had told us that they practiced with large, strange looking, sand-filled bombs. Had they been training to drop this new super weapon? Were they directly involved in this strange and sudden change in the war?

The 393d Bomb Squadron became the 509th Composite Bomb Group, commanded by Col. Paul Tibbets. They arrived on Tinian in June 1945 after I'd been shot down. They did drop the two bombs that ended WW II.

On 12 August another major event happened. Russia could clearly foretell the winning side and they finally declared war on their hated enemy, Japan. Stalin's hordes came pouring over the borders of Manchuria, sweeping Japanese troops out of the way as they attacked south. We had no news about this.

The Japanese PA system was silent during the month of August. Anidatas knew nothing. Sans Souci knew nothing. We waited. . . .

On the night of 14 August there was little sleeping. Everyone, guards and prisoners, was tense — waiting to find out what was about to happen. Something was up, we could sense it. Toward dawn there was a commotion outside our cell. Shorty was yelling orders to a large contingent of Kempei troops. The guards rushed into our dungeon, opening cell doors and ordering the American prisoners to leave the cells. Immediately! There was no roll call. No names were called out.

As the prisoners left the cells there were no beatings, no rifle blows to the head and shoulders. The guards stepped in to push back the natives as they tried to leave with us. Piles of shoes were dumped on the floor outside the cells. We were ordered to find a size that fit and put them on. All shoes were larger than our bony feet.

We were blindfolded, handcuffed, and herded outside into the building's courtyard. We were hurried along but there was no beating by gun butts as was usual. Shorty was screaming, ordering the guards to hurry the prisoners. He wanted us *out* of that dungeon, and we couldn't seem to do it quick enough to please him.

Once out of the dungeon, we joined other Americans. There must have been over a hundred prisoners assembled outside the prison along with that many Kempei guards. A rope was tied around the neck of each prisoner and held by a guard. One guard, one prisoner. The guards and prisoners were all moving about. The guards were yelling and Shorty was giving orders to everyone.

I suspected that that little bastard was taking us to be executed. Well, I had been marched out to my execution once before and it hadn't happened. Maybe it wouldn't this time either. At least this wasn't the "third time."

Several big army trucks were lined up nearby, engines running, the stinking exhaust smoke billowing. We were ordered to get into the trucks. The prisoners were in poor physical condition. We were so weak that guards had to lift us onto the trucks. The Kempei guards didn't hit one prisoner with bats or rifle butts. Very peculiar . . .

Shorty crawled into the back of the last truck and sat next to me. I expected to be kicked, and to have to listen to the usual verbal assault. But instead, he turned to me, stretched his lips into his version of a smile, and asked as pleasantly as he was capable, "How are you?"

How was I? I jerked around to be sure my seat mate was Shorty. *How was I?* I think this was the biggest shock of the morning. Now I really knew that something was very much amiss. I didn't know whether to laugh or choke. I had forgotten how to laugh, so I must have choked because I didn't answer him. All he had wanted since I first saw him was my demise. Now he had cheerfully asked after my welfare. My welfare was awful, thanks mostly to him . . . and he asks, "How are you?"

The prisoners finished loading just as the sun began to appear on the horizon. It was dawn on 15 August. An order was shouted and the trucks started moving. There must have been a column of ten or more Japanese army trucks.

Even with the foul exhaust smoke, the fresh air smelled so good. The rising sun was another treat. I hadn't seen sunlight in so long. *How was I?* I felt better than I had in months. Whatever was ahead, we were leaving Kempei Tai Headquarters. Unfortunately, Shorty was going with us.

I could see beneath my blindfold and noticed that the prisoner next to me had a bloody paper cement sack wrapped around his right foot which smelled very bad. I tried to say something comforting to him. Shorty snapped, "No conversation between prisoners!" But he didn't kick me or have the guard rifle butt me.

Even with my flimsy blindfold, I had a good view out the back of the truck. The scene was one of absolute devastation. Everything was burned to the ground. I noticed burned-out machine tools scattered around. I saw such things as lathes, milling machines, and drill presses abandoned in the ruins of small houses. These machines had been operated by "innocent women and children" engaged in home industries which provided the Japanese military machine with parts to be assembled in larger war factories. Our truck convoy traveled about 15 miles through devastated urban areas that were populated by ragged people living in makeshift shelters made from scrap iron and other scrounged materials. The scenes were awful. I don't know how the Emperor and his military could permit the populace to exist under such abject conditions.

Our Kempei guards were fully armed and ready for trouble, but there were no threats by the few people we saw. As we drove along, I wondered if P-51s or navy fighters might show up and attack our long column of army trucks. They didn't. We saw no aircraft at all in the skies overhead. Except for the noises made by the trucks, there were no sounds at all. The city was dead!

We finally approached a large body of water. It was Tokyo Bay. The convoy parked on the side of the road that ran parallel to the shore and about 100 yards from the water's edge. Between the road and the water was some kind of a vegetable garden. On down the road was a wooden bridge which connected the mainland to a small island in the bay. On the island were several wooden buildings enclosed by a tall wooden wall.

The Kempeis unloaded the prisoners and marched us through the squash plants to the edge of the bay. The ground was soft and sandy and the squash crop made it difficult to walk. Some of the worst-case prisoners couldn't even stand up; they crawled through the tangled vines to get to the water's edge or were dragged by the guards. No one was left in the trucks. Our guards removed the handcuffs, the blindfolds, and the ropes around our necks.

By now the sun was shining brightly overhead. It was blinding to our eyes, which were unaccustomed to light. We were like mules who had lived their whole lives in a mine and saw sunlight for the first time as they were brought to the surface when they got too old to work.

We were overjoyed to be breathing fresh, clean air and seeing the sun overhead. Shorty shouted for us to remove our filthy clothing and wash off in the Bay. I looked back toward the trucks and saw that the Kempeis were setting up several machine guns pointed in our direction. I suspected that they were getting ready to strafe us. I knew for sure that anyone who tried to run would be gunned down.

When we were stripped naked, I looked over the group. I saw starved, bony bodies. I wish I had a photograph of this sorry looking assembly. We were living skeletons. Angry red spots covered our entire bodies from flea bites. Our matted beards and hair were awful looking.

No guards stayed with us at the water's edge. All the Kempei guards moved back behind the machine guns. Our prisoner group was alone in the bay. Many of the prisoners were crying in their joy. We were all laughing and splashing in the wonderful clean water. We

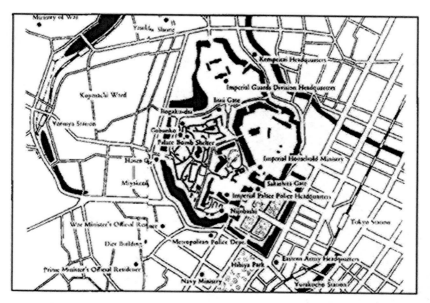

Map showing Emperor's Palace in center and Kempei Tai Headquarters in upper center.

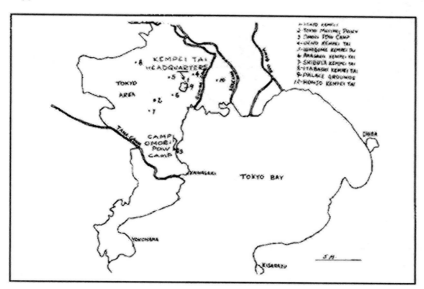

Map showing locations of Kempei Tai Headquarters, satellite Kempei Tai prisons, and Camp Omori on Tokyo Bay.

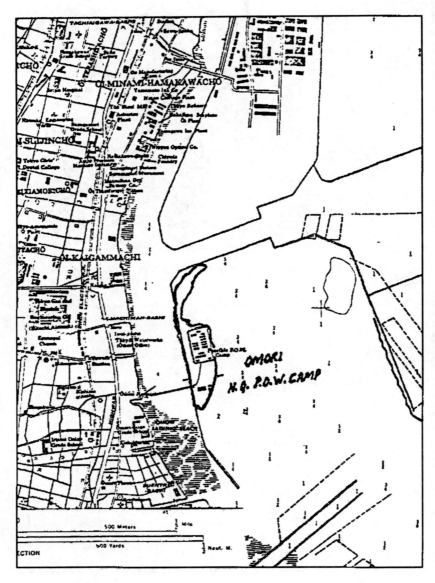

Map showing Camp Omori's locations on Tokyo Bay and outlined area to be reclaimed from the bay's waters.

Camp Omori taken by "POW Supply Drop" B-29. Note camp dock at left center and bridge to mainland.

Sketch of Camp Omori POW barracks by Marcus Worde.

29 August 1945 — POWs at Camp Omori dock as Commander Stassen and Commander Simpson, acting under Admiral Halsey's legendary order, "Those are our boys. Go and get them!" In order to liberate them, Admiral Halsey's fleet entered Tokyo Bay with mine sweepers in the lead, followed by destroyers and hospital ships three days before the September 2, 1945, surrender day on the USS Missouri.

Liberation of Camp Omori on 29 August 1945.

Commander Harold Stassen addressing Camp Omori prisoners. Commander Roger Simpson stands to Stassen's left.

Aerial view of Camp Omori. Note "P.W." and "Pappy Boyington Here" on roofs painted on with toothpowder.

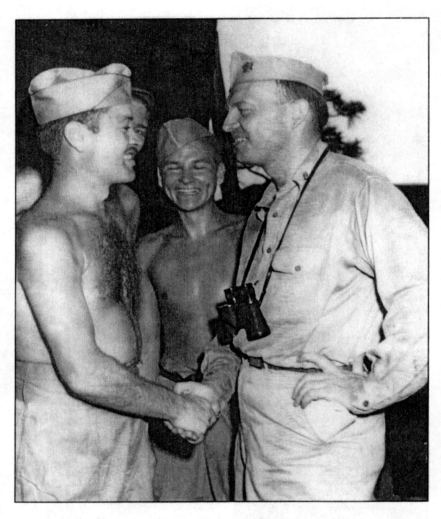

Major Gregory "Pappy" Boyington (USMC) and Commander Harold E. Stassen during liberation of POWs at Camp Omori, Japan on 29 August 1945 when Stassen said, "Pappy, we thought you were dead! I sure am glad to see you!" Pappy said, "I am twice as glad to see you, Commander!"

Author on Honolulu hospital grounds a month after his liberation — still skinny!

Emaciated Camp Omori prisoners.

Telegram, dated 31 August 1945, to author's parents from Dallas newspaper announcing his liberation.

WESTERN UNION

Telegram, dated 22 September 1945, announcing author's liberation.

THE WHITE HOUSE
WASHINGTON

TO MEMBERS OF UNITED STATES ARMED FORCES BEING
REPATRIATED IN SEPTEMBER 1945:

It gives me special pleasure to welcome you
back to your native shores, and to express, on behalf of the people of the United States, the joy we
feel at your deliverance from the hands of the enemy.
It is a source of profound satisfaction that our efforts to accomplish your return have been successful.

You have fought valiantly in foreign lands
and have suffered greatly. As your Commander in
Chief, I take pride in your past achievements and
express the thanks of a grateful Nation for your
services in combat and your steadfastness while a
prisoner of war.

May God grant each of you happiness and an
early return to health.

Harry Truman

Letter from President Harry Truman welcoming author's return home.

Interior view of 504th War Room with stage and sliding panels used in briefings.

504th Bomb Group command staff — L/R: Lt. Col. Howard Hugos/Deputy Group CO; Lt. C.P. Tilton/Executive Officer; Lt. Col. Oren Poage/ Operations Officer; Col. Glen Martin/Group Co.; Maj. Bob Kemp/Intelligence Officer; Capt. Earl Bonham/Supply Officer; Maj. Gene/Adjutant.

504th Bomb Group "Happy Warriors" at briefing.

General Curtis LeMay (deceased) and author at 20th Air Force Reunion.

July, 1995 view of Himeji City, Japan—relatives of bombing victims with Japanese Memorial to over 500,000 killed by bombs. Author presented 504th BG History to city officials.

ATOMIC BOMBS—"Fat Man" and "Little Boy" with author and Larry Smith, 9th Bomb Group historian.

Gen. Paul W. Tibbets, Jr., and the author.

Governor Harold Stassen

Governor Stassen and author during pre-publication visit—St. Paul, Minnesota—January, 1997.

splashed water over our bodies and cleaned up as best we could. This ocean bath was the best bath I had ever had. I knew that I might be machine-gunned any minute but I didn't care. I was so happy to feel like a human again.

The senior Kempei guards were in a huddle by the machine guns. Shorty was dancing around waving his arms and arguing. The others seemed to be against whatever Shorty wanted them to do. I learned later from Al Andrews, who had arrived at the bay after we did, that he'd overheard guards arguing about whether to machine gun the whole prisoner group or not. They evidently decided that it would not be in *their* best interest. They all knew that the war was all but over. And they knew who the victors would be. They were scared enough to defy Shorty.

After bathing, we were ordered to dress again in our vermin-ridden, ragged clothing and marched back across the squash patch. We assembled near the wooden bridge. We were handcuffed, but no blindfolds were tied on us. Each prisoner was guarded by a soldier. We watched as a contingent of Japanese soldiers came toward us from the prison compound on the island.

Shorty shouted at us that the Kempei Tais were turning us over to the regular Japanese army who ran the prison we could see across the bridge. He stepped back and a senior Japanese army officer stepped forward and haughtily told us that we would be marched into his prison, Camp Omori.

He then shouted an order, the guards turned loose of the neck ropes and we moved toward the prison camp at a trot, trying to put as much space between us and our Kempei torturers as we could. I tried to keep up with the rapid pace but soon fell behind. Those prisoners who had crawled into the bay to bathe were dragged by Japanese soldiers into the prison compound.

We left Shorty behind and no one wished him well and no one told him goodbye. If I had looked back and seen the ground open up and the devil reach out and grab him, I would not have been surprised — or cared.

I was winded and could barely walk, so I was one of the last to enter the prison gates. As we moved toward the camp, I saw Hanks. He was limping along and laughing. I saw Al Andrews. He was still wearing the long Japanese army overcoat. He trotted along and looked over at me, grinned and waved. He looked great! I looked around, searching the group to see if I could find any others of our crew . . . but there was only Al and me.

I was no longer caged at the Kempei Tai Headquarters. We were going to another camp, and whatever was ahead, it would be better than the hell hole we had left behind.

For the first time in many months, I had a glimmer of hope that I might live to see the end of the war. I thought that maybe, just maybe, I might see the United States again. I might even get back to Fort Worth, Texas, and see my mother and dad. There was hope.

Chapter 10

Camp Omori

Camp Omori was located on a small, man-made island in Tokyo Bay. The island's major axis ran north-south. It was a Japanese prison camp with wooden buildings surrounded by a tall, wooden stockade fence. A canal spanned by a bridge separated the township of Omori from the island prison. As I limped through the gate of Camp Omori, I felt as if I had entered a "country club." Camp Omori, to its present inmates, may have been a hell-hole. To me, it looked almost like a resort.

I had finally reached a Japanese prisoner of war camp. Here I could breathe clean air, see sunlight, and hopefully receive medical care. It was obvious that we would be in a different environment. There were about 20 or 30 guards surrounding us in the prison compound. Omori guards were not wearing the Kempei Tai armband. They did not have the surly look of our previous tormentors. No Kempei guards entered the camp with us. After turning us over to Omori guards, they dismounted their machine-guns, climbed on the trucks, and departed. Shorty went with them.

We entered the prison camp through its front gate and were marched to the headquarters building. On either side of the street were wooden buildings. Through the window of one of the buildings I saw a medical office. Doctors and medics were busily at work. I could see steam rising from a medical instrument sterilizer. I believed that I was close to Heaven.

Our pathetic looking group milled around in front of the camp's headquarters. We curiously and cautiously examined our surroundings. The prison enclosure was about the size of a city block. Headquarters was also the prison officers' quarters. Behind headquarters was a small dispensary building. Seven prisoner barracks were located on both sides of a dirt street leading to the prison's rear section where a bath house, cook house, and small parade ground were located. Guards were housed in front sections of each barracks. A *benjo* was located at the rear of each barracks against the enclosure wall. The frontmost barracks was surrounded by a fence. It was where Special Prisoners were housed. It was where our group would be housed.

Camp Omori was headquarters for the Tokyo Area POW Prison Camp Command. This command was responsible for POW camps as far north as Sendai in northern Honshu. The commandant was Colonel Sakaba. His prisoners included Americans, Australians, British, Canadians, Dutch, New Zealanders, and Italians. After Italy surrendered, Italian nationals were arrested and sent to POW camps. There were no Chinese. There were about 400 prisoners in Camp Omori before our arrival.

Two Japanese officers came out of headquarters. They were accompanied by two Allied officer prisoners. One of which was the POW camp senior officer. His name was Commander Maher. He appeared clean and in fair health. We must have looked pretty awful to him. He looked us over and sadly shook his head.

An elderly Japanese colonel drew himself to rigid attention and spoke in halting English. "You are prisoners of the Imperial Japanese Army. We have taken responsibility for your imprisonment from the Kempei Tai. We operate a fair and disciplined prisoner of war camp. We have strict rules here. You will be told what these rules are. Swift punishment will be administered when rules are broken. You are still Special Prisoners accused of war crimes against Japanese people, and will be segregated from other prisoners until your fate is decided. You will not work while here. You will receive half-food rations because of your criminal status.You will receive no medical treatment. You will be assigned a Japanese army barracks similar to that which our soldiers use. Your most senior officer will be in charge of your group. He will be responsible to the Allied senior camp officer, Commander Maher. You will respect your guards. The war is not over. Welcome to Camp Omori."

Commander Maher stepped forward to address us. "We Allied prisoners of Camp Omori welcome you. Our hearts go out to you for your suffering at your previous prison. You will find that Camp Omori is one of the best camps in the Japanese POW system. You will receive better care, better food, and humane treatment. We hope your life here will be pleasant until the war is over."

He directed us to line up in an orderly formation and "count off." There were a few more than 100 Special Prisoners in our group. Next, he directed us to strip naked, identify and bundle our filthy clothing, and leave it in a pile. Our rags were to be boiled and washed to rid them of the vermin and accumulated filth and returned to us later in the day. I pretended to scratch at my flea bites as I furtively retrieved the silver dollar from my watch pocket. I clenched it in my fist. I held my breath until I was sure that no one had seen me reach for it.

Our emaciated, naked group was herded into the segregated barracks to be kept apart from the rest of the POWs. Since our barracks was surrounded by a fence, we couldn't communicate with other POWs. We were not allowed out of our fenced area. We were held in a prison within a prison.

Our barracks was divided into three rooms. The frontmost room was the guard quarters. It housed about six guards. We were forced to bow to a couple of guards in the room. We never had to bow to Kempei guards. Omori guards insisted on respectful bows whenever a prisoner approached or passed by. A guard unlocked the door to the second room, we entered, and were excitedly greeted by about 80 Special Prisoners, mostly American submariners and a few B-29 flyers. Guards shouted guttural orders and moved our group through their room.

We were pushed into the farthest room, which was the same size as the middle room. A dirt center aisle ran the length of the building. On each side of the aisle were two wooden platforms, one above the other. The lower platform was two feet above the floor. The upper level was four feet above the lower level. Platforms were about six-feet deep. Windows were spaced along the building's sides between platforms. Ladders provided access to the upper level. Each of us was assigned a two-foot-wide spot on the platforms. We sat in our assigned slot during the day and slept there during the night.

I studied my magnificent prison location. Its two-by-six-foot size was enormous. It gave me twelve-square feet of living space as compared to five and one-half square feet that I had at Kempei Tai Headquarters. I had room to stretch out my skinny frame.

Each prisoner was issued a blanket, soup bowl, tea cup, rice cup, bamboo spoon, and toothbrush. These items were clean and new. We each had our own. We couldn't believe our good luck. We were excited and began laughing and chattering about our good fortune. Guards immediately shouted the order, "Shut up." They knew a few words of English. We were still not allowed to talk to each other. Some things had not changed.

A door at the far end of our room led to a latrine. We were told that we had to get a wooden *"benjo* pass" from our barracks commander before we could go to the latrine. Guards did not want too many prisoners in the *benjo* area at one time. Five at a time was the limit.

I sat on my allotted space and looked out the windows. *Windows!* What a luxury! I could see plants growing against the fence. Prisoners were raising tomatoes, beans, squash, and other vegetables. It was a beautiful sight.

Noontime came. A prisoner mess detail arrived with large, steaming buckets of rice and soup. Mess prisoners ignored the half-ration order and filled our rice and soup bowls to the brim. The rice was hot and clean, with no vermin. The soup was delicious and wholesome. I ate like a starved animal. There was no way to weigh, but I estimated that my weight on entering Camp Omori was less than 100 pounds.

Among the prisoners in the middle room was Maj. Gregory (Pappy) Boyington, a US Marine Corps flying ace. After we had eaten our first meal, he came into our room and briefed us on how to conduct ourselves in order to avoid trouble with the guards. He told us that every morning we were to line up in the center aisle for *tenko* (roll call). We would count off in the presence of Japanese guards. He urged us to be very respectful to the guards. They were to be treated like gods. Lack of proper respect could be deadly. We were to learn that respect, which included bowing to the guards in the proper Japanese fashion. He demonstrated acceptable bowing techniques. Pappy slipped through the door several times during the next few days with suggestions on how to make our stay easier. He seemed to be popular with his troops in the middle room and was their senior officer. He made a lot of points with us.

Major Boyington entered the war as a member of General Chennault's Flying Tiger Group in China. He returned to the Marines and became an ace and commanded a squadron. He was shot down while flying out of Bougainville on 3 January 1944 and captured near Rabaul. He was lucky to be alive. Very few Marine flyers were taken alive in that area. He and the others in his middle room were also classed Special Prisoners because their "superior" fighting embarrassed "superior" Japanese war commanders. Survivors from American submarines were in his section, including Commander O'Kane and the few survivors from the submarine, USS *Tang.*

Our de-loused clothing was returned. Filth had held the fabric together. Our clothes were now just rags. Flak fragments, which I'd saved from my wounds, were still concealed in the lining of Andrews' flight jacket. They survived the boiling operation. Clean clothes, even rags, felt good on my skinny body. My lucky coin went back into my watch pocket.

More food arrived for dinner. My shrunken stomach must have stretched to accommodate the food bonanza. A recently shot down P-51 pilot, whose name was Heinz, evidently did not appreciate the soup and rice as much as I did. He gave me most of his ration. I did not refuse it.

Night arrived. I stretched out in my spacious two-foot-wide sleeping space. There was plenty of room to stretch full length on the hard boards. I could turn over without waking my neighbor. No bony elbows poked at me during the night. No dirty, matted hair was in my face. I didn't need top cover in the August weather so I folded my blanket and cushioned it beneath me. My bony hips did not hurt. I slept luxuriously.

Swiss Red Cross representatives visited the camp and inspected our Special Prisoner accommodations. They weren't the least interested in our physical condition, medical needs, or tales of Kempei Tai atrocities. They acted as if their visit was an unwanted chore. They "did their duty" and left. I never received a Red Cross package during my entire imprisonment. I did, however, get a doughnut and a cup of coffee at a stop en route back to the States.

The next day we heard Canadian and Australian prisoners in the adjacent barracks singing and excitedly calling back and forth. Were they having a party or were the Canadians and Australians just a merry, happy sort of folk? Something was going on over there, for sure! One of our people was able to furtively engage in conversation with one of the Canadians through the fence while visiting the latrine. He came back with exciting news. Canadians learned from a Japanese civilian during their work detail that the Emperor made his *first* radio speech. The Emperor told the Japanese people that the war was over. *Japan was going to surrender!*

Bob Martindale, POW work officer, told me recently that camp authorities and some prisoners knew about the Emperor's speech on the day it happened, which was the day before we left Kempei Tai Headquarters. No announcement was made to POWs that the war was over. We learned the good news through the "latrine grapevine." Neither the officers in charge nor the guards gave any indication that there had been a cease-fire. Omori guards did not relax their attention. In fact, they demanded more bows and respect and administered rifle butt blows more freely for lack of repect. We learned quickly how to pay our respect.

Kempeis rushed us out of their headquarters soon after the Emperor's speech. Now we understood why they were so anxious to be rid of us. They did not want us on their hands at the time of surrender. On the day before the Emperor's speech, Kempei Tai Headquarters commander, Col. Keijiro Otani, issued orders to his deputy, Lt.Col. Ranjo Fujino, to:

"Immediately execute all American prisoners."

Fortunately for us, Fujino did not follow his commander's orders. He knew that the end of the war had come and was afraid that if victorious Americans found that he was guilty of such a massacre, he would pay dearly for this final atrocity. He refused to carry out the order. His solution was to get the Special Prisoners out of the Kempei Tai Headquarters as quickly as possible.

A couple of days after we learned about the Emperor's speech, Omori's commander, Colonel Sakaba, called the entire prisoner population together on the parade ground. This was our first time to mix with the other POWs. He made a speech about the honorable war that Japan had fought against the Allies. He talked about the Greater East Asia Co-Prosperity Sphere and why it was good for Asiatic people. Then he made a very peculiar statement. He said:

"Remember this — after the war ends, Japan will serve as a buffer between America and our common enemy, communist Russia!"

What did he mean? Russia was our ally and friend!

Colonel Sakaba stressed that hostilities had ceased for the present, but the war was not over yet. He did not know when the war would end — that might not happen for years. We were to behave and follow Japanese orders or severe punishment would be dealt out. He announced that the Special Prisoner category was canceled. We new arrivals were now regular prisoners of war. We were elated! When we were dismissed and returned to our barracks, the barracks door was not locked behind us.

Canadians told us that they learned that Colonel Sakaba had been in charge of a POW camp in World War I when Japan had been on our side. His camp held Germans. When he had announced to his German prisoners that the war was over, they immediately broke loose and burned down his house. He did not want a repeat of this, so he made a BIG point that "the war is not over yet."

The next day I went on sick call. I went to the dispensary. I was weighed in the prison hospital. After a week of eating as much rice and soup as I could consume, I weighed in at *ninety-six pounds*. Medics examined my infected wounds, cleansed them, medicated them, and applied bandages. It had been months since I smelled antiseptic medicines. I cannot describe the wonderful feeling of clean bandages on my wounds. An American major, a doctor captured in the Philippines, treated me. He said that he was amazed that as much healing had taken place. He assured me that I had never had gangrene.

Damn Shorty!

Andrews and I were in the same barracks room. We visited and compared notes on our captivity. I learned that he was not held at Kempei Tai Headquarters. He and most of Bill Grounds' crew were taken to small neighborhood Kempei prisons. They were mistreated but didn't receive the ultra-brutal Kempei treatment and interrogations that we'd received. He had been starved on Special Prisoner half-rations and was almost eaten alive by vermin. He had not suffered from flak wounds or cell overcrowding. He was amazed at the extreme cruelty that I described.

There were many interesting, long-time prisoners present in the camp. There were a few survivors of the cruiser USS *Houston* sunk early in the war near Indonesia. I visited with Comdr. Dick O'Kane of the USS *Tang*. O'Kane's sub sank 24 ships, totaling almost 94,000 tons in just over four war patrols. He'd won the Congressional Medal of Honor. He told me about being sunk by his own torpedo. On their last patrol two torpedoes were launched at an enemy ship. One of the torpedoes sank a large Japanese freighter, the second torpedo circled back and sank their own submarine.

Japanese began issuing captured military supplies. We received shirts, pants, and shoes captured during the war's initial months. Brand new US Army blankets emerged. Dutch knapsacks and British bush jackets appeared. I received a pair of pajamas. Bottles of vitamin pills were dispensed. It was amazing what the Japanese had stock piled. Why had they not dispensed these needed items to the prisoners or to their own people?

An Army Air Force colonel, senior to other prisoners, assumed command of the group in our room. I don't remember his name. He was a martinet and disliked by our group.

When supplies of Japanese candy and cigarettes were brought into our barracks our senior officer would not allow an equitable distribution. He divided candy evenly, but ordered that cigarettes be issued only to the prisoners who smoked. Cigarettes made valuable trading goods. One cigarette could be exchanged for one candy bar. Non-smokers, and I was one of them, objected strongly. We, too, could barter. The colonel smoked and thought his cigarette distribution order was all right. It wasn't.

Commander Maher was summoned and quickly corrected the problem. Our senior officer was replaced.

Soap was also valuable. It was in short supply and was even more valuable for trading purposes than tobacco or candy. If there is ever another war, I know what goods to stockpile—cigarettes and soap.

Many airplanes flew over our camp as the days went by. Japanese and our own were in the sky. There were no shots fired and no bombs dropped. Navy aircraft flew over the camp daily and dropped supplies of food and cigarettes. Large TBF (torpedo-bomber-fighter) planes buzzed the camp 100 feet off the ground. They opened torpedo bays and dumped all kinds of goodies along the mud flat adjacent to the prison. Supplies smoothly slid to a stop in the mud. As we enjoyed American food supplies, we paid for our hunger-lust. Our starved bodies experienced nausea and diarrhea. Our shrunken stomachs couldn't cope with the rich food.

Navy flyers, among the prisoners, swaggered around and boasted that their branch of the service was doing the most to aid the prisoners. We B-29 airmen wondered where our people were. Where were our buddies? When they finally came, during the last week before liberation, they came with a vengeance. B-29s dropped tons of supplies by parachute into our camp area. Some parachutes separated from their loads. Heavy boxes plunged and smashed open. A container holding thousands of Mounds candy bars hit in the middle of Omori's *benjo* sewer dump. It was a total loss! To this day, I have an aversion to eating Mounds bars. Two prisoners were hit and killed by falling boxes. Many drops landed quite a distance from our camp. Omori did not possess a truck to use in recovering stray POW supply drops. Military ingenuity common to all armies took place. A detail of guards traveled to downtown Tokyo and "liberated" an army truck. They used it to gather containers dropped on the mainland. I was amazed that guards and nearby citizens didn't appropriate these materials. They didn't. They must have been afraid to steal our goodies.

An event happened during my second week at Omori that sent my hopes plummeting. One afternoon, familiar sounds of a bombing raid were heard. Somewhere down the bay, a terrific attack was being made on a Japanese target. With peace so close at hand, why was a heavy bombing raid in progress? We anxiously tried to find out if the cease fire had been canceled. Australians and Canadians, always the first "in the know," told us what had happened. It was unbelievable!

Fanatic officers at a Japanese naval base aimed a torpedo at an American ship after the cease fire. The American Navy raised holy hell with Japanese peace negotiators. Japanese Imperial Army Headquarters investigated and found out what their navy had done. Our navy was assured that this naval base would be punished. We heard Japanese Army bombers attacking their own navy base. I do not repeat this from hearsay. It happened! I was there! I heard the bombs! I know what a bombing raid sounds like. I had been on the ground with bombs going off all around me. This peculiar and important event has never been reported in any documentation that I've ever read. Why has it been kept a secret?

During daylight hours we observed a constant stream of Japanese fighter aircraft landing at an airfield within sight of our camp. For days this went on. We must have seen several hundred aircraft land nearby. We learned that the Japanese had been ordered to concentrate and deactivate their airplanes at certain spots. Propellers were removed and the planes were pushed forward onto their noses. The airfield became a "bone yard."

Another event happened during my Omori imprisonment which has never been reported to our American public. One day a group of prisoners arrived at Camp Omori. They drove up in Japanese Army staff cars. They were accompanied by ranking Japanese military and civilian personnel. These prisoners were well-clothed, well-groomed, and well-fed. They looked and acted like tourists on vacation. Talk was friendly and easy between the prisoners and their Japanese escorts. Japanese camp authorities seemed to be pleased with their arrival. They were brought into the camp and given special quarters.

These were Propaganda Prisoners. They were traitors!

These Allied prisoners had willingly allowed themselves to be used to help Japanese prepare and present radio and press information for broadcast to the world about the righteousness of Japan's war against the Allies. They helped the Japanese interpret war news for anti-Allied propaganda purposes. They were prisoners from a model prison camp used when the Japanese had to show how they housed and treated Allied prisoners. I recalled that special interrogator at Kempei Tai Headquarters who had interviewed me for recruitment in their society. That same interrogator ordered that my wounds be infected when I didn't measure up. When these Propaganda Prisoners attended camp activities they were shunned by the other POWs. They stayed pretty much to themselves. They were brought to Omori so that they could be liberated as regular prisoners of war. Some were tried for war crimes after the war.

During the second week of our stay, the Japanese paid us according to our rank. They used a pay scale which compared our rank with the equivalent rank in the Japanese military. For some reason, I received 88 yen—not much money then. Today it would be worth almost one dollar. I was told this was pay for a two month imprisonment. A bit short, but what the heck?

One night British prisoners put on a vaudeville show which included scenery, music, and costumes. Several were dressed as ladies. It was almost professionally done. The humor was typically British. Americans didn't always laugh when they were supposed to, but we appreciated their treat. Japanese camp personnel attended and seemed to enjoy the show. Propaganda Prisoners were treated as if they had leprosy!

Prisoners played ball games, card games, sang, exercised, and learned how to enjoy life again. These privileges were strange to those of us that had been imprisoned in dark dungeons. We found that it was actually confusing to see normal life take place, even what passed as normal in a prison camp. We wanted to join in but most of us were still too weak.

One day the Special Prisoners were divided into small groups and taken to the Japanese bath house. First, we stripped bare and soaped off with buckets of warm water. We then entered a large, well-heated, wooden tank and soaked for a long time. This was a treat. I never learned if regular POWs were allowed periodic access to this luxury.

We were allowed out of the camp's walls onto the mud flats during low tide to look for clams. This was good therapy for those of us still in a dazed state. It was not physically tiring. We found a few clams which added to our cuisine. Another day, the Japanese opened up a storeroom where thousands of books, donated by the Red Cross, were stored. None had ever been given to POWs. We were allowed to choose two books each. I still have a mathematics book and a fiction book from this collection.

Prisoners began making American, British, and Dutch flags. They scrounged cloth and coloring materials. The flags looked great. Japanese did not interfere. Toward the end of our stay, the sky was filled with American aircraft, particularly navy planes. The few navy and marine flyers among the prisoners jumped up and down and tried to signal their buddies. POW signs were painted on the roofs of several buildings. A sign, PAPPY BOYINGTON IS HERE, was painted on top of one of the buildings using white toothpowder, the only substitute for paint available. This resulted in a concentration of marine aircraft overhead.

One evening Pappy Boyington entered our section and told us that he'd heard the guards, housed in our barrack's front section, discussing a plan to murder as many Americans as they could before POWs were liberated. Guards were going to start with a drunken saki liquor party and then attack the prisoners, killing as many as possible. After the murders, they planned to commit hari-kari in honor of their Emperor. Pappy told us that prisoners in his section would try to stop the guards by throwing blankets over them and try to disarm the drunken brutes. If they were unsuccessful, then we were on our own. He suggested we prepare some way to overpower the intruders. We made plans to defend ourselves.

The next morning Pappy came back with the news that the guards had gotten drunk on saki and most had passed out. Several of them tried to kill themselves. They botched the job. American doctors had the job of patching them up.

One of the happiest events of my life occurred on 29 August 1945!

American marines landed and liberated us!

Chapter 11

Liberation

On 28 August a navy plane flew over and dropped a message saying that American aircraft had landed the day before at a Japanese airfield called Atsugi. We were to be liberated the next day.

The prisoner who retrieved the note took it to the camp work officer, Bob Martindale, who passed it on to the chief Japanese guard, Watanabe. Watanabe, having been advised that liberation was inevitable, ordered that each barracks commander be notified. Before nightfall, every prisoner had heard the word that tomorrow he would be freed.

There was little sleeping that night. We were excited and anxious to see if tomorrow would bring our liberators. This rumor was based on a lone piece of paper that had fallen out of the sky. Was it possible that this was a hoax?

The morning of 29 August 1945 began clear and quiet. I had slept very little and was awake to watch the sun rise over the horizon. The rising sun was Japan's emblem. I wondered if this was a good sign for the day or an evil one. Would I ever again watch a sunrise and not remember the atrocities and wanton brutality of the Japanese? I promised myself and my Maker that if I could be liberated this day, I would enjoy every sunrise I could witness for the rest of my days. After my prayer I felt an assurance that the sunrise and the beautiful sight it created as it illuminated Tokyo Bay was a *good* sign.

Until the last few days, I hadn't observed any shipping in the bay. Our mines had put a stop to Japanese shipping and sunk most of their remaining merchant fleet. This morning I could see a number of large ships anchored far out in Tokyo Bay. I couldn't tell if the ships were ours or Japanese.

From the first light of day we watched and waited. We watched and waited all morning. After we had our rice and soup at mid-day, we watched and waited.

About mid-afternoon the August sun was bearing down, nothing was happening, so I went back to my barracks and fell into an exhausted sleep. I hadn't been asleep long when I was awakened by shouts and cheers from the bay side of the camp. I ran out of the barracks toward the noise and saw prisoners pointing toward the bay and jumping up and down. Three assault landing craft were heading directly toward our shore. At the same time, streams of navy fighters swooped toward the camp as if pointing the way for the approaching boats. More fighter planes were flying higher in the sky, circling overhead.

The guards did not try to control our enthusiasm. They huddled together and looked toward the bay; most of them headed for the camp gate and ran across the bridge toward the mainland. Guards had been sneaking away and deserting for the last few days.

The entire prisoner population surged toward the camp's dock. We crowded along the pier. We were wild with joy. Those who could jump and yell did so. Singing broke out. National anthems were sung in several languages. The weaker prisoners stood or sat and waved their arms. Handmade flags were unfurled: British, Australian, Canadian, Dutch, New Zealand. The largest and most beautiful flag of all was our *Stars and Stripes*. Captured flyers from the USS *Yorktown* aircraft carrier had made a flag. It was amazing and miraculous that on such short notice such flags could be improvised. A week ago the only flag in the prison was the *Rising Sun* flag of Japan.

By now the boats were close enough that we could see the United States flags streaming back in the wind. What a beautiful sight! We couldn't yet see the 48 stars but the upper left blue patch and the red and white stripes stood out distinctly. Old Glory had never looked in greater glory. These were our fellow fighting men coming to rescue us.

The approaching landing craft slowed and cautiously approached the pier. Some prisoners jumped into the water and tried to swim out to meet the boats. Some overeager prisoners jumped into the water as the boats approached the pier. As they floundered around, strong helping hands pulled them into the boats.

The boats were full of heavily-armed marines. They were veterans of bloody island fights against the Japanese. They appeared ready, willing, and able to handle any opposition. Their guns were at the ready. They were the toughest, meanest-looking combat troops I had ever seen. They looked like avenging angels, come to save us.

Marines jumped off the docked boats. Without a second's hesitation, communication troops deployed into the camp area and set up impressive looking radio equipment and were in instant contact with ships anchored in the bay and aircraft overhead. Orders were barked out. A battle line was established completely surrounding the camp. The operation's speed and efficiency were awesome!

As the perimeter defense was being established, Commanders Roger Simpson and Harold Stassen and their staff stepped onto the dock. They had been assigned by Adm. Bull Halsey to organize a rescue plan for Allied POWs. Simpson was the Liberation Force commander. Simpson barked orders and a command post was set up inside the camp area. American fighter aircraft circled overhead, eager to support the ground troops. Good things began happening.

My position was very close to the command post. I heard the steady crackle of crisp military messages. It was obvious that if more military support was needed, it could be quickly furnished. The speed and efficiency of the landing operation amazed us. We were in safe hands!

The United States Marines had landed! The situation was well in hand!

Not a shot was fired by either side. Capture of the camp was immediate and complete! A US Naval officer, obviously one of the officers in command, had finished his initial duties and was standing relaxed and smiling as the many prisoners gathered in awe around him. I approached him and asked if I could get his autograph. I apologized and explained that the only paper I had was a piece of toilet paper. He laughed and pulled out his pen and signed while asking who I was and how I was doing. I thanked him. When I read the signature, I realized that this was Comdr. Harold Stassen, Assistant Chief of Staff to Admiral Halsey, Governor of Minnesota, on leave, and future presidential candidate. He was as happy to be here as we were to have him. He had come on this first rescue operation as Halsey's staff observer. I had the privilege 50 years later to shake his hand and thank him again.

Camp Omori was the first prison camp liberated on the Japanese mainland.

I later learned, from a friend on Admiral Halsey's staff, that General MacArthur had ordered that no prisoners were to be liberated until after the signing of peace. Admiral Halsey knew that there was a high risk that prisoners could be slaughtered before the formal surrender three days away. He disregarded MacArthur's edict and ordered that our camp be liberated immediately. The order from Halsey to Simpson and Stassen was, *"The prison camp can be seen on the shore on Tokyo Bay. Those are our boys. Go get them!"*

The Japanese commandant had come out of his headquarters at the first sound of shouting. He was obviously very angry and agitated. He called ranking POW officers and together they marched toward the pier. Commander Stassen told me 50 years later, that Colonel Sakaba shouted at him, "I have no authority to turn these men over to you." Stassen looked at him coldly and said, "You have no authority, *period!*" He back-armed him aside and walked on toward the camp.

Colonel Sakaba was placed in the protective custody of a couple of marines who towered over his small body. He was ordered to command his remaining troops not to interfere. By now there were no remaining troops. The guards had fled. The little Japanese stood alone.

There were navy medics accompanying the task force. These specialists rapidly searched for and identified the sick and wounded prisoners. Acutely ill and wounded prisoners were given immediate medical attention. They were the first to be loaded on the landing craft and taken to the hospital ship anchored in Tokyo Bay.

Prisoners were examined and separated into groups of 30. I

was designated "ambulatory" by the medics. I didn't know then what ambulatory meant, I just kept close to the pier so that there was no chance that I would be left behind. Weakened Kempei prisoners had found during our limited freedom that we couldn't run without falling down. If necessary, I was ready to crawl to that landing craft, but I was glad that I was able to walk on deck with my head held high.

Within the hour after our liberators' arrival the first landing craft were headed toward the large naval ships anchored in the middle of Tokyo Bay. We shouted and cheered as the boats left the dock. The landing craft ran a shuttle service from the camp to the ship waiting in the bay until all were liberated.

My boat was the last to leave the camp. Al Andrews and I were on the same landing craft. The boat was packed with happy prisoners. The Coast Guard helmsman steered us straight out into the middle of the enormous bay. He was laughing with us, sharing our happiness. As we plowed out into the bay, clean and sweet smelling ocean spray showered us. The American flag flapped defiantly in the breeze. I had never before known such elation.

I looked back as my boat pulled away from the dock. The marines guarding the perimeter were still in place. The camp appeared deserted and quiet. There were no Japanese guards to be seen. The elderly Japanese army camp commander stood alone on the dock.

In a short time, we pulled alongside a large white ship with red crosses painted on the sides. We looked up and saw the USS *Benevolence* lettered on the prow. It was a navy hospital ship. Smiling, white-uniformed nurses and crew lined the rail above us as we tied up. What a beautiful sight! A ramp of many steps went from the water to the deck of the ship. To me, they looked like the golden steps to Heaven.

After the landing craft was secured, our raunchy and emaciated group struggled up the steps and climbed on the deck of the surgically clean ship. After all the filth that we'd endured, it was hard to believe that anything could be so clean. The ship was spotless! The white-uniformed nurses and doctors broke into cheers as we came aboard. We'd forgotten what friendly, humane treatment could be like. No guttural shouts, no club blows, no rifle butts! We felt like human beings again.

I was under United States protection! I was liberated! I was going to live! I was not going to be executed on the first of November when the Allies invaded Kyushu Island. I was not going to starve to death. I was not going to die of gangrene.

Shorty must be very, very disappointed.

Press reporters accompanying our liberators to Camp Omori were free to roam around the camp. Later, I read some of their eyewitness stories. They reported Camp Omori to be a "Hell Hole," the prisoner treatment to be brutal, and the condition of all the prisoners to be pathetic. I wondered what they would have written if they had seen the Kempei Tai dungeons. They would have had a field day. Omori was no vacation resort, not even a nice place, but compared to Kempei Headquarters it was a country club. Press photos taken during our liberation showed prisoners who were nothing but skin and bones. Those were the Kempei Tai transfers.

A few days after the peace signing, reporters tried to enter Kempei Tai Headquarters. Heavily armed Kempei Tai guards, with their distinctive red armbands, would not permit access to the building. The reporters were told that there were no prisoners there. "They have been freed."

The Kempei Tai were still in control, as is their successor organization today.

Chapter 12

To the West Coast

29 August 1945

A motley assortment of American, English, Dutch, Australian, New Zealand, and Canadians stumbled onto the deck from the gangplank steps and were directed to several lines leading to tables where navy personnel were logging us in. With great efficiency, our citizenship, name, rank, serial number, and branch of service were noted. Next, we moved on to another line where medical personnel determined just what help we needed. Most of us looked much worse than we actually were, others needed immediate medical aid and were moved or directed to the dispensary.

When the medics realized that we were contaminating their sanitary hospital ship with fleas and lice, they rushed us on to a shower room where we stripped bare and were handed a bar of antiseptic soap. We were allowed to shower as long as we wanted. I can not describe the luxurious feeling of standing under that smooth hot water, rubbing down with the fragrant soap; antiseptic it might have been, but it smelled wonderful. I scrubbed until I knew that no flea, no lice, no filth, or unwelcome varmints could possibly survive my attack on them. Next, I was given a razor, and I shaved for the first time in six months. Our prison clothing was collected and burned.

We were issued crisp, new navy-issue denims. The feel of clean underwear and outer garments was indescribable. I looked at myself in the shower room mirrors. I no longer looked like the mangy, filthy animal that the Japanese wanted me to be. I had rejoined the human race.

Navy doctors gave us cursory physical examinations. I was weighed and found that I had gained eight pounds on Camp Omori's food. I now weighed 104 pounds. The doctors decided which men would remain hospitalized and which could leave the ship. I was relieved when I was told that I could leave with the group headed for the next leg of a trip toward *home*. The time must have been around seven or eight in the evening when we finished our physical exams.

While we were going through this registration process the doctors were conferring, trying to decide how these emaciated, starved men were to be fed their first meal out of captivity. Could the shrunken stomachs and damaged digestive systems stand the shock of regular fare? Should they continue with the soup diet and gradually ease them toward a regular fare of solid foods? Since they knew we were all looking forward to our next meal, they hated to disappoint their "guests."

The final decision was: How can we withhold food from these poor devils? Load up the tables and turn them loose. They would monitor us and see that we stopped short of "suicide by eating." They knew that we would certainly become temporarily ill, but felt the psychological good would outweigh the gastric shock.

The cooks went to work and by the time we were logged in, cleaned up, and had our first physical exams, the tables were groaning. They really fed us! I had never before seen such delicious and beautiful looking food. There was a never-ending supply of it. Navy mess personnel went out of their way to assure that anything we wanted was available. I knew from meals eaten with Navy Seabees on Tinian that the navy ate well. This was the best of the best. We ate and we ate and we ate. We would eat, go back for more, go to the railing and throw up, then go back and eat some more.

The mess attendants were very tolerant. They kept the tables loaded and stood back and grinned while the medics observed and attended those who got sick. We were allowed to eat for several hours. It wasn't until the last man no longer came back for more that they shut down the operation.

As the men left the mess hall, those in need of immediate medical aid were directed to the dispensary and stayed on the *Benevolence*, the others were taken by landing craft to the USS *Reeves*, an attack transport anchored a short distance across the bay. By then it was around midnight.

We were welcomed aboard the USS *Reeves* by the ship's commander and cheering sailors. They had everything ready and waiting for us; their ship-to-ship radios had been busy. We were told that if we needed anything, anything at all, to let the nearest sailor know.

We were immediately taken to our assigned bunks. To provide for their guests, they had hung extra canvas hammocks, spaced so close that when you turned over, you nudged the man sleeping above and felt the presence of the man sleeping below. No one complained. For the first time in six months, I had clean white sheets and a pillow. What luxury!

30 August 1945

There was no wake up call, no *tenko*, no shout of *"sho."* I had slept so hard that I woke up later than many of our group. I went to the mess room and ate a bountiful breakfast. American fare of scrambled eggs, bacon, cereal, and milk were in abundant supply. That morning I ate a full loaf of excellent fresh baked navy raisin bread, spread with a full pound of butter. I was surprised that I was still hungry after my eating orgy of the night before.

After breakfast I went topside to see what was going on. The morning was another beautiful day. Our ship was surrounded by American warships. The bay was literally blanketed with them. I had never seen so many ships in all my life!

The skeleton-like POWs were given the run of the ship. We were exploring, laughing, and enjoying life. There wasn't a complainer on board. The air force troops got a charge out of the nautical language we heard coming over the ship's PA system. We heard: "Now hear this. Clean sweep fore and aft." Stairways were called "ladders." Walls were called "bulkheads." We were told to "stow our gear." That was a joke. None of us had any gear — except

— I had my lucky silver dollar which was stowed in my new watch pocket. Later, each of us was issued a navy sea bag stuffed with two complete enlisted seaman's uniforms, underclothes, shaving gear, toothbrushes, and other shipboard gear. We were delighted to have these things and to have something to "stow."

As I milled around on the deck visiting with fellow POWs and ship's crew, I heard the ship's PA announce "Lieutenant Hanley please report to the ship's stern." The message was repeated several times before I recognized that they were calling me. I couldn't believe my ears. Why was my name being called? Had I been rescued by mistake and they were returning me? Had all this been a dream and I was really back in Kempei Headquarters and I was being waked up to go to an interrogation? I was worried.

I knew that the stern was the back end of the ship, so I moved aft. I found several naval officers gathered there with a civilian dressed in suntan clothing. He wore no insignia. On the left shoulder of his shirt was a patch which said "Press." I marched up to the group in my best Air Force style, saluted and announced, "Lieutenant Hanley reporting." The senior Naval officer, a commander, introduced himself, his staff, and Mr. Ted Dealey, the civilian. Mr. Dealey was an owner and editor of the *Dallas Morning News*.

Mr. Dealey smiled and asked me if I was from Texas. I wondered how he knew this and answered, "Yes, I am Fiske Hanley from Fort Worth, Texas." He had seen my home state listed on the list of POWs. The ship's officers questioned me on Japanese treatment of Special Prisoners. I expressed my bitterness against the Kempei Tai. They said that they felt the same way about the Japanese kamikaze pilots who had killed so many of their men and their friends. I didn't know what they were talking about. What were kamikaze planes?

After the officers went back to their duties, Mr. Dealey and I were left alone. He congratulated me on my liberation and asked if my parents knew that I had been freed. I told him that I did not think that they knew that I was alive. He said that they would be notified within the hour by his staff in Dallas.

He and I talked for some time. It was like being with a friend from home. It was certainly my good fortune to have been on the same ship with Mr. Dealey. He questioned me in depth about my prison treatment and experiences. He had been present at Camp Omori when I was liberated. He said that he couldn't believe the inhumanity and squalor of the place. I told him that he should see the dungeons of the Kempei Tai in downtown Tokyo.

Mr. Dealey's son, Comdr. Samuel David Dealey, was on the submarine *Harder* when it was lost at sea in 1944. Mr. Dealey was hoping that he would find his son alive when the prison camps were evacuated. It was his first heart-breaking disappointment when his son was not with the POWs freed from Camp Omori.

We were on the USS *Reeves* for three days, eating, sleeping, and trying to adjust to the idea that all this was not a dream but a reality. I wandered around just being excited and happy. *The sun was beautiful, the air smelled wonderful. I was not caged! I was not being beaten every day! I was not hungry! I was not filthy! I was not being consumed by vermin! I was glad to be alive on God's good, wonderful ocean!*

2 September 1945

When we came topside 2 September we noticed hundreds of ships of all sizes and types. There were battleships, aircraft carriers, cruisers, destroyers, tugs, mine sweepers, freighters, transports, and tankers. There had been many ships in the bay for several days, but this morning the bay was "carpeted." The sky above us was covered with maneuvering American warplanes of all sizes and descriptions. It was a wonder that there were no collisions. We could feel excitement in the air!

We were told that the peace treaty was to be signed on board the USS *Missouri* that morning. We couldn't see the *Missouri* from our ship but knew that important things happened over there. We watched as over a thousand B-29s flew over. That was the exact time of the surrender ceremony. Our ship was within sight of that ceremony. Minutes after our ship's PA system had announced that World War II's formal surrender ceremony had taken place, we heard the sound of ship whistles and horns erupt. The sound was almost ear-shattering. *World War II was officially over!*

That same morning we were taken to another ship in the bay, a very large ship with enormous front-end doors. I had never seen a ship like this before. It was an LST (Landing Ship Tank), the largest landing craft ship in the navy. The ship was over 300 feet long. The cargo deck had been designed to hold tanks, artillery, and vehicles, but this day it was set up with more than a thousand cots and staffed with navy medical personnel. I had never seen so many doctors in all my life. Throughout the day, liberated POWs were brought to this ship to be examined, diagnosed, and treated.

The authorities and the medical people did not know exactly what to do with us. Camp Omori was the first POW camp to be liberated and we were their first POWs to deal with. Nearly every POW went through a treatment of doses of castor oil and paregoric. Two of our main health problems were diarrhea and constipation caused by our eating orgies. Our shrunken stomachs couldn't cope with the rich diet and the amount we were consuming in such a short period. When we were constipated, doctors prescribed castor oil. That led to diarrhea, and the doctors prescribed paregoric. Then we went back to constipation and more castor oil. We underwent several cycles of this treatment before we had normal, healthy body functions.

And still we ate and ate and ate.

3 September 1945

Our LST pulled anchor and got under way. It made its way to a naval base near Yokohama. We docked, unloaded, and were placed on new US Army 6 x 6 trucks. Having seen, smelled, and ridden on the Japanese trucks, I couldn't help comparing these beautiful machines to theirs. Our US trucks looked good, felt good, smelled good, and ran good.

Our well-protected truck convoy drove over badly damaged roads for about ten miles. We traveled though burned and bombed out Japanese urban areas. We saw total destruction. Nothing remained but a chimney or concrete ruin here and there. I hadn't been able to get as good a view of these sights during my previous travels in Japan while blindfolded. Now I had the whole picture. I saw the enormity of what our fire raids had done to the population and its dwellings. The Japanese military leaders and their "Son of Heaven" had known for some time that the war was lost to them. Why hadn't they saved their people this last torture?

We bumped over the sorry Japanese roads and finally arrived at the large Japanese airfield, Atsugi. This was the airfield where the first Americans had landed earlier, and where General MacArthur had landed. As we approached, for miles around the airfield, we observed hundreds of fighter airplanes concealed from aerial observation under trees. These airplanes didn't have propellers and were pushed onto their noses. They had been deactivated as part of General MacArthur's cease fire orders.

Our truck bounced onto the field, over and around many bomb craters. We stopped in front of a badly damaged hangar building. Very few American troops were in sight. We observed many unarmed Japanese military standing around sullenly glaring at us. I was nervous and fearful that trouble could erupt at any instant.

Even before we arrived at the airfield, we began to notice the constant stream of landing and departing transport aircraft. They were landing at the rate of one every two minutes. When we pulled up in front of the hangars, we could see that the apron in front of the hangar was packed with large transport aircraft discharging heavily armed American soldiers. The aircraft were instantly refueled and readied for quick departure. The planes were mostly C-47 Dakotas (lovingly called "Gooney Birds" by GI soldiers) and C-54 four-engine transports. It was apparent that all this hustle and bustle meant that our army was rapidly building up occupation capability.

We dismounted from our trucks and entered the hangar. High-ranking military officers from most of the Allied nations involved in the Pacific War were present. We were served Red Cross doughnuts and coffee. I asked one of the pretty Red Cross girls if she had stationery and stamps. I told her that I had not been allowed to write home in over six months. She told me that the Red Cross did not furnish such things. Their mission was to furnish doughnuts and drinks only. Doughnuts and drinks from the Red Cross were more than Special Prisoners had received before now. Except for the one perfunctory Omori visit, we never had any contact with the Red Cross. This cup of coffee and that one doughnut was the only thing I got from the Red Cross during all my Atsugi visit.

We were told that we would be flown out of Japan as soon as transport aircraft became available. We were divided into airplane loads and given an airplane number with an approximate waiting time. Efficient Air Transport Command (ATC) operations officers were directing this operation. I remembered that in early 1944, when I was asked my first choice for assignment, I had stated "ATC Engineering officer." My last choice had been Flight Engineering

Officer. I did not know then that the Air Force assigned by last choice *first*.

> On the 28th of August, Lt. Gen. Seizo Arisue was present at the large Japanese airfield, Atsugi, to surrender the airfield to the Americans.
>
> A couple of hours before the American Army landings, American Navy planes dropped a 15-foot banner saying,
>> "WELCOME US ARMY,
>> COURTESY OF THE US NAVY."
> Wanting to avoid trouble, the Japanese hid the sign.
>
> Forty-five C-47s, loaded with the American advance party, landed at Atsugi a few hours later. They were commanded by Col. Charles Tench, a member of MacArthur's staff. Soon after, the 11th Airborne Division came in. When the US Army arrived, they brought their own paint and splashed it across the biggest hangar.
>> "WELCOME TO JAPAN.
>> COURTESY OF THE US ARMY."

My flight was finally called. Together with a crowd of happy POWs, I approached a large, four-engine transport aircraft. It was the relatively new Douglas C-54, which became operational late in the war. This was my first time to see one. On board, there were bunks along the length of the airplane instead of the usual bucket seats. It was a litter plane with flight nurses and medics aboard. I was surprised because we were ambulatory and could have traveled in seats very easily. The military authorities did not know what to expect and wanted to assure our safe travel. We let out a big cheer as we lifted off Japanese soil.

After take-off, the airplane climbed to cruising altitude and droned southward. The engines sounded great to my engineer's ear. Our route took us over the southern part of Honshu Island, Shikoku Island, and then Kyushu Island, where the bloody November invasion had been planned. We flew just east of the little village where I had been captured and very near the Shimonoseki Straits where Al Andrews, myself, and our lost crew had laid our last mines. This was my first time since our last disastrous flight that I had flown in a plane. I missed my buddies.

Finally, *finally*, we left the Japanese mainland far, *far* behind.
We arrived over the island of Okinawa after a couple of hours of
smooth flight, no flak, and no enemy threat. We were free men in a
United States airplane. It was an exhilarating feeling. Night had
fallen by the time we arrived over Okinawa. We could see that the
large, narrow island was ablaze with lights.

Our airplane landed at Yontan Airfield near the town of Naha.
We were picked up by a convoy of army ambulances with their distinctive red cross markings. We were still being treated as casualties.
We were driven along a newly built "superhighway." Mountains of
war materiel lined the road. There was evidence of recent heavy
fighting. The enormous preparations visible made us proud of our
country's build-up aimed at defeating the Emperor and his brutal
and suicidal troops. The invasion of the mainland had been planned
to take place in just a few weeks. Okinawa had been captured at a
terrible cost for this purpose. Now it could be used as a safe, peaceful island for the return of the first POWs . . . *us.*

*BOCK'S CAR, which dropped the second atomic bomb on
Nagasaki, had diverted to Yontan Airfield because of fuel manage-
ment problems. Capt. Jacob Beser, a friend of mine, and the only
crewman to fly on both planes carrying the atomic bombs, reported
that their bombardier missed the Nagasaki aim point by over a mile.
The bomb still had enough energy to cause terrible damage.*

We stopped at a camp, a tent area of eight-man tents with
wooden floors. The camp's PA system welcomed us to Okinawa
and said that we were the first POWs liberated since the invasions
of the Philippines and Okinawa. We were the first liberated prisoners to arrive from the Japanese homeland.

After we were assigned quarters, we went to a field kitchen and
were treated to a big meal of wholesome army chow. We were
served fruit cocktail, ladled from a new 30-gallon garbage can.
Seeing that container somehow affected the taste. We had been
spoiled by the outstanding navy cuisine and were already returning
to our picky ways.

During the flight from Japan, I had become increasingly
uncomfortable. I was in real pain by the time I prepared to bed
down for the night. I couldn't sleep because of the intense pain. My

discomfort got to the point where I could no longer stand it. Several of my tent mates awakened and tried to comfort me and finally helped me to the dispensary located near our tent. The doctor on duty examined me and said that my problem was hemorrhoids. He recommended an operation as soon as possible. He called the nearest army field hospital and was advised that they could not operate until the next morning. I had just returned from six months of torture by the Kempei Tai but, and so help me, this was worse. I was in such pain that if given a knife, I would have operated on myself.

4 September 1945

The dispensary doctor applied cold packs to the area, and the next morning an ambulance carried me about a mile to the large, tented Army 75th Field Hospital. It was one of many hospitals set up to handle the casualties expected during the Kyushu invasion. I was examined by an elderly army colonel, with medical insignia on his collar, who told me that they would operate immediately, if I desired, but he firmly recommended that I wait until returning to a stateside hospital where the operation conditions were better. By now, the ice pack treatments had given me some relief so I told him I would wait to make my decision. Hot packs and antibiotics were administered by the beautiful nursing staff. I had a moderate temperature of some 101 degrees. Blood work was done, but revealed no other problems. My pain level slowly decreased. The doctor assigned me to a surgical ward where I was with other returning POWs. Many were in pretty bad condition, much worse off than I.

I was stuck in an army field hospital. I wanted to go home! I knew that the POWs with whom I had come from Japan were to be air evacuated to the Philippines on the first available air transport. There we would receive a complete medical examination, treatment, uniforms, and military pay. There we would be allowed to communicate with our families. I wanted to go with them and did not want to stay behind in an army field hospital.

The army medical staff, led by the colonel, visited my ward every morning. Each case was discussed in detail by the group. My case was baffling them. They didn't seem to know why my temperature was elevated or why I was in such pain, which at times was unbearable. There obviously was infection. This bothered them and they would not sign my release until the temperature dropped from 101 degrees to normal. They were frustrated; *I* was frustrated!

One of the nurses asked about my rank. I was in an officer's ward and was addressed as Lieutenant Hanley by the personnel. I looked like a navy gob. I explained that I was an Army Air Force second lieutenant. The only clothing I had was that which the navy had issued on the USS *Benevolence*. I hadn't been able to replace them or buy new rank insignia because I had not been paid and I had no money.

The nurse smiled and left the tent. She returned shortly with shiny second lieutenant bars. She had just been promoted to first lieutenant and these were her old bars. She pinned them on the collar of my hospital pajamas and saluted me. I thanked her for the snappy salute and she said that was the least she could do.

The fellow in the next bed was a civilian contractor captured on Wake Island. He was in very poor physical condition. The nurse whispered to me that he was not expected to live. I enjoyed visiting with this poor fellow. I doubt that he lived long after I left him there in the army field hospital. He was given medical whiskey three times a day to improve his spirits.

He told me about his captivity. After Wake Island was captured, many of the prisoners were tortured and murdered by their guards. Prisoners were forced to work endless hours while enduring a starvation diet. They sabotaged with human cunning anything that could be ruined. He told me about one unique act of sabotage that totally confounded the Japanese. Before Wake's capture, the marines were well-stocked with fuel for their fighter aircraft. The fuel was stored in thousands of upended 55 gallon barrels. An ingenious prisoner conceived a subtle sabotage scheme. If the barrel's screw-in plug was slightly loosened, rainwater from the frequent showers caught on the barrel's top would slowly seep around the plug into the barrel. Water, being heavier than gasoline, would force the lighter fuel up and out of the barrel. The barrels would be contaminated with rainwater and eventually be nothing but rainwater. Soon, the entire captured fuel dump was composed of contaminated fuel barrels. Bad fuel caused airplane crashes. Japanese wondered why the dumb Americans stored so much contaminated fuel.

I lay on my hospital bed all day with nothing to do but visit with the nurses and the patients. My hemorrhoids had quit hurting. I felt all right but couldn't bust out of the hospital because my temperature went to 101 degrees every afternoon. Every morning the doctors seriously discussed my case while at my bedside. I asked when I could get out of the hospital and received cold stares as an answer. The colonel said, "Lieutenant, we can't release you until we know what's wrong with you." I protested to no avail. I was getting nowhere!

I was kept on a meager hospital diet. My clothing was kept under lock and key. I didn't like this. My days dragged slowly by. The middle of September arrived, and I was still stuck in the hospital. I had to do something drastic to gain my hospital release. It had been over two weeks since my liberation.

I decided to make myself an undesirable patient and maybe they would kick me out of the hospital. I would start by insulting the doctor in charge. I concocted my dismissal insult and waited for the morning staff visit. As the medical team gathered around my bed and started their discussion, I told the colonel that I wanted an immediate dismissal from his hospital. I added that I didn't think he knew what he was doing.

I held my breath as I watched him grow red in the face and started huffing, "What do you mean, Lieutenant?"

I said, "Either your hospital or the dispensary doctor's treatment of my hemorrhoids is wrong. The dispensary used cold packs. This hospital uses hot packs. My hemorrhoids are no better and I still run a fever every afternoon. I need someone who knows what the hell he's doing."

The red-faced colonel looked around at his staff as they quickly wiped the grins from their faces. He turned to me and said, "Lieutenant, you are insubordinate." He turned on his heels and stormed off with his staff running after him. My pretty nurse, the giver of second lieutenant bars, came over and told me, "You did it. I'll bet that you will be out of here in an hour." I was!

I was given new army-issue khakis, escorted to a waiting ambulance, and returned to tent city. I found it full of liberated POWs. Al Andrews and the rest of my Kempei group had left Okinawa and were on their return home. I was placed in a tent with Army Air Force POWs who had been liberated from Formosa. One had injured his arm during bailout. His upper left arm was completely out of the joint. The sadistic Japanese never reset the bone. He had suffered with this awful condition for over a year.

There was a weather forecast that a typhoon was headed our way and was expected to hit sometime during the night. I looked at the flimsy tent and could see that it could not withstand the typhoon winds. I had no intention of coming this far only to die in a typhoon.

I looked around for a place to survive. Next to our tent area were quonset huts housing a large army supply depot. These buildings were firmly anchored to the ground with cables. They looked like they could ride out a pretty good storm. I walked over to the nearest depot hut and approached a grizzled army sergeant who appeared to be in charge. I introduced myself and asked if my tent mates and I could sleep on the floor of his building during the typhoon. He grinned and said, "I've stocked a lot of things in my depot, but never skinny guys like you. Go get your buddies." I went back to our tent and invited the men to join me and the sergeant in the quonset hut; to a man they accepted.

The typhoon, with winds over 150 mph, hit about dusk. Our quonset rocked and shook but stayed in place. When we returned after the storm we found the tents in shambles; the whole tent area was destroyed. Army crews moved in, quickly stripped the whole area, and erected new tents. By nightfall, the tent area was resurrected. My buddies and I survived the storm, thanks to that kind army sergeant.

My tent mates were happily anticipating how long it would take them to fly home. I was puzzled by their talking about flying all the way home. My current mates said that the Army Air Force directed that all liberated air force personnel be flown back to the United States and asked why I hadn't already flown back to the States, since my camp had been the first liberated. I told them about the delay that my hospital experience caused. I added that we had been told that our Camp Omori group would return by ship from the Philippines to the West Coast — a long, slow trip. We discussed my situation and decided that when they flew home, I would go along.

18 September 1945

The next morning trucks came by and picked us up and off we went to Okinawa's Yontan Airfield where we boarded a C-46 transport airplane. This was the first time I had ever seen one of these planes. It had been used to fly supplies "Over the Hump" into China. The C-46 had a reputation as an unsafe airplane. No matter! We were heading toward home.

Unlike the C-54, no litters were aboard this time. This plane had bucket seats. The "rest rooms" were relief tubes. Flight nurses accompanying us joked, "Engineers didn't think about us when they designed the relief tubes for nature's call, but we manage." They did not elaborate, and we didn't ask.

Our plane did a refueling stop on Iwo Jima. We had a couple of hours to spend on the ground while our airplane was being serviced. The island was truly a miserable place — hot, with very little vegetation. Volcanic gases seeped from the black, sandy soil. The airfield was adjacent to Mount Suribachi, where marines had raised a flag of victory after capturing the summit. The photo of the flag and marines raising it became a symbol of the bloody fight where there were 22,000 United States casualties. Almost the entire Japanese garrison lost their lives in the battle.

I remembered that Iwo Jima was the first target that our plane had bombed. It was a practice mission. The bomb aim point was the Japanese airfield runway intersection. Our large formation of B-29s dropped bombs based on the lead aircraft's bomb drop. There were 97 aircraft in the bombing formation. The key bombardier badly missed the target! Ninety percent of our bombs exploded harmlessly in the ocean. Japanese defenders must have thought that with an enemy like this they would have no trouble winning the war.

But they did not win the war, and now we were roaming freely around the airport like happy tourists. We examined the bulletin board located in the airfield's operations hut. It was hard to believe some of the announcements posted there. Most concerned court martials on petty charges such as lost article of clothing and personal gear. Severe sentences were handed out for very minor offenses. We felt sorry for the poor victims of some over-zealous commander. He must have been a martinet to permit such trivial charges and sentences — six months in prison for losing a pair of socks? We couldn't wait to get away from this unhappy, tainted island.

Our plane taxied onto the hot runway and took off for our next destination, Guam, which was located about 100 miles south of Tinian. We arrived just as the sun was setting. Guam was a beautiful island covered with lush, tropical growth. We were trucked through heavy jungles to a large army hospital. It had many wooden buildings which were joined together.

20 September 1945

I knew that several of my friends were stationed on Guam. I was looking forward to surprising them by walking up, *alive.* I'd heard while in prison that Col. Glen Martin, the 504th's commander, had been promoted to General LeMay's staff and was based on Guam. Ed Frederickson, a cadet friend, and Jerry Nash, a fellow Texas Tech student, were also here. After processing into the hospital, where we underwent more POW physical exams, I slept through a pleasant Guamian night.

21 September 1945

After breakfast I called Guam's military locator service. I'd found this service outstanding. I asked for Ed Frederickson's office and was connected immediately. Ed was an engineering officer of one of Guam's B-29 squadrons. He dropped everything and drove his Jeep over to the hospital. I begged permission from the medical authorities to spend the day visiting the island with him. Permission granted.

Ed drove me over to see "Nig" Nash, my buddy from Lubbock. We found him shaving outside his quonset hut. He was standing nude and staring into a mirror propped on the quonset wall. I approached and slapped his backside and said, "Hi, Nig." He saw me in his mirror and dropped his towel and razor and cried, "Fiske, you're *dead!*" The expression on his face was one of disbelief. He thought that he was seeing a ghost. We had a good visit. At Texas Tech, Nig and I had been friendly rivals for the same girl's affections. We both lost.

Next, Ed took me to General LeMay's 20th Air Force Headquarters to visit Col. Glen Martin. The colonel had flown with our crew during our Nebraska training period and had developed a great respect for our crew, particularly our airplane commander, John Brown. We found Colonel Martin's office and were promptly admitted when he found out that I'd come to see him. I marched to the front of his desk and presented a sharp military salute and announced, "Lieutenant Hanley reporting for duty, sir!" He carefully looked me over and without cracking a smile said, "Lieutenant, you are out of uniform." I looked down at my emaciated figure clothed in the ill-fitting army issue khakis. I really didn't look very sharp! I apologized for my appearance. The colonel broke into a big smile and came around his desk. He shook my hand and said, "Fiske, you look great, but your rank insignia is incorrect. You are wearing second lieutenant's gold bars. You should be wearing silver first lieutenant's insignia."

I told the colonel that everything I had on was given to me after liberation. I knew that all POWs were to be promoted one rank as soon as the system could take care of the administrative details. Anyhow, I had not been paid yet. I certainly couldn't buy better clothes. Colonel Martin asked me where I was assigned while on Guam. I didn't know, but Ed was able to identify the hospital as the 204th General Hospital. The colonel said, "Fiske, when you get back to your bed, if your promotion orders are not on it, call this number." He gave me a slip of paper with his phone number written on it. Colonel Martin asked how long I'd be on Guam. He wanted to arrange for me to fly to Tinian, which I wanted to do, but I was only to be on the island about two days for extensive medical testing. He arranged for me to receive a partial pay advance in his headquarters. I now had pocket money. It was a good feeling!

Ed and I went to the officer's club, where we had a few beverages stronger than water. I hoped my hospital tests wouldn't reveal my secret. Ed dropped me off at the hospital in time for dinner.

When I went to my room, to my surprise I found face up on my bed official orders promoting me to first lieutenant along with two shiny silver bars. People like Colonel Martin win wars and the hearts of their troops! He later rose to three-star general and deputy chief of staff of the air force.

We were the first POW patients the staff of Guam's Army Hospital had processed. There was a lot of medical overkill on our small group. It was fun, though! I faced my first psychiatrist since being given combat crew screening in Nebraska. This fellow seemed fresh out of an asylum, lost and puzzled by my answers to his questions about prison life. I was glad when I was rid of him.

We stayed on Guam three nights, then enplaned for Hawaii. Dates changed as we flew east.

23 September 1945

We flew from Guam to Johnston Island on another C-54 medical transport airplane. We stopped at Johnston Island to quickly refuel and be on our way. This island was a tiny speck in the immense Pacific Ocean and was a major refueling stop for air traffic flying across the vast Pacific. After dark that same day, our plane landed at Oahu Island's John Rogers Field. It was a special, comforting feeling to be on United States soil again.

The POWs were taken to Triplett General Hospital, located on a hill overlooking Honolulu. We spent two days here with more medical check-ups. I received my second psychiatric examination after liberation. Its purpose, I guess, was to determine the mental and psychiatric effect of Japanese imprisonment, but mostly they seemed to want to satisfy their own curiosity.

The counseling seemed hollow and meaningless to me. I was so full of hate for all Japanese. They talked about forgiveness. They had not been where I had been. They had not known the sadistic, inhuman beasts, as I had. They had not been exposed to Japanese acts of cruelty, as I had. It was too soon to probe. I needed time to do some self-healing. These sessions did a lot of harm. These green psychiatrists opened up wounds that had begun to heal in the last three weeks.

One evening was spent seeing the sights in downtown Honolulu. We toured the Waikiki Beach area along with thousands of other uniformed sightseers. This should have been an enjoyable evening, but after an all day session with psychiatrists, it wasn't. The next morning we left on the last leg of our return to mainland USA.

26 September 1945

When we reached the West Coast, our pilot flew the C-54 very low across the Golden Gate Bridge. What a wonderful sight! This was our country. We'd fought to preserve its freedom. It was safe again from predators.

I was very aware, as I looked at this first peaceful, beautiful view of our country, that the prisoners who had been captured alive, then murdered, and starved to death, should have been with us. If the Japanese had followed the Geneva Convention Rules, these missing patriots would be flying over the Golden Gate Bridge — flying *home!*

The plane touched down on the runway at Hamilton Field north of San Francisco. After the airplane taxied onto the ramp and shut down its engines, we let out a whoop and a holler! I couldn't wait to walk down the steps and touch the ground. I was on the United States mainland!

I was on my homeland's soil. It was an even greater feeling than when we had touched down in Hawaii. This was the moment that I had prayed for and had almost lost hope that it would ever happen! I bounced down the steps and fell to my knees and kissed the ground of *The United States of America! I was alive! I was home! I was an American citizen! I was going to have a life beyond a dungeon prison!*

Chapter 13

Home at Last

We had watched eagerly for the first sight of the West Coast of the United States of America. We had flown over the Golden Gate Bridge and touched ground just north of San Francisco. I could see *Old Glory*, my beloved flag, flying in the California breeze. The good Lord had looked after me this far. I did not doubt for one second that He would stay with me the rest of the way home — all the way to Fort Worth, Texas.

26 September 1946

I was loaded on a waiting army bus and was driven south toward San Francisco. The bus rolled over the Golden Gate Bridge. It was beautiful in the morning sunlight. I remembered flying over the bridge less than a year ago, on my way to the war. It was symbolic to me that this bus took me over this famous structure during my first trip on home soil. On Tinian, I'd heard a popular saying, *"Golden Gate in Forty-Eight!"* Fortunately for me and others, the war didn't last that long. Too bad the Japanese military did not agree to surrender sooner. They could have stopped the fighting before the last bombing was necessary. My bus turned off the highway and entered the army's *Presidio,* a large military complex located on the heights overlooking San Francisco Bay. The Presidio, named by the first Spanish settlers, was a beautifully landscaped area containing the West Coast army headquarters. My bus stopped in front of a large, imposing Spanish-style building, Letterman General Hospital. If I had to be hospitalized, this was the best place. It was the finest hospital that I'd ever seen. I entered, was taken to the commissioned officers' ward, and signed in.

Here, I was taken to the Red Cross office and allowed to place a call to my mother and father. Mr. Dealey had promised me that he would notify my parents that I was alive and liberated, and I had written from Okinawa but I did not know if Dealey's call or my letters had reached them.

It was unbelievably wonderful to hear them answer the telephone and to hear their voices. This was the first time I'd talked with them in almost a year. Through her tears my mother said that they had never given up hope that I had survived being shot down. My folks wanted me to come home as soon as possible. I couldn't wait to see them.

Mother told me later that letters from my bomb group told them that no parachutes had been sighted coming from our burning airplane and that no one had survived the crash. Then, on 30 August 1946, they had been notified by *The Dallas Morning News* that Mr. Dealey had seen and talked to me. A week later, the army telegraphed that I was alive and on my way home. They waited another three weeks for my call.

At Letterman Hospital I was assigned a beautiful room with a window that looked out on an immaculate landscaped garden. I shared the room with a Colonel Cushing. He, like me, had no love for the Japanese. We discussed our war experiences. I told him about my being a Special Prisoner and about experiencing the sadistic, brutal Japanese treatment. He had a personal knowledge about unending and horrific Japanese atrocities in the Philippines.

Colonel Cushing was about fifty years old, a most interesting person, a true war hero. Before the war, he had been a civilian contractor on Cebu Island in the Philippines. After war was declared, our army commissioned him a colonel, a rank equal to his civilian position as head of a large civil engineering operation. When the

Japanese invaded Cebu Island he avoided capture and recruited guerrilla troops from Philippine scouts and natives.

During the war years his resistance military organization grew into a potent 65,000-man fighting force. His troops conducted resistance throughout the war against the murderous Japanese occupation troops. His guerrilla outfit had artillery, infantry, engineers, intelligence, supply, personnel, and plans. The whole works! His troops fought regular battles with the Japanese. They built a well-camouflaged airfield so as to better receive supplies. Colonel Cushing showed me his organization chart which would have made General Patton proud. He even had a military historian post.

His outfit survived by trickery and deception. If a Japanese Cebu commander became too dangerous, Cushing told me that he would carefully compose a folksy and friendly letter to that Japanese commander, who never received the letter. Instead, a copy of the bogus letter was allowed to fall into the hands of the commander's military leader in Manila. Pretty soon the bad guy would be transferred. This elimination scheme worked several times.

Colonel Cushing noted that I was in the Army Air Force. He asked if I knew about a magazine called *Air Force*. I told him that it came out monthly and was available to air force personnel. He asked if I could obtain the latest issue for him because he'd heard that his Cebu exploits were reported in it. I searched and found an Army Air Force Liaison Officer in the hospital. He said that the September edition of *Air Force* had just been received and showed me a whole stack of them. We looked through the magazine and, sure enough, there was the story of Colonel Cushing's exploits. I asked for two copies of the magazine and was told that I could have them all to take to Colonel Cushing. The colonel was delighted to get them.

While the colonel was my roommate, he received orders directing him to return to the Philippines. His health was poor and he should have remained hospitalized, but he was needed immediately to return to Cebu and demobilize his army. His thousands of troops were still armed, organized, and presented a threat to the postwar Philippine government. This was going to be a real challenge for him.

While at Letterman, ex-prisoners who had been wounded due to enemy action were awarded Purple Heart Medals. There was a formal ceremony and the hospital's commander, General Hillman, made an impressive presentation. We returned to our ward wearing the medals pinned to our hospital pajamas. The nurse in our ward was very impressed with her bejeweled patients. She had never seen this medal before. For that matter, neither had I.

When I learned that the first returning POWs were to arrive at the army Presidio dock I got permission to meet the ship. I figured that these troops might be my friends from Camp Omori who had left me behind in the hospital in Okinawa. If so, I had beaten them to the USA. I was on the dock when the ship tied up. Along the ship's rail overhead, I spotted several of my fellow Kempei cellmates. As they came down the gang plank, they were shocked to see me there waiting for them and gasped, "How did you beat us here?"

All across the Pacific they had been sorry that they had left me behind and that I would be delayed coming home. Their ocean voyage had been slow and uncomfortable. My flight home had been a pleasure.

The next day a message was delivered to my room to report to the Red Cross office in the hospital. I wondered why. It couldn't be my parents; I had just talked to them. They were both just fine. I couldn't believe anything could be wrong there.

The RC representative informed me that my immediate departure for home was being arranged. He told me that he had bad news, that my father was dying. "But I just talked to them. They said they were fine," I said. I argued with him that he must be mistaken — he had the wrong Hanley. He assured me that it was true.

After my call, my mother had contacted the Red Cross in Fort Worth who, in turn, had notified him. The Red Cross had issued a request for the army to send me home as quickly as possible. After talking to the Red Cross rep, I again called home. Mother was within hearing range of Dad and did not want to discuss his health. I told her I was being sent to San Antonio but would come home as soon as possible. She asked me to hurry home but suggested that I first stop off in Austin and see my sister, Edna, who was a student at The University of Texas. Edna would fill me in on the facts she could not tell me in front of Dad.

I was rapidly processed out of Letterman General Hospital. My orders were to go directly to Brooke General Hospital in San Antonio, where I would be given leave.

I left early on 7 October on the only transportation available, the railroad. I arrived at Brooke General Hospital in San Antonio late the next evening. On 9 October an army surgeon interviewed me and prepared a brief medical history for their records. He asked me whether I wanted a 30-day or 60-day leave. I told him that I wasn't crazy, yet, and I wanted a 60-day leave. He grinned, said I'd passed the nut test, and issued orders for a 60-day medical leave. At Fort Sam Houston an army paymaster granted me the maximum pay and allowances possible. I didn't know there were so many rules that could favor an officer's pay. I was given very generous pay for my six months as a guest of the Emperor, certainly more than the 88 yen I had been paid at Camp Omori. I had one *big* gripe, though. My check was taxed for the time I was imprisoned in Japan. If I'd been imprisoned in the Philippines, there would have been no tax. Figure that one out. I never have, to this date.

On 10 October I entrained for Austin. The train carried civilians and troops. The cars for non-military passengers were loaded to standing room only. I'd noticed that the troop-train cars were hooked onto the rear of the train. I strolled aft through several crowded passenger cars to the troop cars where an armed sentry stopped me. I told him my problem. He grinned and said, "Lieutenant, we have room for one more troop. Come on back. We're serving lunch. Have some."

The train crept toward Austin, which was only 80 miles away. It took almost three hours to get there. I was anxious to see my little sister and I wanted to find out more about Dad before I reached home.

As I climbed off the train, I looked at my shoes and uniform. My clothes were caked with mud from the Fort Sam Houston temporary barracks area. This was the first time I had visited Edna at her school, and I wanted to present a decent military appearance. I stopped at a cleaning shop near the railroad, undressed in a waiting room, and had my whole uniform cleaned. I found a shoe shine stand where the operator cleaned my shoes and made them presentable. I caught a taxi to the dormitory, hoping that my sister would be out of class. She was, and we were able to have a real visit. My sister told me that Dad had an incurable cancer. Until I told her what the Red Cross had relayed to me, she hadn't realized that he was as sick as he was.

We had time to go out to dinner before my train left. Her dorm manager recommended *Hoffbrau*, a steak house. There, I ordered their biggest steak and ate it all. It was so good that I ordered and ate another. They were both excellent.

I told my sister goodbye and took another slow train two hundred miles to Fort Worth, arriving at home, by cab, after midnight.

It was 11 October, over a month since my liberation from Camp Omori. I had been a long time coming home. It had been an eventful, *long* year since I last stepped onto my front porch. I kissed the front door and rang the bell. I heard Mother run through the house and throw open the door. We held each other a long time before either of us said a word.

Chapter 14

Sequel

My mother and I stood on the porch and held onto each other. She said, over and over again, that she never doubted that I was alive and would be coming home. I told her that there were times when I wasn't so sure.

We tiptoed in to look at my father and let him sleep. He was heavily sedated with pain killing drugs. He had terminal cancer. His wish to live until I returned home had kept him alive. The human body is capable of survival by pure determination, as I'd seen and experienced over and over again in Japan.

My father and I had several weeks to be together — not long enough. I was grateful for the time we had left. He passed away on 10 December 1945 and was buried in Fort Worth's Rose Lawn Cemetery next to his father, Fiske Hanley I.

Dad's affairs were in good order. He had arranged that Mother would live comfortably for the remainder of her days. I was glad that Mother did not have to face losing him alone, while she worried about the war and her three sons who were serving their country. My brother "Juney" was flying P-51 Mustang fighters in Europe. My brother "Doc" was in the navy. My liberation and my arriving home at this time eased her stress considerably.

I was still feeling the shock of the past year and the results of Japanese torture. I couldn't yet shake the awful nightmares, but I was determined to rejoin the human race as quickly as possible. With a 60-day leave ahead of me, I set out to organize my transition to civilian life. I ordered a new car. I was granted a veteran's priority and quickly received a spanking-new Ford convertible. I bought civilian clothes to replace my uniforms. Civilian clothes were as scarce as new cars, but I was reasonably clothed by understanding store owners and clerks. With my shiny new convertible and my fine new clothes, I began my program of recuperation.

Many of my friends in the service had not yet returned home. I learned that most of the beautiful young ladies that I'd known before the war were married or had moved elsewhere. Bill Grounds, my Kempei Tai cellmate, arrived home shortly after I did. I saw a lot of him and his lovely wife, Dorothy. Dorothy was acquainted with a few American Airlines stewardesses and arranged for me to have blind dates with them. I quickly became acquainted with many of these delightful young ladies.

American Airlines based about 250 stewardesses in Fort Worth. Whenever I heard that a new crop of stewardesses arrived in town, I'd arrange an introduction, pick the prettiest, and we'd go out on the town. I quickly earned an unusual reputation. Stewardesses who dated me soon became engaged to other eligible bachelors and married. This didn't bother me. There were plenty of beautiful young ladies left among American Airlines' stewardess pool. My "date Fiske and get engaged" reputation along with my sporty Ford convertible gave me the pick of the prettiest of the pretty.

One afternoon I went to the apartment of stewardess friends with whom I had a "brother/sister" relationship. They invited me to drop by and meet "the new crop" who had transferred to Fort Worth. When I arrived, the group of beautiful young ladies were visiting and enjoying airline-issue drinks. Their small living room was full of stewardesses. Some were sitting in chairs and some on the floor. As I was introduced to the new crop I looked around and spotted an especially pretty young lady sitting on the floor. It was love at first sight.

That was the beginning of my courtship with Betty Baker from Tulsa, Oklahoma. This one didn't get away. We became engaged that summer of 1946 and married in August 1947.

I got out of the air force in June 1946 and immediately became an engineer, working for Consolidated-Vultee Aircraft's Fort Worth plant. The company's name changed to Convair, then General Dynamics, and is now Lockheed-Martin. I pursued an interesting and challenging engineering career during my 44 years. I helped design and flight test the B-36 Peacemaker bomber. I trained and checked out the first air force crews on this monster, ten-engine bomber at nearby Carswell Air Force Base.

The air force must have missed me, for they recalled me during the Korean War. Convair and the air force fought over my services while I wore my ill-fitting World War II uniform for two-weeks. I was pleased when Convair won and I stayed a civilian. I had all the war experiences I wanted. I also had a wife and two small daughters at the time. My industrial career was more important to our country during that "police-action" war than my flying in a military airplane.

My company assignments included high-tech work in advanced design, where weapon systems ten or more years in the future were developed. I spent a couple of years in nuclear engineering, involved in development of a nuclear-powered bomber.

Many years were spent in Manufacturing Technology, where I managed the Instrument Unit stage of NASA's Saturn V Moon Rocket and pioneered the use of advanced composite materials for aircraft. I was deeply involved in design and development of the F-16 Fighting Falcon fighter, which is the world's finest fighter. I traveled world-wide and provided technical support for the F-16's European users.

In 1989 I retired from General Dynamics. I had enjoyed a rewarding, long-lived career with the same company. For three and a half years following retirement, I researched and wrote *The History of the 504th Bomb Group (VH) in World War II*. The book was published by a company owned by Art O'Hara, a fellow survivor of the Kempei Tai and a member of our 504th Bomb Group. As the historian of my 504th Bomb Group I attend yearly reunions and also serve as a director of the 20th Air Force Association.

My wife, Betty, passed away after 45 happy years of marriage. Our three wonderful children, Fiske III (Tommy), Barbara, and Diane have grown up to be a great source of pride. They completed their educations through college, married well, established themselves in careers, and have presented me with five delightful grandchildren.

In January 1993 Ann Dana and I were married. She added two daughters, their husbands, and five grandsons to our combined family. We enjoy our home. We delight in our children and grandchildren and spend much time traveling around the world.

In 1995 Ann and I flew to Tinian Island with four of my B-29 comrades to celebrate the 50th anniversary of the end of WW II. I had previously flown to Saipan and Tinian, in 1991, with members of the Memorial Dedication Committee of the 504th Bomb Group Association to dedicate a memorial to the memory of our fallen comrades who gave their lives to defeat the Japanese enemy in World War II. Tinian Island has returned to a tropical paradise. Signs of the awful war are almost entirely erased. The scars are overgrown with lush growth and flowers.

We went to Tokyo to visit the site of the Kempei Tai Prison where I was held and Camp Omori where I was when liberated. The bay-side has been filled and the site of Camp Omori is now a boat racing arena.

The Kempei Headquarters Building has been replaced with a modern high-rise, but I had an eerie feeling that it was still the Kempei Tai Headquarters, and that the evil Kempei Tai organization is still alive and operating full-force.

While in prison in Tokyo, I swore that if I could survive my imprisonment by the Japanese Kempei Tai, and be returned to a normal life, I would enjoy living to the fullest. I have!

Appendix A

Japanese vs. American POW Treatment

During the recent Nimitz Museum's World War II Symposium, *"December 7, 1941 — The Gathering Storm"* held in Fredericksburg, Texas, I met and briefly discussed POW affairs with Ens. Kazuo Sakamaki who was the first Japanese military prisoner captured by United States forces during Pearl Harbor's "Day of Infamy."

Sakamaki had the distinction of becoming POW #1. He had served as an ensign in the Imperial Japanese Navy. He commanded a two-man Japanese midget submarine, one of five suicide subs attacking Pearl Harbor. These small submarines operated as part of the Imperial Navy's Special Attack Unit, whose mission was to sink US naval targets. He was the only surviving crewman of these five subs. He tried, unsuccessfully, to commit suicide before capture.

Ensign Sakamaki wrote a book, *I Attacked Pearl Harbor*, published in the US by Association Press in 1949.

Ensign Sakamaki's humane POW experience, such a contrast to the horrors I lived through in Japan, is summarized for the reader's appreciation of a completely different POW story.

FOUR YEARS AS
PRISONER OF WAR #1

Ensign Kazuo Sakamaki, US Prisoner of War #1, left Pearl Harbor in late February of 1942 aboard the internment ship *Etlon*, one of three ships

219

taking Japanese internees and American evacuees to the US mainland. The trip was uneventful.

Sakamaki spent one week at Angel Island, near San Francisco. It was here that war prisoners and internees were classified and then grouped according to destination of their imprisonment or detention. Sakamaki was assigned to Camp McCoy, Wisconsin.

The journey by train from Oakland took them through the snow-covered Rockies, Salt Lake City, Denver, and on into Wisconsin. He wasn't blindfolded and could watch the scenery. The entire area around the camp, covered with snow, brought back memories of home to Sakamaki.

His first night at Camp McCoy was spent among Japanese internees from California. Their words of encouragement brought some comfort to Sakamaki, but he was not in a joyful mood. He kept thinking of his countrymen who were fighting and dying, and this brought a sense of guilt to him.

During these early days of confinement, Sakamaki was thought to be a little demented; otherwise, why would anyone insist on wearing only light, summer time clothes in the dead of winter. He wouldn't permit himself to use hot water for showers. He preferred the cold showers of his training days at the Naval Academy. The stove provided for his comfort remained unlit. Sakamaki reasoned he had no right to enjoy these comforts so long as his fellow countrymen were suffering and dying in the war, and he had all the comforts he could ever imagine. The generally uncooperative attitude of Sakamaki in not taking advantage of the few comforts offered caused the American commanding officer of the camp to be concerned about his prisoner, and he tried to help Sakamaki. But Sakamaki, instead of accepting anything that would assure personal comfort, chose pencils, paper, magazines, books, and the daily paper. He decided he would spend his prison time learning to improve his knowledge of reading and writing the English language.

Whether or not Sakamaki was "normal" was a matter of opinion. In the eyes of an American he was not. From the time he first entered the Naval Academy, every moment of his life had been devoted to strict conditioning of his mind and body. This process caused him to lose all sensitivity to temperature changes, he says, and to restrict his understanding of human beings only to those, like himself, who were in the military.

During 1942, when the fall of Bataan was announced in the papers, Sakamaki thought it very strange that such news should be made available to the general public. He couldn't understand the criticisms about our government, pertaining to its conduct of the war.

There was also the news of Japanese victories, which Sakamaki knew would be the cause for celebrations by his countrymen. But he wondered if such celebrations would have occurred if the Japanese had known of the tremendous resources that were available to America. Sakamaki was well aware that the American people and their government, despite set backs such as Bataan and the Allies' loss of the British and Dutch East Indies, were firmly united with the desire to wage this war to the finish. The war would be a long, hard road for his country to follow, and he dreaded the thought of the outcome if Japan should not be able to take quick advantage of her recently gained resources in Southeast Asia.

Doolittle's raid on Tokyo in April 1942 came as a shock to Sakamaki. He hadn't dreamed such a raid was possible, at least not so soon.

He was completely puzzled as he became aware of the humanity of the Americans around him. He was beginning to have a slight change of heart, and his thoughts of suicide gradually changed to a desire for life. At first, he couldn't believe this was happening to him. Yet, he couldn't seem to stop dreaming that it was real. Could it have been the green valleys and hills of Wisconsin that brought back his memories of the home he knew as a child? Even the setting sun of Wisconsin spoke of home to him, and the desire to live became very strong. Becoming so overwhelmed, he dropped to his knees and prayed. He wanted to return to the kind of life he lived before he entered the Naval Academy; he wanted to be a human being again.

During the latter part of May 1942, Sakamaki and 250 other Japanese internees left Camp McCoy. The train carried them from Chicago through Illinois and south into Kentucky. Marvelous land! The train continued on into Tennessee to Nashville. There the "Gray Ladies" greeted the soldiers and prisoners with refreshments of fruit, candy, and postcards. They seemed to be really interested in offering what comfort they could to the soldiers, including the prisoners. Sakamaki was surprised at the women's friendliness. The fact that they gave him these gifts was more than he could understand. As Sakamaki noticed, some of the women were young, some were old, but most were middle-aged. Dressed in their aprons, they looked neat and tidy. Sakamaki wondered if the women of Japan realized that American women were not all like the women shown in Hollywood movies.

Life at Camp Forest, Tennessee, was quite different from Camp McCoy. Here, there were a few Italian prisoners who kept to themselves. At Camp McCoy he had had his own bunk in the corner of a mess hall. Here at Camp Forest he shared a hut with five other Japanese internees. The Japanese, including the West Coast repatriates, held classes every day. Subjects included English, geography, agriculture, Buddhism, and theology. Sakamaki didn't miss a session. (Sakamaki is a member of the Shinto religion; he never became a Christian.)

From a radio broadcast, Sakamaki learned of the Battle of Midway and what a disastrous defeat it was for Japan. He blamed this on the fact that, as earlier reported, the United States had broken the secret Japanese code.

From Camp Forest, Sakamaki was moved to Camp Livingston, Louisiana. This camp was different. In addition to being an internment camp for about 1,200 Japanese, mostly displaced US citizens, it was also a jungle warfare training camp for US soldiers who were headed for the South Pacific. There was much more freedom for Sakamaki at Camp Livingston. His hut was near the main gate. He was allowed to spend daylight hours with the Japanese civilian internees. Sakamaki was impressed by the Japanese civilian internees. Their orderly life was a constant source of inspiration for him. He felt he could learn a lot from these people who had spent most of their adult life in the United States.

More and more, Sakamaki was being swayed by the human kindness bestowed on him. Yet, he said, "If anyone had tried to change me or my mind, or had shown the slightest sign of trying to convert me, I would have reacted with extreme skepticism."

Sakamaki's lack of responsibility came to an end in November 1942 when he was moved to another area of Camp Livingston where he would be among other Japanese combat prisoners who had just arrived as survivors from warships that had been sunk in the Midway battle, the attack at Wake Island and from submarines in the Aleutian campaign. These compatriots of Sakamaki were unruly and showed signs of hostility toward Americans.

Not wanting the men to get out of hand, Sakamaki called a meeting to explain the rules of the camp and to convince them they would be well treated.

As the senior Japanese prisoner of war at the camp, and as their superior officer, Sakamaki then organized these men into groups and set up a daily schedule and started evening classes to keep them physically and mentally active. These men were prisoners of war, a fact that made them very ashamed and dejected. Moreover, they expected to be killed. It was shameful to be taken prisoner, and no doubt their captors, knowing this, felt nothing but disgust for them, and at a suitable time would kill them all. Sakamaki, however, soon convinced his fellow prisoners that the Americans had no intentions of killing them; and from these men Sakamaki learned a little more of the progress of the war, which seemed ever more in doubt for their beloved Japan.

At Camp Livingston Sakamaki was successful in keeping the combat prisoners under control. No serious disturbances broke out.

In May 1943 Sakamaki and the other POWs at Camp Livingston were sent to Camp McCoy. In the Wisconsin camp, they were given various jobs to do in accordance with the Geneva Convention pertaining to prisoners of war, as they had been in the previous camp. At Camp McCoy a favorite task was the privilege of planting and raising their own vegetables. The men were very happy and proud when these vegetables appeared on their tables in the mess hall.

It was about this time when Sakamaki's midget submarine was brought to a nearby town for display during a war bond drive. Sakamaki was very embarrassed. His submarine, instead of sinking an American warship, was now raising money which would be used to fight Japan. He didn't ask to visit the submarine. Actually, he didn't feel too badly about the sub's new mission. Reflecting on that, Sakamaki realized how much he had changed.

In September 1943 additional Japanese war prisoners arrived at Camp McCoy. By the end of the year, the total had grown to 100. The battles at Tarawa and the Marshall Islands found more prisoners winding up at Camp McCoy. The camp became very crowded. Eventually, the officer prisoners were separated from the group and were housed in a section of the infirmary.

Then, when 250 new prisoners arrived in February 1945, it was imperative for the US Army to find room for the POWs elsewhere.

Sakamaki, along with his fellow prisoners at Camp McCoy, again boarded a train. Their final move was to Camp Kennedy, Texas.

The war was fast coming to an end. There was the report of the dropping of the atomic bombs — then a surprise report of Russia entering the war against Japan. The prisoners at Camp Kennedy were shocked and dumbfounded. They took personally the blame for losing the war. Some of the men couldn't believe their country lost the war, but Sakamaki tried to convince them it was so. He spoke of the job they all had to do after they returned to their homeland. There would be much work to do, and they all resolved to do their best to help rebuild Japan.

All of them would soon be going home, and Sakamaki would recall that life in American prisoner of war camps as no real hardship in the sense he had been taught to believe. It had not always been a bed of roses. As an officer, he always had certain responsibilities for the supervision and good order of those of his countrymen of lesser rank. At times, arguments occurred which stretched his persuasive abilities.

Once, he had to settle a dispute in the recreation hall about who had priority on use of the pool tables. Some of the younger officers who were newly arrived in the camp felt that they, as officers, should have the privilege of being first. This was disputed by the enlisted men who had spent many months in prison camps and felt they should have first use because of their "seniority." Sakamaki settled it by convincing everybody that in this and similar situations rank and seniority should be parked at the door, and it was first come, first served.

Sakamaki was also able to convince his fellow prisoners of war the value of learning the American language and making use of all of the educational facilities which had been provided for them. Sakamaki explained that it would be to Nippon's advantage for the prisoners to cooperate to the fullest with their captors, whenever consistent with their loyalty to their beloved Japan, in order to get as much out of their internment as possible.

December 1945 found 800 anxious Japanese prisoners of war leaving Texas for their trip home. On the train trip to the West Coast, during the few days in the repatriation center, and then during the sailing of the broad Pacific, Sakamaki and his comrades had much time to think about what their status in Japan would be when once they arrived home. There would be monumental adjustments for each one of them. No doubt about that.

At home there would be bitterness, humiliation, and the exhaustion of defeat. As for Sakamaki, and no doubt for countless others who watched the Japanese islands rise on the horizon, there was a resolve to help build their beloved country into something even greater than it was, and rebuild their own lives in the process, if possible.

Thus ends the story of Ensign Sakamaki's American prison experience. It is obvious that there are two greatly different cultures and national attitudes presented here. My treatment by the Japanese was deadly, brutal, and evil. Sakamaki's was civilized and humane. What a world of difference.

WHY THE DIFFERENCE?

The only explanation that I can make is that Japanese culture considered *all* other world peoples as barbarians and sub-human, to be treated as such. They have tortured, mutilated, and murdered Asian peoples, as well as Western captives. Historically, they have believed themselves to be a superior race. The Japanese were not a civilized people.

I hope that returned Japanese POWs have positively influenced Japan's brutal culture.

I pray that such a change will take place.

Appendix B

POW Massacre

This is an account of the massacre of 62 American prisoners of war (POW) who were moved from Kempei Tai Headquarters (in downtown Tokyo) to the Tokyo Military Prison on 9 May 1945, and massacred, to the last man, at the Tokyo Military Prison on 25-26 May 1945. I shared cell life with some of these unfortunate victims of the murderous Japanese before they were selected to make that fatal prison transfer.

Kempei interrogators continually assured me that my incarceration in this overcrowded and death-threatening prison was only temporary, and that all Special Prisoners would be moved to a Japanese army POW camp soon. The thought of this upcoming transfer was all that offered hope of survival to our miserable and slowly dying American prisoner group. I was told during an interrogation just prior to that fatal 10 May 1945 prisoner transfer that there was a shipment planned in the very near future of all Special Prisoners, and that I would be amongst those shipped out.

During my Kempei prison stay, I was moved many times from cell to cell and cell block to cell block. I had shared the same cells with Tony Scalero, John Meagher, Otto Marek, and Doug Bannen in the overpacked Kempei cells. All these unfortunate Special Prisoners perished at the Tokyo Military Prison. The account of their terrible deaths are recorded in the *War Criminal Trial Account* which follows. Their story will live in infamy and will always remain an indictment of the Japanese war time treatment of their Special Prisoners.

On 9 May 1945 we were awakened earlier than usual by much activity around our cells and the shouting of many excited Kempei guards. All cell doors were opened and the names of most American prisoners were called out. My name was not included.

Sixty-two Americans were on the transfer list and were handcuffed and blindfolded and led off to be taken to their unknown, but supposedly much more humane army POW camp.

None of these 62 prisoners were ever seen alive again.

At my next interrogation, I asked why I hadn't been included and where they had been taken. I was told that they had been shipped to a "nice" prison camp. I complained as best I could that I had been promised to be included on the next prisoner transfer, the last of which I'd just missed when I arrived at Kempei Tai Headquarters around 12 April 1945. I was told that I had been scheduled for the shipment, but my name had been left off the list because of a mix-up with that of a fellow prisoner whose last name, Hanks, was similar to mine in Japanese. As a result, neither of us were included in the shipment orders. Junior, who was my interrogator at the time, assured me that both Hanks and I would be included in the next shipment. Time passed, we starved, brutal interrogations continued, prisoners were beaten, prisoners died, and more B-29 survivors arrived.

Finally, on the morning of 15 August 1945, all American prisoners in Kempei Headquarters were awakened before the *sho* call. We were herded onto smelly, wood-burning trucks and taken to Camp Omori Prison located on Tokyo Bay near Yokohoma. At the time, we Special Prisoners thought that this was the long hoped for shipment to the "nice" prison camp. Little did we know that World War II was over, and we were not told this good news.

After our arrival at Camp Omori, I looked over the hundred or so Special Prisoners for my friends who had been removed from Kempei back in May 1945. Not a one of them was amongst the Omori prisoners. I asked about those POWs taken earlier from Kempei Tai Headquarters prison. No one had seen or heard of them!

I was puzzled by their absence.

The fate of those missing Special Prisoners bothered me, until quite by chance, I learned their terrible fate.

While reading John Toland's excellent book, *The Rising Sun*, published in 1970, I noticed on page 919 of Volume II a brief statement, "During a fire raid on Tokyo, the Tokyo Army Prison was burned down, killing sixty two Allied airmen." No details were given as to how they died. The number of prisoners matched! Could these unfortunate prisoners be those who were removed from Kempei Tai Headquarters in May 1945?

Soon after seeing Toland's account, I stumbled across the exact story of their fate during an encounter at General Dynamics Convair, where I was employed after the war, while spinning war stories with a company attorney. When he learned that I'd been a Japanese prisoner, he asked where I had been imprisoned. When I answered his question, he asked if I had heard about the Tokyo Military Prison massacre. I told him that I didn't know what he was talking about.

Unfortunately, I don't remember the attorney's name. He had participated in prosecuting the Tokyo War Crime Trials. He searched his records and found a copy of the trial summary relative to the 62 missing American airmen.

The following is an exact copy of those proceedings. If it had not been for the Hanks/Hanley name mix up, I would not be alive today. By a stroke of fate, I was spared from this awful tragedy!

The good Lord had looked after me once again.

The tragic story:

GENERAL HEADQUARTERS
SUPREME COMMANDER FOR THE ALLIED POWERS
LEGAL SECTION
    Tokyo, Japan
    APO 5000
    26 March 1948
    File No. 014.13

    Legal Section Informational Summary No. 249
    SUBJECT: US vs Toshio *Tashiro* et al

Charged with the responsibility for the murder of 62 captured American fliers who were either slashed, stabbed, or burned to death when Tokyo Military Prison was destroyed by fire following a heavy US air raid, five Japanese war criminals are presently on trial before a Yokohama Eighth Army Military Commission.

In charges and specifications signed by Alva C. Carpenter, Chief of the Legal Section, Supreme Commander of the Allied Powers, the accused are alleged to have failed to let the Americans leave their burning cells and to have cut down 17 of the Americans who attempted to do so.

Responsible for the tragedy are Toshio *Tashiro* who was warden of the Tokyo Military Prison, also known as Shibuya Military Prison and Masao *Koshikawa*, who was chief jailer. Matsuaki *Kambe*, Keiji *Kamimoto*, and Mataishi *Okubo*, all of whom served as prison guards, are alleged to have killed 8, 6, and 3 unidentified prisoners respectively. All of the accused were civilians, but

Tashiro later became a captain in the Japanese Army. All pleaded not guilty to the charges brought against them by Legal Section prosecutors Andrew A. Adinolfi of 3015 Roberts Avenue, Bronx, NY and Grey Anderson of 310 Stuart Drive, Galax, VA.

"The study of wartime atrocities perpetrated by the Japanese has brought to light numerous fiendish and barbaric acts" said Adinolfi in his opening statement before the court, "but few of these can attain the diabolical depths reached by the acts surrounding the tragedy that took place in May 1945 at the Tokyo Military Prison in Tokyo. On that fateful night of 25-26 May 1945, there were confined in this prison at Shibuya, Tokyo, 62 American fliers, ranging in rank or grade from private first class to lieutenant colonel, all of whom had been shot down while engaged in bombing operations over Japan. Of this number, 45 have been positively identified — at the same time there were also confined at that prison some 450 to 500 Japanese military and political prisoners.

"On the morning of 26 May at 0300 hours there was not an American alive of these 62. All had perished by fire or sword during a fire brought about by an incendiary air raid that burned the prison to the ground. Of all the Japanese prisoners incarcerated in the prison at the time, not a single one of them perished, since all had been safely evacuated to places outside the prison area during the night."

Adinolfi went on to describe the previous arrival of the prisoners who had been brought blindfolded to the prison in trucks and never allowed out of their cells from the time of their arrival. Since a 7 foot wooden fence surrounded their particular cell block, the prisoners were never even permitted to view their immediate surroundings at the prison. All the Americans were being held pending investigation of charges accusing them of the crime of indiscriminate bombing, Adinolfi continued.

He went on to describe the scene of the tragedy, stating that the prison proper consisted of an outer and inner prison compound. A large gate and a smaller side entrance permitted passage from one compound to another. Surrounding the inner prison area was a 12 foot brick wall. Within this area were the cell blocks, six in number, one of which was occupied by the Americans. The cell block where the Americans were confined was a wooden building with a tile roof. It had 17 cells, each one about 12 feet long by 6 feet wide. The front end of each cell was covered with wooden lattice-work, and the sides of the cells were built of pine boards. Each cell had a door equipped with a large iron lock that could not be reached from the inside of the cell. There was a passageway running completely around the cells which were located in the center of the cell block itself. "One thus can readily see that the entire cell block was a veritable fire trap," Adinolfi said.

He went on to describe the part of each of the accused in the series of events on the night of 25 May. Sometime late in the night of 25 May, an air raid alarm sounded over Tokyo, and eventually the Allied bombers came over and bombed the city. Fires first broke out outside of the prison grounds. This was followed by incendiaries falling upon prison buildings and installations, causing the prison area itself to become a sea of flames.

"The guards, *Kambe, Okubo,* and *Kamimoto,*" Adinolfi stated, "are charged with the outright acts of murder in that they willfully and unlawfully killed 17 American prisoners by piercing and cutting them with swords during the time of the fire.

"*Tashiro* as prison warden, is charged with ordering his subordinates to kill any Americans that might escape from their cells during the air raid, such orders resulting in the killing of 17 Americans Prisoners of War. He is also charged with failing to provide for the safety of the American prisoners, failing to protect them from the hazards of war, and failing to authorize their release during the air raid and fire. Not only did he fail to furnish his subordinates with a plane for the release of the prisoners in the event of an air raid or fire, but he specifically ordered his subordinates not to release the Americans, thereby causing the deaths of 45 American prisoners by burning. *Koshikawa,* as senior chief jailer and second in command, is also charged with failing to release the 62 Americans from their cells. He and *Tashiro* in conjunction with others, are also charged with a common plan or conspiracy to fail to release or cause the release of prisoners in the event of fire, air raid, or other common disaster, and also with a conspiracy to with hold information concerning the incident from the Government of the US of America. They alleged to have suppressed information and to have fabricated other false and misleading information concerning the incident.

"As may very well have been surmised," Adinolfi continued, "the Prosecution finds itself with no live American witnesses for the simple reason that of the 62 Americans who were present at the prison during the time of the fire, not one of them survived to tell the tale of atrocities that took place that night. The Prosecution will conclusively and beyond a reasonable doubt prove its case against all of the accused herein though the live testimony of Japanese Nationals, both prisoners and prison employees alike, present at the Tokyo Military Prison at the time of its destruction — Eyewitnesses will place *Kambe* and *Kamimoto* present in the cell block of the Americans with swords in their hands and lunging and stabbing at the American prisoners there. Other eyewitnesses will place *Okubo* in the vicinity of the inner gate with sword in hand, shouting threats concerning the Americans and further he will be shown to have killed Americans as they attempted to escape from the fiery inner prison area through this inner gate."

Concerning the attempt to conceal the crime, Adinolfi said that evidence would be introduced to show that *Tashiro* and *Koshikawa* had devised a plan to give false and incomplete reports of the events to the occupation authorities. *Koshikawa* is said to have ordered the guards to say that eight Japanese prisoners had perished during the fire, whereas in actuality none died. This distortion of fact is alleged to have been made in an attempt to help the defense of the parties guilty of the murders of 62 Americans.

In conclusion, Adinolfi stated, "The nature of the crimes committed by the five accused — is such as to warrant the imposition of the death penalty upon them. They will be shown to be wanton and deliberate murderers. They are deserving only of that same consideration that they gave to those boys who perished during the night of 25-26 May amidst the flames and at the points of swords. It is for this reason, that at the termination of this case, after all the evidence has been called to your attention, that the Prosecution will call upon you to bring in a verdict of death by hanging, upon each of the accused."

Names and hometowns of the 45 identified Americans who perished in the fire are as follows. (Asterisks note victims who were my cellmates or I knew were present at Kempei Tai Headquarters.)

2d. Lt. Clifford Manning	Covington, KY
Sgt. John W. Welsh	Saginaw, MI
Sgt. Robert K. Sedon	Warren, PA
Pfc. Edwin P. Lund	E. Stanwood, WI
2d. Lt. Justice J. Buttala	Chicago, IL
*S. Sgt. Anthony P. Scolaro	Chicago, IL
Sgt. Wm. W. Sutherland	Rosenberg, TX
Maj. Ralph H. Chapel	Jackson, MI
2d. Lt. Harvey M. Glick	Grand Rapids, MI
2d. Lt. Harold J. Nelson	Minneapolis, MN
2d. Lt. James A. Reinhart, Jr.	Wichita, KS
1st. Lt. Edward Sullivan	Somerville, MS
Pfc. John T. Hosey	Mechanicsville, NY
*Sgt. John W. Meagher	Ligonier, PA
T. Sgt. Frederick E. Hulse	Circleville, OH
Lt. Col. Doyne L. Turner	Muskogee, OK
Capt. Elmer G. Hahn	Idaho Falls, ID
2d. Lt. Eugene J. Redinger	Wanaque, NJ
2d. Lt. John T. Price	Salisburg, MD
2d. Lt. David M. Gerhardt	Springfield, OH
Sgt. Donald W. MacNiven	Waterbury, CT
2d. Lt. Andrew J. Litz	Bassett, NE
Cpl. Walter G. Grubb	Marietta, PA
2d. Lt. Eugene A. Homyak	Denver, CO
2d. Lt. John R. Jennings	Gibsonia, PA
S. Sgt. Allan K. Hill	Eureka, CA

*Sgt. Otto J. Marek	Chicago, IL
S. Sgt. Alfred J. McNamara	Julesberg, CO
Cpl. Darwin J. Muller	Bassett, NE
2d. Lt. Wm. F. Muhlenberg	Wyomissing, PA
2d. Lt. Theodore C. Reynolds	Peterborough, NH
Sgt. Donald L. Schubert	Westbrook, CT
T. Sgt. Jim W. Verhines	Danville, IL
Sgt. Thomas L. Klingensmith	Arnold, PA
Sgt. Gilbert C. Stockinger	Philadelphia, PA
S. Sgt. Chester A. Johnson, Jr.	Houston, TX
Cpl. Allen L. Morsch	Enderin, ND
2d. Lt. Donald L. Bartholmew	Union City, IN
1st. Lt. Alpheus G. Carle	Shreveport, LA
2d. Lt. Ray E. Harry	Chicago, IL
S. Sgt. Lawrence T. Duffy	Falls, VT
*Sgt. Douglas Bannon	Portland, OR
Cpl. Calvin R. Raymond	Brooklyn, NY
Henry L. Younge	Copague, NY

This is not the only massacre of groups of B-29 prisoners. Special Prisoners were executed several places in Japan toward the war's end. In William Craig's fine book, *The Fall of Japan*, on page 297, he reports that "fifty airmen were beheaded by vengeful Japanese soldiers."

Lt. Marcus McDilda, a member of that Kempei prisoner lot, escaped death by being brought to Kempei Headquarters just before V-J Day so that he could be questioned about his wild tale of nuclear bombs about which he knew nothing. He hoodwinked the Japanese Kempeis and unknowingly saved his life.

The Kempei Tai Headquarters commander, Colonel Otani, on 14 August 1945, ordered his deputy, Lt. Col. Ranjo Fujino, to execute all American prisoners. Fujino elected to disobey the direct order because he knew the war's end was imminent and that he'd be better off with his American captors holding live prisoners than by being a party to their execution. The good Lord looked after me again.

To my knowledge, the story of B-29 prisoners in World War II has never been researched and documented. I estimate that a maximum of 200 survived imprisonment. Not a good record. The Japanese did not foster Special Prisoner survival.

Appendix C

Air Raids

As a Special Prisoner caged in a dungeon in the middle of Tokyo, I was sensitive to air raids which targeted the Emperor's city. Such attacks were positive indications that the war was being vigorously pursued. I wanted air raids — I welcomed the sound of our planes overhead.

Even though I was at high risk from the bombing attacks, I hoped and prayed for frequent air raids to hit Tokyo. My life was in extreme jeopardy. I didn't care whether the bombs hit near or far, as long as they kept coming. I wanted the Japanese to be bombed into oblivion. I expected to be tried and executed, or massacred, when Kyushu Island was invaded in a couple of months. My future did not appear promising.

The more air raids, the better! My crew, in its short combat life of seven missions, bombed Tokyo three times. The Emperor's city was a prime target for B-29s. A third of its urban area had been destroyed with fire bombs during my March mission. I knew that our navy's aggressive battle groups would soon hit the city with swarms of carrier fighters and bombers.

I'd been briefed by senior intelligence officers about the awesome offensive power that America was building to destroy the Japanese will to fight.

Our forces were escalating punishment of the Japanese nation for "The Day That Will Live in Infamy," as President Franklin Delano Roosevelt called the dastardly Japanese Pearl Harbor attack.

Understandably, our Kempei Tai captors were not happy about these air raids. Their personal lives were affected by the casualties and destruction resulting from the bombings. They lost family members and friends. I was concerned about what effect their reaction to these losses would have. Fortunately, rigid Japanese army discipline saved us from their vengeance.

As a form of torture and punishment, during air raids, Kempei guards forced prisoners to stand at attention with arms extended to the ceiling throughout the long raid alerts. This amounted to many hours of torture. Weaker prisoners passed out and slumped to the floor. Guards poked bayonets into the cell to rouse them to their feet. Buckets of water were thrown on prostrate bodies to revive those who didn't move when pricked with bayonets.

Guard reaction during air raids was interesting. These battle hardened Kempei troops calmly showed no emotion. They removed the steel helmet stowed on their backs, placed it on their heads, and continued as if nothing was amiss during bombings. Apparently, dying for the Emperor was the greatest thing that could happen to them. I was amazed at the mental attitude of these sadistic savages. When the air raids ended, their helmets were restored to the stowed position, and the guards went about their duties as if nothing had happened.

The Japanese air raid warning system was very efficient. There was plenty of time to prepare for an incoming raid. Approaching planes were detected by Japanese observers on outlying islands and picket boats. Our prison was wired into the Japanese Imperial Headquarters information network which supplied the public address system with up-to-the-minute combat announcements, including air raid information. Our cell areas could hear these messages. They were a morale booster for us. The more Japan was bombed, the more we liked it. I never thought I'd be happy to be on the receiving end of an air raid. I was! I wanted more air raids.

A typical raid started with a continuous blast of sirens sounding the alert. Many sirens covered the entire city. We heard them sound off from far away. Sirens began sounding about two hours before the attackers arrived over the city. For a navy carrier raid, the warning could be just moments before low flying fighters could be heard hitting the city. Sirens were easily audible in our cell areas.

Sirens warned the populace to seek air raid shelters and for anti-aircraft and fighter defenses to prepare for action. Air raid wardens, fire fighters, and civil defense people prepared for whatever was coming.

The PA system reported on the threat. Type and quantity of aircraft were announced. We prisoners became proficient at understanding these messages. *Bee-Nee-Ju-Coo* meant B-29. *Pee-Go-Ju-Itchee* meant P-51. I don't remember what the navy designations were. They had many different types of fighters and small bombers hitting the city.

Counting in Japanese is fairly easy if you know how to count from one to ten. Eleven is ten-one. Twelve is ten-two and so on. Twenty is two-ten. To interpret B-29, the Japanese call out *Bee* for bomber, then *Nee* for two, *Ju* for ten and *Coo* for nine.

A typical quantity of aircraft could be announced as *Hutch-Ju-Sichee* (eight-ten-seven) or 87 aircraft approaching.

When the Japanese determined that Tokyo was the target, a series of short siren blasts sounded, meaning that the raid was about to happen. During the raid, it was obvious that the attack was in progress. The sounds of destruction were awful, even in my dungeon cage.

Nearby flak batteries defended the Emperor's Palace and Kempei Tai Headquarters. They opened up with terrific flak barrages. B-29 attacks occurred mostly at night. Naval raids hit during daylight hours. As the attackers roared overhead, continuous pounding of the heavy caliber flak guns was heard. These guns were so near that smells of their burning cordite explosives seeped into our dungeon area. In the horse stalls, the din was deafening. I don't know why, but die-hard Japanese crowds gathered in the streets near the flak batteries. I could hear their babbling excited voices. Every now and then I heard banzai cheers which could only mean that the guns had hit one of our airplanes. Unfortunately, I heard these cheers too many times. I related to those poor crewmen in their stricken aircraft. I prayed for their survival.

During B-29 and naval airplane attacks, bombs and bullets hit close enough to our building that I heard impacts of shrapnel against the structure. I wondered how the Emperor and his family, across the moat from me, were taking these raids. I was elated that our mighty air power was striking Tokyo. If a long period elapsed between air attacks, my morale suffered. I prayed for frequent bombing and strafing missions.

The raids against the Tokyo area that I'm aware of are listed below.

TOKYO AREA AIR RAIDS (JANUARY-AUGUST 1945)
*** *Raids in which I participated*

NOTE: On 20 January 1945 General Curtis LeMay assumed command of 21st Bomber Command (Marianas based B-29s).

27 January	73 B-29s from Saipan's 73d Wing hit Musashimo (Musashi) and Nakajima aircraft plants near Tokyo
10 February	84 B-29s hit Nakajima plant
11 February	9 B-29s fly reconnaissance for Navy
12 February	8 B-29s fly reconnaissance for Navy
14 February	B-29s fly reconnaissance for Navy
19 February***	119 B-29s bomb Tokyo port and urban area
25 February***	172 B-29s bomb Tokyo urban area

| 4 March | First B-29 makes emergency landing on Iwo Jima; 2400 emergency landings will be made later. |

4 March — First B-29 makes emergency landing on Iwo Jima; 2400 emergency landings will be made later.
159 B-29s bomb Tokyo urban area when primary target, Musashimo (Musashi) plant, was obscured by clouds. 20 B-29s hit other alternate targets.

NOTE: *Previous B-29 bombing was done during daylight at 25,000 to 30,000 feet altitude with poor results. General LeMay changed this mission strategy to carry full bomb loads and bomb from 4,000 to 8,000 feet altitude at night.*

9 March*** — 279 B-29s blast Tokyo from low altitudes at night with full bomb loads. First of five *Incendiary Blitz Missions* directed by General LeMay. We thought he was crazy. I was on this mission. More than 83,000 people killed. 15.8 square miles (about one quarter of urban area) obliterated; 267,000 buildings destroyed.

NOTE: *During March, five Incendiary Blitz Missions were launched. I participated in three of the five.*

11 March — 313 B-29s hit Nagoya. *Incendiary Blitz Missions #2.* 2.05 square miles destroyed. Disappointing results.

13 March — 274 B-29s blast Osaka. *Incendiary Blitz Missions #3.* 8.1 square miles destroyed. 135,000 houses burned.

16 March*** — 307 B-29s hit Kobe. *Incendiary Blitz Missions #4.* 2.9 square miles destroyed. 66,000 houses burned. 42,500 homeless. 3,000 killed. 11,000 wounded.

18 March*** — 290 B-29s blast Nagoya. *Incendiary Blitz Missions #5.* 3 square miles destroyed.

27 March*** — Shimonoseki mining mission. (Our plane shot down.)

2 April — More than 100 B-29s bomb Nakajima Tokyo plant.

3 April — 68 B-29s bomb Koizumi aircraft factory and Tokyo urban areas. 100 plus B-29s strike Tachikawa air craft plant near Tokyo.

7 April — 101 B-29s hit Nakajima aircraft engine plant near Tokyo. 91 P-51s accompany B-29s for first time.

12 April — 94 B-29s blast Nakajima aircraft factory escorted by P-52 fighters.

13 April — 330 B-29s bomb Tokyo arsenal area.

NOTE: *Until 17 April B-29s carried out high priority bombing of kamikaze airfields on Kyushu island at navy's request to cut down on murderous attacks on ships participating in the Okinawa campaign.*

15 April	109 B-29s hit Tokyo urban area.
25 April	101 B-29s strike Hitachi aircraft plant at Tachikawa near Tokyo.
5 May	86 B-29s drop mines in Tokyo Bay.
24 May	Large number of B-29s bomb Tokyo urban area.
26 May	464 B-29s pound Tokyo urban area immediately south of Imperial Palace, including financial, commercial, and governmental districts. 26 B-29s *shot down*.
29 May	454 B-29s accompanied by 101 P-51s (first night escort) bomb Yokohama, which is very near Tokyo. Nine square miles destroyed. 7 B-29s (including Marcus Worde's) and 3 P-52s are lost.

NOTE: *There were no B-29 air raids on Tokyo during the entire month of June. We were worried and dejected by this lack of bombing activity. The B-29s were busy plastering other major targets and conducting mining missions as part of* Operation Starvation.

| 6 July | Major B-29 incendiary strike at Chiba which is across Tokyo Bay. |

NOTE: *There were no additional reportable B-29 strikes on Tokyo until 10 August. The B-29 fleet was busy bombing and mining other targets. General LeMay even gave advance warning to selected targets that they were to be bombed so that civilians could be evacuated. The 20th Air Force was running out of targets.*

On 6 August Colonel Tibbets dropped the first atomic bomb from his *Enola Gay* B-29 on the city of Hiroshima. On the 9th of August, Maj. Charles Sweeny hit Nagasaki with the second atomic bomb.

The Emperor at all times was in charge of Japanese war operations, was convinced that it was useless to continue the war and directed that Japan surrender.

8 August	60 B-29s hit aircraft and arsenal targets in the Tokyo area.
10 August	70 B-29s bomb arsenal complex in Tokyo, last B-29 raid on Tokyo area targets.
15 August	504th Bomb group airplane drops last weapon of war and World War II fighting ends.
29 August	First prison camp, Camp Omori, Liberated.
2 September	Peace was signed on deck of USS *Missouri*.

WORLD WAR II ENDS

Appendix D

Affidavits

Special Prisoner affidavits were obtained from Robert H. Neptune, Special Prosecutor of Kempei Tai war criminals responsible for the horrors inflicted on American prisoners held as *Special Prisoners.*

Shortly after the war, Army Criminal Investigation Division (CID) and Federal Bureau of Investigation (FBI) agents were given names of known survivors of the Kempei Tai prison. Sixty-nine Special Prisoner survivors were found and provided depositions for use during the criminal prosecutions.

Neptune provided the author original copies of the depositions along with war crimes court records of the trial.

These depositions provide individual horror stories of the privations, tortures, beatings, starvations, and murders of American flyers by the Kempei Tai during the last few months of World War II.

The lengthy depositions were condensed by the author. Summaries include the name, B-29 combat unit, airplane crew position, hometown, date shot down, and the names of cellmates, if given in the depositions.

Individual horrors experienced are italicized. The reader is encouraged to study these depositions in detail in order to better understand the animal-like Japanese culture as practiced on a particular group of unfortunate POWs. These highlights are offered in the voice of the individual POW, not the author. Your attention is directed to the deposition of Marcus E. McDilda, who avoided murder by the Osaka Kempei Tai by professing knowledge of the atomic bomb.

HAROLD ANDERSON: Brooklyn, NY, 6th BG. Downed 25 May over Tokyo. Radar-Navigator-Bombardier. Cellmates — Boyko, Costello, Evans, Gorrie, Hill, Johnson, Jones, Lounsbury, Macomb (504th), Mitchell, Moritz, Sasser, Thomas (504th), Worde (504th), Mansfield. Interro — 18 times. Horse stalls. Senior military interro not so brutal. Radar questions. Japanese knew more than he did. Told execution ordered when invasion started.

MICHAEL BOYKO: Chesapeake City, MD. Downed 25 May over Tokyo. Lounsbury crewmate. Broken ankle. Japanese kicked wounded area. Caught diphtheria. Became paralyzed. Macomb's fractured left arm was not set. Worde was cellmate. Worde's beating injuries so bad he was unrecognizable. Guard smuggled mercurochrome, ¼ inch in bottle. Horse stalls. Cellmates — Sasser, Mitchell, Lounsbury, Worde, Jones, Anderson, Macomb.

JOHN B. BOYNTON: Chippewa, MI. Downed 25 May over Tokyo. Eluded capture for two days. Captured by civil police. Heidlebaugh was Co-pilot. Interro — "Shorty" ordered brutal beating by *kendo* bat. McQuade had bad burns. Beaten on wounds. Raw meat protruding. In Horse stalls, only 4 cellmates at first — Burkle, Evans, Franz, Grant, Heidlebaugh, Hoffman, Lyons, McClure, McQuade, Orzilli, Phillips, Romoser, Ryan, Slater, Townsend, Trump. *Fox in Cell #3 — Bleeding from mouth and rectum — Delirious in cell six hours, died in O'Hara's arms.*

GORDON BRANSTROM: Russell, PA. 505BG. Downed 25 May over Tokyo. Gunner. Interro — Centered on P-61 "Black Widow" fighter. Beatings. Horse stalls. Cellmates — Babica, Bloodgood, Briscoe, Decker, Downing, Forystek, Halbert, Jelgerhuis, Jones, Lamon, Olsen, O'Mara, Pell, Reams, Ryan, Shelton, Strelnik, Unterman. *Brutal Torture.* Japanese kneel position. Kneecaps hurt. Passed out. Beatings. Stand at attention with arms raised. *Stanley Forystek had bad burns — died in cell after two days on 28 May. Warren Olsen had bad burns and welts — was beaten — removed from cell — infected neck wound — guards stabbed with bayonets.*

CHARLES J. COUCHMAN: Harrison, OH. 505BG. Downed 25 May over Tokyo. Captured by civilians. Tied to tree for five hours. Truck pick up. Others on truck - Leavitt, Lurvey, McGuire, Jensen. Stood in sun all day. Jensen — badly burned. Lurvey — broken jaw. Brutal beatings. Interro — "Shorty" was writing book about Manchuria. Beatings with *kendo* bat. Caught talking — punished by severe beatings. One Christian guard. *Jensen murdered after about three weeks.*

KENNETH ESTEL CREECH: Knoxville, TN. Radar Operator. 6 BG. Downed 25 May over Tokyo. Captured by civilians. *Snellz — bad burns —*

beatings — could not stand up — kendo *bat — Murdered.* Cellmate — Mansfield. Interro — "Shorty" responsible for beating up Snellz.

LOREN E. DECKER: Bartley, NB. Downed 25 May over Tokyo. Interro — *kendo* bat beatings — black and blue — Beaten by "Shorty." Forystek — bad burns face, arms, sides — "Shorty" and guard gave continual beats — out of his head — died in cell on 27 May from two days of beatings — beat to death — Japanese grin at conditions. Olsen — bad burns — continual beatings — Neck swollen from beatings — murdered — beaten by Fujino with *kendo* bat. Jensen — beaten by "Shorty" — murdered on 8 June. Theodore H. Fox — died 2 June in next cell — fighter pilot — out of head — Internal Bleeding. Frank Carey Massey — broken leg. Glidden Carey Lurvey — next cell — broken jaw. Cellmates — 19 of them — George Forystek, John Lanon, Wesley Halbert, Melvin Unterman, William Strelink, Scott Downing, Robert P. Jones. Ring in next cell.

JOHN DEEB: Boston, MS. 29BG. Downed 25 May over Tokyo. Central Fire Control Gunner. Captured and mobbed by civilians who tried to hang him - saved by soldier - bad cut on head - bleeding like "stuck pig." Interro — brutal beating with *kendo* bat — Navy officer asked if civilian targets intentionally bombed. Saw Mansfield, Jorgenson, Michaelsen, Ring, Unterman, Jones of his crew alive. Crewmember — Edward I. Karna held in another Tokyo prison. Beaten by "Shorty" — *Kendo* bat — "Make you a cripple by beatings." Horse stalls. Cell #1 directly across from guard room. Cellmates — *Charles W. Snellz (murdered)*, Charles E. Couchman, Okean, OH; Kenneth E. Creech, Knoxville, TN; Milam M. Dananay, New Kensington, PA; Robert M. Humphreys, Wausau, WI; Robert M. Mansfield (asked by "Shorty" to correct his book about Manchuria), Thorman D. Jorgenson, Austin, MN; Harold Leavitt, University City, MO; Glidden C. Lurvey, Springfield, MO; John M. McGuire, New Haven, CT; Harry D. Magnuson, Minneapolis, MN; Richard M. Mansfield, Craig Field, AL; Robert F. Michelsen, Minneapolis, MN. *Snell — badly burned face, arms, and body — Extreme pain — Jap doctor examined, gave kick and left — Murdered. Francis Jensen — badly burned face and body — same doctor as with Snellz — examined Jensen and left — carried from cell 18 days later and murdered. McGuire developed dysentery but lived. Lurvey broken jaw from civilians. Ring bad thigh cut. Other crewmembers were murdered — Robert McKenzie, Edward C. Coughlan, and Dwight Knapp — they bailed out — didn't survive war.*

WALTER DICKERSON: 6BG. Downed 20 July over Nigata City. Captured by civilian mob — beat up entire crew who bailed out. Train ride to Tokyo with Gordon Jordan, George E. McGraw, Robert J. Burkle, Robert Grant, Walter W. Wiernick. Horse stalls — 16 cellmates — David Glenn

Farquhar, Floyd F. Fielder, Robert L. Fink, Nick Gazibara, Franklyn S. Green, Frank Massey, George E. McGraw, Abel Soto, Dennis E. Tyring, Marvin S. Watkins, Walter W. Wiernick. Interro — bad beatings — Hikida speaks excellent English gave *kendo* bat beating. Hikida visited cells and tortured Frank Massey. Sheridan (died at Omori), Franklyn Green, and Maynor Hanks already in cell. *Japs liked to see bloody heads. Paul Trump badly beaten during capture. POWs at Nihata prison camp heard that four of his missing crew members were murdered and hung by civilians.*

JACK GERALD EVENS: Charleston, WV. Downed 2 April over Tokyo. "Shorty" beatings. Accused of bombing innocent women & children. *On 18 April — Happy M. Glick dragged into cell — cellmates — William Henry Osborn, Ray F. Hoope. Glick taken from cell on 17 April — Tied to post downtown Tokyo — Bayonetted several times in front of civilians — suffered water torture — simulated execution — cigarette burns — nose and ears — murdered on 4 May.* On 26 May in cell #4. Cellmates — John B. Boynton, Robert Glenn Phillips, William Howard McClure, Robert Joseph Burkle, Joe Louis McQuade, John Francis Ryan, Ward Byron Lyons, Harry Junior Slater. *Theodore Fox — cell #3 — died in cell.* Frank Carey Massey — Cell #5 — broken ankle — survived — *Shinagawa.* On 1 June — moved to cell with Maurice San Souci, Siliva LaMarca, Francis Reynolds, Patrick Pellecchia, Delbert W. Miller, Arthur P. O'Hara, John Harvey Newcomb, James P. Martin, Glen B. Guyton, Sherwood C. Kiernon, Dale Lavern Johnson, Robert Neal. *Pellecchia and Miller caught talking — beaten unconscious. On 2 April — John S. Houghton — next cell — bad burns — six days of interro — 9 April — out of mind — murdered by medical officer who gave injection — Arthur A. Gora his cellmate and witness. At Shinagawa Hospital with Joe Louis McQuade — Bad burns — was told he had gangrene and was going to die. Robert Fink — arrived good condition — Tortured to near death.*

FLOYD F. FIELDER: Tyler, TX. Downed 25 May over Tokyo. *Kendo* bat beatings. Not allowed to lie down in daytime. Had to sit at attention. "Shorty" brutally tortured him.

ROBERT L. FINK: Youngstown, OH. Downed 1 June over Tokyo. Cell #6 cellmates — Walter Dickerson, David Glenn Farquhar, Floyd F. Fielder, Nick Gazibara, Franklyn S. Green, Maynard B. Hanks, Frank Massey, George E. McGraw, Donald Press, Harmon Reeder, George Sheridan, Abel Soto, Dennis E. Tyring, Marvin S. Watkins, Walter W. Wiernick. *Notation on cell wall — date of death 14 Feb 1945. Hanks, Gazibara, and Watkins missed massacre shipment of 12 May. Snellz and Jensen in nearby cell were murdered. Massey and Sheridan were paralyzed — both died due to lack of medical treatment. Tyring and Fink beaten near death for talking by five guards outside of cell.* Press evaded capture for 11 days — black and blue from Kempei beatings. *Torture of Hanks and Gazibara — made to stand with hands over head — bad shape — passed out — no food. Interro — beatings — personal history — good detail on P-51 pilot, Fox, murder. Murder victims were cremated — saw roomful of boxed ashes — Kempei records destroyed.*

ROBERT A. FRANZ: Belmore, OH. Downed 24 May over Tokyo. 6 BG. Evaded capture for 8 days. Captured by civilians. All of crew parachuted from plane. Crew listed. Horse stalls. *Six blankets — 16 men — had to sleep two deep —* benjo *overflowed. Good cell description.* Cellmates — Townsend, Boynton, Romoser, Heidlebaugh, McQuade. *McQuade couldn't walk — had to be carried on way to the Camp Omori. Had Beri Beri, trench mouth, swollen ankles. Was fed two-inch diameter rice balls — sometimes less than inch diameter. Given ¼ water each meal. Sometimes given Daikon Pickles. Food thrown on floor. Never saw sun. Lost 55 pounds in two months. Tortured by forced into Japanese kneel position. Kendo bat beatings.*

VINCENT A. GANDIANI: Downed 6 August over Tokyo area. Captured by civilians near Tachikawa Airfield. He was P-51 pilot. *Placed in cell with four Japanese prisoners — two civilians — two soldiers. Dungeon cells. Gives good cell description. Water never enough. Guards wore face masks. Tells about McDilda missing prisoner massacre at Osaka. Interro — personal history — morale — no tech — badly beaten until unconscious for no reason.*

NICK GAZIBARA: Export, PA. 9BG. Downed 16 April over Tokyo. Kawasaki the target. Captured 28 April. Harvey Glick on train to Kempei — never saw him again — *probably murdered. Many beatings by guards. Forced to kneel on floor. Kendo bat beatings. Mock execution with sword. "Shorty," guards, and Japanese officer beat him. He pleaded, "Please don't beat me anymore. Please kill me." Shorty shouted, "You want me to kill you?" "Yes, please kill me." "Stick out your neck." Shorty pulled sword. I did not dare move my eyeballs. Whop, he hit me with the flat of the sword on the back of my neck. "Silly boy, get up." I have permanent scar marks. Made to stay awake in our cell. Cellmates — Warren Ransler, Syracuse, NY; Maynar Hanks, Sweetwater, TX; Fiske Hanley — Witnesses in cell on 11 May 50 to 60 prisoners were transferred from Kempei Tai Prison. They were all massacred.* Cellmates — last days — David Glenn Farquhar, Floyd F. Fielder, Robert L. Fink, Franklyn Stanley Green, Maynar Ben Hanks, Jr., Harry E. McGraw, Frank Carey Massey, Donald R. Press, Harmon Reeder, Jr., Abel Patrick Soto, Dennis E. Tyring, Marvin S. Watkins, Walter W. Wiernik, Ollin Walton Williams, and George L. Sheridan. *Known May massacre victims — Muhlenburg, Morsch, Price, Ralph H. Chaple, Harvey Glick, John T. Hostey. Frederick Hulse, John Meagher, Anthony F. Scolaro, Bertram L. Ware. Robert Williams — P-51 pilot murdered* *by injection. Sheridan died due to brutal treatment. Fink beaten with Kendo bat and pistol. Tyring and Fink badly beaten for talking.*

AUTHUR A. GORA: Downed 7 April. *Kendo* bat beatings. *Cellmate — Houghton murdered by injection.* Cellmates — Allen L. Morsch, Price, Ware, Hulse, Norman Sellz, Ferdinand Spacal, Arthur Beckington, and Sam Smith. *Hulse tied to post by Japanese Cavalry and horse-whipped by every man in hut.* Only four of his crew survived bailout. Meagher & Marek massacred. Spacal and Gora survived Kempei imprisonment.

EDWARD GORRIE: Downed 24 May over Tokyo. 504th BG. Cellmate — Lounsbury with broken ankle taken to Shinegawa when others went to Omori.

JAMES L. GREEN: Downed 25 May over Tokyo. 6 BG. Evaded capture four days. Captured on the Chiba Penninsula. Dungeon cellmates — Japanese civilians. Interro — *Forced to sign war crime confession without knowing what it said. "Shorty" threatened death if questions not answered and confession not signed. Taken out of cell. Tied to cement cross in downtown Tokyo. Bayoneted in neck. Beaten with swords.* Guards hit wounds with kendo bats. Moved to horse stalls. Six cellmates — Fink, Dennis Tyring, John Schroff, and Herbert L. Law (Navy flier). *Fox died in next cell. Kink and Trying beaten unconscious for talking. Vermin bites — ulcerated mass of wounds — lifetime scars. Weight loss down to 87 pounds in two months. Massey and Lounsbury in next cell. Sheridan paralyzed by beatings — almost lost mind.*

GLEN BERTUM GUYTON: Tulsa, OK. 444th BG. Downed 25 May over Tokyo. Badly burned. Captured by civilians — Beaten unconscious — Awoke in Tokyo jail — Saw Michael J. Robertson, crew gunner. Given missing crewmember jacket. *Crew listed. Interro — Execution Threats — Lied about missions — kendo bat beatings like baseball bat swings — caused hip wound open to bone — covered with benjo paper cement sacks, magazines, newspaper, book. Horse stall cell #6 with O'Hara cellmates listed. Harold E. Halidorson entered cell on 28 May — badly wounded 20-30 flak wounds and burns — delirious — died in cell on 6 June. Theodore Fox died in cell from wounds and kicks and blows and internal injuries — passed blood.* Only two of his crewmembers survived — Robertson and Guyton.

WESLEY CLARK HALBERT: Murtaugh, NB. Downed 25 May over Tokyo. Airplane Commander, Homer Hinkle, gave bailout order. He was third man to leave forward cabin. Captured by civilians. Beatings — permanent scars-tied up for 15 hours — displayed to crowds. Horse stalls —

19 cellmates. *Interro — accused of burning Emperor's palace.* Kendo *bat beatings — couldn't eat for days.*

FISKE HANLEY: Fort Worth, TX. 504th BG. Downed 27 March over Shimonoseki Straits. Captured after near murder by civilians — Saved by policeman. Dungeon cells until 12 April — Then horse stalls — Cellmates — Otto Marek, John W. Meagher, Douglas Bannon, Anthony F. Scalero, Ferdinand Anton Spacal — *All died in massacre / 10 May POW transfer to Camp-Random selection of about 60 POW's — Record Mix up (Hanks-Hanley) saved both of us from shipping out on 15 April with 62 others who were massacred — Roland Nelson brought to cell block with third degree burns over most of his body — died in cell. Robert Williams murdered. Fox died in O'Hara's cell. Peterson's gangrene — loss of toes. Three Doolittle fliers executed at Kempei Tai Headquarters.*

ROLLIN E. HEIDLEBAUGH: Lexington, OH. Downed 25 May over Tokyo. *Interro — kendo beating — 50 blows with fists and Hobnail boots* Horse stalls — Cellmates — Roger Townsend, John B. Boynton, Albert S. Romoser, Robert G. Phillips, Roger J. Orzilli, Joe M. McQuade, and Robert A. Franz. McQuade badly burned. Two and one-half month weight loss 53 pounds. Food thrown on floor.

HARVEY H. HOFFMAN: Illinois. Interro — *kendo* beatings. Horse stalls — 13 cellmates. Heidlebaugh — chair broken across his back. McQuade badly burned and beaten, tripped, and kicked by "Shorty" — blood running down his legs. Fox was first P-51 pilot from Iwo captured. He paid with his life — died in cell after surviving parachuting and capture in good shape. He was beaten to death by Kempeis.

ALVIN JELGERHUIS: Downed 25 May over Tokyo. In same horse stall cell with his crewmembers — Peel, Ryan. Reams, Halbert, Shelton, and Lamon — Other cellmates — Chester Bobicz, Donald Bloodgood, Gordon Branstrom, Glenn Briscoe, Loren E. Becker, *Scott Downing,* Wesley C. Halbert, Robert P. Jones, John C. Lamon, Edward F. O'Mara, Thomas W. Peel, Clarence Reams, Donald E. Ryan, Arthur M Shelton, William Strolnik, and Melvin Unterman. Forystek and Olsen — *Forystek was badly burned and out of his head — his skin was burned away — He screamed and hollered — "Give me water or shoot me" — He died in cell on 27 May. Olsen was also badly burned — badly beaten — murdered.*

DALE LA VERNE JOHNSON: Rio, IL. 40th BG. Downed 25 May over Tokyo. *Weighed 90 pounds after Kempei imprisonment — had Beri-Beri, Scurvey, and Pellagra.* Describes dungeon cells. Interro — bad wounds from beatings. He was one of my cellmates. Other cellmates were Bill

Grounds' crewmembers who survived 25 May fire in North Tokyo jail when Guards left them to burn to death — three Japanese cellmates — Anihatas (Communist College Professor whose father was Japanese lieutenant general and governor of Java), Japanese black marketeer, and a Korean youth arrested for attack on Japanese soldiers. Peterson — gangrene caused by stick bound behind his knees for days cutting blood flow to his toes.

ROBERT P. JONES: Norfolk, VA. Downed 25 May over Tokyo. 29th BG. *Placed on public exhibition for 5 hours. Kicked, stoned, and beaten unconscious by civilians, women and children included. Most of beating directed at his flak wounds. Interro — more beatings into unconsciousness by "Shorty."*

GORDON P. JORDAN: Monroe, LA. 6th BG. Captured on 20 July near Niigata by Japanese Home Guard. Interro — five hours — Beaten — made no difference whether questions answered or not. During 28 days in prison — questioned 24 times. Placed face down on floor — stomped all over body — concentrated on head area. "Junior" born San Francisco.

SHERWOOD C. KIERNAN: Hartford, CT. 39th BG. Downed 25 May over Tokyo. Evaded capture for two days. *Kendo* bat beatings by "Shorty." *Cellmates — Dale Johnson had enormous cyst on hip from beating — the bone could be seen,* John Newcomb, Delbert Miller, Michael J. Robertson, Walter Ostriech (fellow crewman), Lloyd Hill and Halldorson who died in cell.

SILVIO LA MARCA: Staten Island, NY. 498th BG. Downed 2 April. Radio Operator. Interro — Nine times. "Shorty" gave beatings to head — no reason. Cellmates — Maurice San Souci, J.W. Evans, T. Fox, G. Guyton, R. Hopper, D. Johnson, A. Beckington, K. Peterson, J. Martin, J. Newcomb, D. Miller, A. O'Hara, P. Pellechia, F. Reynolds. I Arthur K. Hill along with approx 65 others transferred 12 May — supposedly to a better camp — Massacred. Nelson murdered. Fox died in cell in O'Hara's arms. Interro — Senseless questions.

JOHN C. LAMON: Chicago, IL. Downed 25 May over Tokyo. 498th BG. Four crew members killed in plane. Seven captured and placed in same Kempei cell. Four crew members killed — Homer Kinkle (Pilot), Fred Dunham (CFC), Lewis(Gunner), Willis White (Flight Engineer). *Interro — "Shorty" beat him with kendo bat until it broke — accused him of lying. Horse stalls. Forystek and Olson badly burned, knocked heads on bars and walls — were beaten by guards — were delirious. They were both murdered. "Shorty" writing book* Mr. Korea goes to China. Cellmates — Chester Babicz, Donald Bloodgood, Walter G. Branstrom, Oren G. Briscoe, Loren

E. Decker, *Scott M. Downing*, Stanley Forystek, Wesley C. Halbert, Alvin Jelgerkins, Robert P. Jones, Warren Olson, Edward F. O'Mara, Thomas W. Peel, Clarence Reams, Donald E. Ryan, Arthur M Shelton, William Strelnak, and Melvin Unterman. *Interro — Kempeis tried to get confessions about bombing of women and children.*

ALBERT P. LOUNSBURY: Baldwinsville, NY. Downed 25 May over Tokyo. 6th BG. Gunner. Captured by civilians. Broke ankle when parachuting. Beaten and stoned. *Beaten again when requesting splints for ankle.* Imprisoned first in dungeon with five others. Moved to horse stalls. 16 cellmates — Harold Anderson, C. Babicz, Michael Boyko, J. Evans, E. Gorrie, J. Macomb, A. Mitchell, W. Moritz, R. Sasser, M. Worde. *Taken to Shinigawa hospital on 22 August. Liberated on 29 August. Frank Massey in next cell was paralyzed and had diptheria. James Macomb had broken leg tried to splint. Robert Evans in nearby cell — guards kicked and hit flak wounds. Heard groans from beatings in nearby cells. The more one groaned — the more the beatings. Three prisoners in adjacent cells died. Brutal torture — hands over head at attention. Contracted diptheria along with five others.*

GLIDDEN G. LURVEY: Downed 25 May over Tokyo. *Captured by civilians — bad beatings with bamboo poles, one of which was stuck through jaw and broken off— six-inch piece left sticking through mouth, jaw, and neck — left in place for days at Kempei. Made to sit in sun while display to public — rough handling. Fellow crewmember Jensen — badly burned — delirious for eight to ten days — doctor murdered him. Water hard to get. Guards taunted prisoners — finger to head — "bang, bang." Cellmates — Charles W. Snellz — bad burns all over — taken from cell after seven days — doctor murdered him. Jensen had third degree burns — doctor murdered him. John W. MacGuire had dysentery and pneumonia — murdered by doctors.*

WILLIAM H. McCLURE: Chicago, IL. Downed 25 May over Tokyo. *Interro — "Shorty beat him with kendo bat — Permanent disabilities — when senior officers present — no beatings — little bearing on military subjects — personal life — told that after Japs won war all Americans would be slaves of the Japanese.* Horse stall cellmates - Robert Joseph Burkle, Jack G. Evans, Robert A. Franz, Rollin Heidelbaugh, Harvey H. Hoffman, Joe L. McQuade, Ward, B. Lyons, Roger J. Orzilli, Robert G. Phillips, Albert Romoser, John F. Ryan, Harry J. Slater, Roger L. Townsend, and Paul A. Trump. *Charles W. Snellz brought into cell with bad burns — waist up — worst I've ever seen — He was murdered by Japanese doctor. Fox died in nearby cell. Stanley Forystek — in next cell — I was put in that cell in error — observed Forystek — bad burns — waist up — died in cell — not removed for hours. Halldorson also in that cell — Flak & bullet wounds — died in cell. Three to four days after Forystek's death. Fink in nearby cell — removed from* *cell — beaten by seven or eight guards. Macomb arrived his cell and developed diptheria. McQuade — my cellmate — badly burned — state of shock — guard smuggled mercurochrome — no help. Paul A. Trump badly beaten before arrival — covered with blood.*

MARCUS E. McDILDA: Dunnellon, FL. Captured near Osaka during P-51 strafing mission. *Beaten by civilians and soldiers during Osaka Public display. Osaka interro about Iwo Jima based P-51 fighters and Atomic Bombs. Intense interro about Atomic bomb — Jap general pulled sword and struck McDilda in face — "If you don't tell me about the Atomic Bomb, I'll cut your head off." He had heard someone on Iwo talking about splitting of atoms, negative and positive charges. He told the Osaka Kempeis this meager info. He enlarged on it including next target to be Tokyo or Kyoto. Kempeis called Tokyo — General Anami, chief of staff of the Imperial Japanese army, ordered that McDilda be flown immediately to Tokyo. He became VIP to Kempei Tai/ see pages 73-74, 116, 134, 297,* The Fall of Japan *by William Craig/10 August-flown to Tokyo — interro by graduate of CCNY — Kempei interro recognized hoax/ bruised and bleeding put in dungeon cell — cellmates — Lester Morris & 6 Jap prisoners. His life saved by this guessed at story — Other 50 prisoners in Osaka beheaded, one at a time by Osaka Kempeis murdered after Nagasaki Atomic bombing. Cellmates Lester Morris — leg cut half in two after bailing out of engineer's hatch — terrible infection — ate nothing — wound full of maggots — saved by transfer to Omori on 15 August.*

JOHN W. MacGUIRE: New Haven, CT. 505th BG. Gunner on Alva A. Brooks crew. "In the Mood" airplane. Downed 25 May over Tokyo. Eluded Japanese farmers armed with farm implements — Captured by soldiers who allowed civilians to beat him up — almost to death — Saw four other crewmembers — Frank Jensen, Charles C. Couchman, Harold Leavitt, and Glidden C. Lurvey. Interro — Officers educated in U.S. — *Told they could expect to be executed because Emperor's palace bombed that night.* Horse stalls — *Next door to Kempei soldier's barracks holding about 150 men. Hogs fed better than POW's. Jensen and Snellz suffering third degree burns — both taken out of cell after eight and fourteen days respectively — murdered by Japanese doctors. No talking — bad beatings by guards. Interro — Jap privates educated in US had diptheria. After liberation — put on hospital ship U.S.S.* Benevolence.

JAMES THOMAS MACOMB: Staten Island, NY. Downed 25 May over Tokyo. Gunner. — 504th BG. *Gran's Crew* — Only three crew members survived — himself, Gorrie, Jones. Airplane blew up. His arm was broken — splints were applied after capture by civilians. Interro — *Told to sign confession of bombing innocent women and children. Fox allowed to die in cell. Olsen and Forystek taken to dispensary and murdered by injec-*

*tion.*Cellmates — Albert Lounsbury, Harold Anderson, Edward Gorrie, Henry Jones, Ralph, Sasser, Wallace Moritz, Michael Boyko, Joseph Costello, Mitchell, Marcus Worde, Michael. Sheridon, Allan Keniston. *Albert Lounsbury in cell on arrival with broken ankle — Japanese guard smuggled in two boards to splint ankle. Contracted diphtheria. Interro — "Shorty" beat him badly — senior officers also directed beatings with kendo bats — told he was to be executed. Japanese attitude changed near end of war.*

JAMES PFOHL MARTIN: Mayodan, NC. 504th BG — Worde's crew. Downed 29 May near Tokyo on the Chiba Penninsula along with O'Hara. Captured by civilians - Beaten unconscious — Injured right leg. Horse stalls. *Harold B. Halldorson — 58th wing — died from mistreatment. Fox died in cell.* Interro — Beaten by "Shorty" and guards. *Bayonet thrusts through bars. Taken out of cell and beaten. Treated like cattle. Always hog tied and blindfolded outside of cell.*

FRANK CAREY MASSEY: Williams, AZ. 6th BG. Boynton's crew. Downed 25 May over Tokyo. Eluded capture for four days. Captured by a soldier. Marched through streets. Stoned and beaten. *Transferred from Camp Omori to Shinegawa hospital "which was supposed to be a hospital, but was as bad as the prison camp" with diphtheria spread by all prisoners drinking from same cup. Liberated from there. End of war saved his life. "Japanese let prisoners lie in cells until they died." Fink and Tyring caught talking and were kicked with Hobnailed boots and beaten unconscious by many guards outside cell — then thrown back into cell bleeding and suffering head injuries.* Horse stall cellmates — Walter Dickerson, David Glenn Farquhar, Floyd F. Fielder, Robert F. Fink, Nick Gazibara, Franklyn S. Green, Maynard B. Hanks, George E. McGraw, Donald Press, Harmon Reeder, George Slheridan, Abel Soto, Dennis E. Tyring, Marvin S. Watkins, and Walter W. Wiernick.

ROBERT F. MICHELSEN: Captured and tied to a post. Fellow crew members — Jorgenson, Ring, Mansfield, Unterman, Jones, Deeb. *After had D.H. Knapp's ring returned (all bent out of shape). Deeb had rope burns on neck after Japs tried to hang him — also had hole in head. Jones had bad flak wounds. Ring's leg torn open — hip downward 18 inches and two and a half inches deep. After arrival at Kempei — made to sit Japanese fashion — beaten repeatedly into unconsciousness.* Horse stall cellmates — Snellz and *Jensen were badly burned — examined by Japanese doctors — both were murdered by Japanese doctor applied injections. Japanese doctors would do nothing for Ring's leg.*

DELBERT W. MILLER: Bombardier. Downed 25 May over Tokyo.

Andrew C. Papson crew. *Crew listed. Bailed out of co-pilot's window. Others in front cabin asphixiated by smoke and couldn't get out. Survivors — Pellecchia, Oestreich, Bertsch.* Captured and beaten by civilian mob with bottles and poles. They tried to hang him — rescued by soldiers. *Believes Bertsch was killed by Kempeis. Beaten by Kempeis. Interro — Kendo bat beatings - English speaking interro. Oestreich badly wounded in hip by severe beatings caused chipped bone and abscess* Horse stall cellmates — O'Hara, Martin, Newcomb, Johnson, San Souci, Reynold, Kiernan, three orientals. *Two prisoners died in cell — Peter Fox on 7 August and Harold B. Halldorson on 3 June. No Red Cross Supplies.*

LESTER C. MORRIS: South Belmar, NJ. 29th BG. Captured 9 August. *Bailed out of engineer's hatch. Propeller severed Achilles tendon right heel. Gangrene — leg swollen all way to hip. Semi-conscious most of time in cell. Dungeon cellmates — McDilda and some Japanese. Interro — Atomic bomb questions — high ranking interro.*

WALLACE MORITZ: Brooklyn, NY. 504th BG — *Worde's Crew.* Downed 29 May near Yokohama. Radar Bombardier. *Witnessed Worde's terrible beating with kendo bats to the point that his whole head was so swollen that no one could recognize him — he was black and blue all over his body. "Shorty" directed the beating. "Shorty" shouted that he was going to cripple Moritz — tried to force signing a confession of bombing innocent women and children.* Horse stall cellmates — H. Anderson, M. Boyko, J. Costello, E. Gorrie, H. Jones, A. Lounsbury, J. Macomb, W. Mitchell, R. Sasser, M. Worde, L. Hill, W. Johnston, R. Grant, O. Thomas, A. Keniston, and Jordan. *Fox died in next cell. Macomb had broken left arm. Lounsbury had broken ankle and developed diphtheria. Mitchell and Anderson also developed diphtheria. Hill had dysentery. Was told that prisoners were to be executed for bombing civilians.*

JOHN H. NEWCOMB: Downed 25 May over Tokyo. Saw three parachutes of fellow crewmembers. All perished except for Donald D. Bloodgood. Vincent Pittari bailed out but was probably killed on landing. Horse stall cellmates — James W. Evans, Theodore H. Fox, Glen B. Guyton, Harold E. Halldorson, Dale L. Johnson, Sherwood C. Kiernan, Sylvio La Marca, James P. Martin, Delbert W. Miller, Arthur P. O'Hara, Jr., Patrick E. Pellecchia, Francis E. Reynolds, Michael J. Robertson, Maurice W. San Souci, Ray F. Hoppe. *Fox died in O'Hara's arms in our cell. Harold B. Halldorson — badly burned — wounds infected — interro even while dying — murdered.* "Shorty" tortured, kicked, and beat all prisoners and ordered brutal guard treatment. *Interro — naval officers interested in mines and mine laying — He was one of six senior prisoners taken to Imperial Army headquarters to stand trial as War Criminals — Fate of all prisoners were based on* *this event — He stood before about 50 Japanese military officers for questioning — the Japanese group was divided into teams of about ten officers each. Each prisoner was questioned by one team at a time. Then interchanged between teams until all teams had interro each of six prisoners — they were told this was trial for lives of all prisoners — high quality technical and military questions were asked — prisoners complained of Special Prisoner treatment and were told that was the responsibility of prison commander — all prisoners were to be shot as war criminals.*

WALTER W. OESTREICH: Downed 25 May over Tokyo. He and fellow crewman Elmer H. Bertsch were captured by civilians — Badly beaten — Rescued by soldiers. Horse stalls. "Shorty" beat him unconscious with *kendo* bat blows directed to his head — Permanent scars — Guards kicked him in his ribs — Spit in his face. *He suffered an abcess on his right hip due to beatings. The wound went all the way to the bone. Fox died in his cell.* Horse stall cellmates — J.W. Evans, Dale LaVerne Johnson, Sherwood C. Kierman, James P. Martin, Delbert W. Miller, John Harvey Newcomb, Silvio La Marca, Arthur P. O'Hara, Patrick Pellecchia, and Michael J. Robertson. *Harold B. Halldorson in same cell — badly burned and flak wounds — dying — kicked in ribs by medical officer — removed from cell — left on ground outside cell all night — murdered by medical officer by injection.*

EDWARD F. O'MARA: Jersey City, NJ. Downed 25 May over Tokyo. 444th BG. Radar Operator on "Her Majesty" airplane. Harold B. Halldorson — only other surviving member of his crew — Badly beaten during capture. Captured by civilians — Badly beaten — Saved by civil policeman. "Shorty" beat him with *kendo* bat for no reason. Horse stall cellmates — C. Babicz, D. Bloodgood, W. Branstrom. O. Briscoe, L. Decker, S. Downing, S. Forystek, A. Jelgerhuis, W. Halbert, R. Jones, J. Lamon, W. Olson, T. Peel, C. Reams, D. Ryan, A. Shelton, W. Strelnik, and M. Unterman.

THOMAS WILLIAM PEEL: Champaign, IL. Downed 25 May over Tokyo. 468th BG. Sprained ankles in bailout. Evaded capture one day. Captured by soldiers. Interro — Naval officers — Told that all crew died in crash. Fellow crewmen imprisoned at Kempei — Arthur Shelton, Wesley Halbert, Clarence Reams, Alvin Jelgerhuis, Donald Ryan, and John Lamon. Willis White was beaten on head and shoulders and put on public display — Stoned and beaten by civilians — Recognized voices of fellow crewmen, Jelgerhuis. Horse stalls — Nineteen men in his cell. Smelled burned flesh. His copilot in cell. Horse stall cellmates — Chester Babicz, Donald Bloodgood, Walter Branstrom, Oren Briscoe, Loren E. Decker, Scott Downing, Stanley Forystek, Wesley Halbert, Alvin Jelgerhuis, Robert P. Jones, John Lamon, Warren Olson, Edward F. O'Mara, Clarence

Reams, Donald E. Ryan, Arthur M. Shelton, William Strelnick, and Melvin Unterman. *Forystek and Olson were badly burned — blood and pus seeping out of their bodies — Forystek died in cell — his body was dragged onto ground outside cell and left lying for hours — Olson's burns were worse than Forystek — Ropes around his wrists cut through to bone — He was in cell about three weeks — no food — wounds smell awful — He was murdered out of cell. Fox was in the next cell — died in cell from Kendo bat beatings.*

PATRICK EDWARD PELLECCHIA: Philadelphia, PA. Downed 25 May over Tokyo. 40th BG. "Shorty" shouted death threats. Interro — Always beatings for no reason — Personal life questions.

ROBERT G. PHILLIPS: Downed 25 May over Tokyo. 73rd Wing. Plane exploded. Never heard of any crew members during captivity. Crew listed. Landed in water. Captured by soldiers in boat. Kicked and beaten. Mobbed by civilians. Interro — Beaten by "Shorty" with *kendo* bat. Dungeon cell for two days. Cellmates — Hoffman, McClure, and one other American. Moved to horse stalls. Cellmates — McQuade, Harry Slater (not Slater on his crew), Roger Townsend, Robert Franz, Rollin Heidlebaugh, Paul Trump, Robert Burkle, Albert Romoser, Rodger Orzilli, William McClure, John Boynton, Ward Lyons, John F. Ryan, Jack Evans, and Harry Hoffman. *Albert Lounsbury in cell #5 — broken ankle — made to stand for long periods. Fox in cell #3 next to his kicked by guards before dying.*

WARREN H. RANSLER *(One of my cellmates)*: Syracuse, NY. Downed 15 April over Kawasaki (near Tokyo). *Evaded capture 19 days. Captured on 4 May by a marine patrol.* "Shorty" *made him kneel and beat him unmercifully with* kendo *bat. Made him sign confession of war crimes — bombing innocent women and children. Horse stall cellmates — Fiske Hanley — badly injured with infected flak wounds, Nick Gazibara, Bill Grounds, Jack Hobbie, Ferdinand Spacal, Neal Cooper, Tribble, Arthur Gora. Robert Williams (P-51 pilot) with bad head wound — left side paralyzed — murdered by doctors. Fox died in horse stall cell block.*

CLARENCE P. REAMS: Bakersfield, CA. Downed 25 May over Tokyo. 468th BG. Fellow crewmembers who parachuted — Wesley Clark Halbert, John Charles Lamon, Arthur More Shelton, Alvin Jelgerhuis, Thomas William Peel, and Donald E. Ryan. Four crew members were lost with airplane. "Shorty" *kendo* bat beatings. Horse stall cellmates — Melvin Unterman, William Strelnik, Arthur More Shelton, John Charles Lamon, Wesley Clark Halbert, Loren E. Decker, Robert P. Jones, Scott M. Downing, Chester Babicz, Alvin Jelgerhuis, Edward F. O'Mara, Thomas William Peel, Donald E. Ryan, Donald Bloodgood, Walter Gordon Branstrom, Oren Glen Briscoe, Warren Olson, and Stanley Forystek. On 26 *May Forystek and Olson were pushed into cell — they had been badly beaten*

— *Olson was forced to walk to interro* — *Olson cried, "Give me water or shoot me! Please stop the pain." Both were murdered by the Japanese.*

HARMON REEDER: Gibson, OK. Downed 25 May over Tokyo. 504th BG. *Hitt's Crew.* "Shorty" threatened to behead — Hit with back side of sword on neck. Interro — Eight times — Beaten by guards on head and face. Dennis Tyring and Fink in his cell were caught talking — Badly beaten with clubs and rifle butts.

FRANCIS E. REYNOLDS: McDonald, PA. Downed 2 April over Tokyo. 498th BG. Captured by police. Moved three times on way to Kempei Tai. Kicked and beaten at each place. *John Houghton (his crew)* — *badly burned* — *died. Fox died. Forced to stand and kneel which was torture.*

ROBERT E. RING: Lafayette, IN. Downed 25 May over Tokyo. Leg badly injured in bailout. Horse stall cellmates — *Charles Snellz* — *bad burns* — *Died in next cell. John McGuire* — *good shape but contracted diphtheria* — *murdered. Lurvey* — *badly beaten* — *jaw fractured* — *kendo bat broken* — *splinters in jaw. Robert Jones* — *good shape* — *contracted dysentary* — *no food.*

MICHAEL J. ROBERTSON: Port Arthur, TX. Downed 25 May over Tokyo. *Broken leg and bad flak wounds* Civilian mob beat him up — Rocks, sticks, fists, kicks — Rescued by Kempeis. *Only surviving crewmate* — *Glen B. Guyton* — *large hole in head* — *captured at same time. Interro* — *beaten 25 times with* kendo bat — *told he would receive same punishment as his bombardier, whatever that meant. Horse stalls* — *eighteen cellmates* — J.W. Evans, LaVerne Johnson, Sherwood Kiernan, James P. Martin, Dilbert Miller, John Newcomb, Silvia La Marca, Arthur O'Hara, Patrick Pellcchia, Bertrum Guyton, Theodore Fox (in cell 12 hours — died), Harold B. Halldorson, Maurice San Souci, Francis Reynolds, Clarence Pressgrove, and O.W. Williams. *Guard stuck bayonet into fellow cellmate because his wife was killed by bombings. Cellmates beaten for lying down during day. Acute dysentary. Kneel Japanese fashion* — *paralizes legs. Fox died in cell. Went from 160 to 90 pounds in 81 days.* Halldorson — severe flak wounds and burns — murdered on 5 June.

WILLIAM P. L. ROSENTHAL: Chicago, IL. 462nd BG. Downed 24 May over Yokohama. Blown out of airplane. Flak wounds. Only co-pilot, Walter Tribel, and he survived. *Crew listed.* Captured in middle of Tokyo. Beaten by civilian mob who would have killed him. Saved by soldiers. *Horse stall cellmates* — *Japanese priest, Rev. Paul Sasaki, Majiro Church, Yodobashi, Tokyo requested med aid for his flak wounds* — *refused, Walter Tribel* (his co-pilot), *Gordon Scott - Morris in nearby Cell. Interro* — beaten and threatened with trial and execution. *Fox in nearby cell with Jap civilians then moved to Newcomb's cell where he died. Williams in nearby cell — carried in on stretcher — beaten many times with kendo bats while guards stood on feet and neck.*

JOHN FRANCIS RYAN: Portsmouth, NH. 504th BG. *Worde's Crew.* Downed 29 May near Yokohama. *Crew listed.* Captured by Japanese Home Guard. Horse stall cell #4. Initial cellmates — Jack G. Evans, Rollin Heidelbaugh, Roger J. Orzilli, Robert G. Phillips, Albert S. Romoser, Harry J. Slater, Joe L. McQuade, William Howard McClure, John B. Boydston. Later cellmate arrivals — Ward B. Lyons, Roy Washington, Robert J. Burkle, Robert Franz, Paul A. Trump. Interro —three to four hours — beaten. *Talking — bad beatings by guards. Marcus Worde (His airplane commander) brought to next cell was so badly beaten and head swollen that he couldn't be recognized. "Shorty" beatings. Jap "Turkey" — only one with cell keys — always accompanied guards when they entered cells. Getting drinks of water always a problem. Told by interro, "When we Japanese are ill, we refrain from food and water" — so seriously ill prisoners were denied food and water.*

ALBERT S. SOMOSER: Baltimore, MD. Downed 25 May over Tokyo. Evaded capture several days. *Horse stalls — pigs & chickens.* Fellow crewmen — Massey, Farquhar, and Green in nearby cell. *Green in good shape when captured — infected insect bites — bad dysentary — weak — made to stand up — badly beaten all over. P-51 pilot — Robert Williams — in next cell — flak wounds and internal injuries — died in cell Massey contracted diphtheria — paralyzed — beaten McQuade — badly burned — landed in water — wiped infected wounds — dirty* benjo comme *(toilet paper) used to clean wounds.*

MAURICE WILFRED SAN SOUCI: *Volunteer* benjo *soldier (collected sewage)* Central Falls, RI. 498th BG. Downed 1 April over Tokyo. Evaded capture one day. Captured by civilians. *Witnessed beatings of Roland Nelson, Fox, John Houghton. Pete Fox died in same cell — interro and beaten — had been there five days when first saw him — no food allowed — all good health on arrival — injuries caused by Japanese beatings. Houghton — badly burned — died about 14 April — kicked by "Shorty" who called Japanese doctor who gave lethal injection — body found in grave. Kenneth Peterson (on his crew) evaded capture three weeks — right food gangrenous — bad beating by "Shorty" who shouted, "You stole food from Japanese farmers, therefore you get no medical attention." — denied food for a couple of days — "Shorty" used rusty razor blade to lance gangrenous leg which drained for five days and bled so much Peterson became weak — "Shorty" said Peterson to be sent to camp for treatment — massacred at Tokyo Military prison / Many beatings — some-*

times by up to eight guards and "Shorty" — clubs, fists, boots — all over, including crotch area. Cellmates — Silvio LaMarca, Francis Reynolds, J.W. Evans. Observed beatings, Arthur O'Hara, James Martin, Milford J. Robertson, Dale J. Johnson, Delbert Miller observed Fox mistreatment and death / Guard's food — heaped bowls of rice, fish, vegetables, all they wanted. "Shorty" attended University of Ohio — in charge of intelligence.

NORMAN SELLZ: Omaha, NB. Radar Operator. Downed 7 April over Tokyo. Only five aft cabin crewmen survived Flak wounds. *Captured by mob of 500 civilians — beaten into unconsciousness — dragged through streets — then put in 1937 Ford car with about 12 Japs piled on top of him — hands wired together — still has scars. Zero fighter shot at him. Taken to Kempei Tai headquarters (Gestapo). Tortured with cigarette burns and matches. Put in a dungeon cell. Prisoner initials on walls with days marked off — some as high as 70 days. Japanese civilian cellmate awaiting trial. Japanese prisoner got two to three onigres and tried to get Sellz's. Had guard beat Sellz awake at 5 A.M. Interro — every three or four days — ropes, handcuffs, blindfold — bad beatings. After a week in dungeon — moved to horse stalls. New prisoners badly beaten. Beatings for talking. Nine P.M. sleep (shoto). On 10 May shipment of about 65 prisoners made to Tokyo military prison where they were massacred. Gore, Spacal, and about 10 Americans left in Kempei. "Remaining prisoners to be shipped a little later." Moved back to dungeon. Cellmates — Arthur Beckington (P-51 pilot), Robert Williams — in very bad shape — completely paralized. Japanese prisoners complaining couldn't sleep because of groans of American wounded. Four Japanese and four Americans in cell including Samuel Smith (Marine pilot) who arrived 12 June. Had to sleep on top of each other. Gora and Spacal in bad shape. Gora served as "Benjo soldier" saw some Swedish, German, and Japanese women prisoners in another cell group. Bad diarrhea and trench mouth. If rice kernel fell on floor, it was carefully recovered and eaten. A few guards talked to prisoners. Baseball, hot dogs, ice cream and movies are discussed. 15 August — moved to Omori Camp — bathed in ocean. Prisoners suffered from Beri-Beri, scurvy, diarrhea, trench mouth, and pellagra. American doctors (Bataan, Corregidor) at Camp Omori. English, Dutch, Italian prisoners. No other survivors of his crew. Robert Williams, Hulse, and Price were massacred at Tokyo Military prison.*

ARTHUR M. SHELTON, JR: Ithaca, NY. Downed 25 May over Tokyo. Navigator. 468th BG. *Gave war crime depositions on USS Benevolence to naval intelligence and at Letterman Hospital. Bad infected left leg — swollen to eight times size. Denied food — beaten on bad leg repeatedly — lanced with splinter — drained for a month hole in foot afterward — ulcers on leg. Saw plane crash while still in parachute. Only Survivor. Horse stalls —*

Eighteen cellmates — Chester Babicz, Donald Bloodgood, Walter Branstrom, Oren Briscoe, Loren Decker, Scott Downing, Stanley Forystek, Wesley Halbert, Alvin Jelgerhuis, Robert Jones, John Lamon, Warren Olson, Edward O'Mara, Thomas Peel, Clarence Reams, Donald Ryan, William Strelnik, and Melvin Unterman. *Forystek — bad burns and in shock — screaming for water — died in cell. Olson bad condition — walked out of cell block — murdered. Interro — twice.*

JOHN HENRY SHROFF: *US Navy — Air Group 85 — USS Shangrila.* Corsair pilot. Downed 8 June by Japanese fighter planes. Southern Kyushu. Landed in ocean. Captured by civilians. Arrived Kempei Tai 15 June. Dungeon cellmates — Leonard Green — Boil on neck — guards hit wound — Ankle wounds — Infected. Another Navy Pilot — Herbert Lincoln Law — F6F Pilot — Captured 1 August. Gordon H. Scott, William P. Rosenthal, Vincent A. Gaudiani (P-51 Pilot), Gordon P. Jordan. *Political prisoner wing of Dungeon — James Leonard Green and Shroff in cell from 15 June with four or five Japanese political prisoners — no other Americans in this wing. 15 July — transferred to another wing. Herbert Lincoln Law (navy) put in cell about 1 August. Eight Japanese in cell — mostly Americans in this wing. Gordon Scott and William Rosenthal in adjacent cell Theodore Homer Fox brought into left adjacent cell 1 August — in good shape — put on "Benjo soldier" detail — must have been horribly beaten — after about five or six days became violently ill — no medical attention — moved to another cell block — died in cell. Interro — beatings — Japanese doctor — questions about medical facilities on ship — Japanese study of malnutrition on ability to concentrate. Torture — Japanese kneel position for hours — beatings with kendo bat into unconsciousness. Starvation diet.*

HARRY SLATER, JR.: Pasadena, CA. Gunner. Downed 25 May over Tokyo. Horse stalls. Fifteen cellmates — James Evans, John Ryan, Boynton, William McCall. Interro — Beaten with *kendo* bats — No reason — Concentration on head. "Red" McQuade — Gunner — Severe burns — Bad wound odor — Beaten during interro. *Eleven dirty blankets for sixteen prisoners. No shoes and socks. Pig fed better than prisoners.*

SAMUEL S. SMITH: Minneapolis, MN. 2d Marine Air Wing — VMF-312-Corsair. Downed on 1 July. *Fighter Mission from Okinawa to Kyushu.* Drifted ashore in dinghy. Captured in Tokana Shima by soldiers placed in cave cell — handcuffed all time 10 to 12 days on Kyushu. Saw no other American prisoners. Taken to Kempei Tai Prison on 12 July. Arrived Kempei Tai political cell wing. Cellmates — Arthur E. Beckington, Arthur Gora, Ferdinand A. Spacal. *Interro — training questions — beatings for no reason. P-51 pilot (probably Fox) — saw him beaten up. Fox had diarrhea.*

Not fed food. About 50 American prisoners present during his stay. Lost 40 pounds in one month — food cut off for sick prisoners. No Red Cross supplies.

FERDINAND A. SPACEL: Chicago, IL. Downed 7 April over Tokyo. Radar Operator. 499th BG. Shot down by Japanese fighters over Chosi Point. Only he and Tail Gunner got out of airplane which blew up. Captured by soldiers. Heard fellow crewman Otto J. Marek on way to Kempei Tai. Interro — Beaten with *kendo* bat by "Shorty" who screamed threats — Many interros — Many beatings — Personal life questions. *Horse stalls — cell #2 — San Souci, Peterson, Arthur Beckington cell #3 — Don't remember cell #4. Arthur Gora only one remembered. 10 May — large POW Group transferred to another prison — about 65 in group. Known to be in group — Douglas Bannon. Harvey M. Glick, John T. Hostey, Frederick Hulse, T. Price, Theodore C. Reynolds, Anthony F. Scolara, Henry L. Younge, Bertram L. Ware — all called out by F. Scolara, Henry L. Younge, Bertram L. Ware — all called out by name — number put on backs with chalk — no system in selection — many radar operations were kept at Kempei. 14 April — Roland Nelson and John S. Houghton arrived — both badly burned — Nelson died two days after arrival. Don't know Houghton's fate. 25 May — Robert Williams arrived — paralyzed in left side — in spite of poor condition interro four times. On 28 July he was removed and murdered. Fox died in his cell on 21 April. Peterson arrived — "Shorty" threatened him — Gangrene set into his foot and leg — toes dropped off. Fiske Hanley arrived — flak wounds in back posterior, and legs. Doctor examined him — no medical help.*

ABEL P. SOTO: San Francisco, CA. Downed 25 May over Tokyo. Flight Engineer. Fellow crewmen — Fielder, Reeder, and he were badly beaten with rifle butts during capture. "Shorty" beat him many times about face and head — knocked out teeth — mouth badly cut — a torture to eat.

WILLIAM B. STRELNIK: Anaconda, MT. Heard beatings of others. Beaten himself. "Shorty" beat him while kneeling Japanese style. Torture - Japanese kneel position — Leg paralysis. Horse stalls. *Fox in next cell — died. Arrived with Forystek and Olson — both badly burned — beaten in truck to Kempei. Forystek particularly for asking for water. Forystek died in cel. Olson taken from cell and murdered.*

ROGER LEE TOWNSEND: Ohill, IL. 6th BG. Downed 25 May over Tokyo. Flight Engineer. Horse stalls — 16 *cellmates — too crowded to lie down to sleep* — John B. Boynton, Robert J. Burkle, J.W. Evans, Robert A. Franz, R. Heidelbaugh, Harvey H. Huffman, Ward B. Lyons, William H. McClure, Joe L. McQuade, Rober J. Orzilli, Robert G. Phillips, Albert S.

Romoser, John F. Ryan, Harry Slater, Jr., and Paul A. Trump. Frank C. Massey, Radio Operator, — Interro several times. Joe L. McQuade — Severely burned back & legs — Wounds kicked — Forced to walk to interro — Blood running from wounds. *Cells alive with fleas and lice — sprayed with something which did no good.*

DENNIS E. TYRING: Millersburg, IN. Downed 25 May over Tokyo. Horse stall cellmates — Walter W. Dickerson, Floyd F. Fielder, David Glenn Farguhar, Jr., Robert L. Fink, Nick Gazibara, Jr., Franklyn Stanley Green, Maynard Ben Hanks, Frank Cary Massey, George E. McGraw, Donald R. Press, Harmon Reeder, Jr., George Sheridan, Abel Patrick Soto, Walter W. Wiernick, and Marvin S. Watkins. *Fellow crewman — George L. Sheridan — navigator — cruelty and neglect resulted in deaths. On arrival needed no medical treatment — got sore throats — couldn't eat — got no food — dysentery. Couldn't kill his fleas and lice. Looked no longer human. Made it to Omori. Diagnosis — Diphtheria — died before liberation. Frank Massey — cellmate — condition similar to Sheridan's. James T. Nacomb — next cell — broken arm — caught talking to Robert L. Fink — both almost beaten to death with rifle butts, kendo bats, boot kicks — lost conciousness — given dirty rags to soak up blood. Maynor Hanks brought into cell 10 after my arrival. Hanks really in bad condition — a skeleton — grew so weak he could hardly sit up — tortured by forced standing at attention until fainting — then beaten — pitiful to see life ebbing away — would not have survived another two weeks at Kempei. Franklin Green — poor condition — weak — intensified by fleas bites — body one solid scab. "Shorty" and guards laughed. Interro — beatings for no reason — threatened with execution by beheading.*

PAUL A. TRUMP: Phoenixville, PA. 6th BG. Downed 20 July over Niigata. Captured by civilians — beaten with sticks, stones, and long poles with knives on the ends until unconscious with three knife wounds. Rescued by Japanese soldier who heard screams and rifle shots. Fellow crewmen bailing out — Gordon P. Jordan, Walter W. Wiernick, George E. McGraw, Walter Dickerson, Robert J. Burkle, Robert A. Grant. All survived Kempei. Missing crew members listed. Horse stall cellmates — John B. Boynton, Rollin Heidelbaugh, Harvey Hoffman, William McClure, Roger Orzilli, Robert Phillips, Albert Romoser, Joe McQuade, Jack G. Evans, Robert Franz, John Ryan, Harry Salter, Robert J. Burkle, plus two forgotten names. *Theodore Fox in next cell — suffering immensely — died — interro eight times.*

MARVIN SIDNEY WATKINS: Church Road, VA. 6th BG. Downed 5 May over Tachairai Air Depot, Kyushu. Arrived Kempei Tai on 10 May. Solitary confinement until 26 May. Next day had *Fifteen cellmates — Frank*

C. Massey and George L. Sheridan got diphtheria — both made it to Omori prison camp were treated by American doctors. Robert L. Fink and Dennis E. Tyring were caught talking and beaten almost to death by many guards. Franklin Green — after 30 days — body covered with infected flea and lice bites. Maynor B. Hanks — at Kempei long time — forced to stand at attention for hours — very poor condition. Continual "Shorty" beatings and threats.

Appendix E

War Crime Trials

Robert Neptune, War Crime Prosecutor of Kempei Tai war criminals, preserved a considerable file on his Japanese war crime trial work. He generously furnished me with Special Prisoner affidavits and prosecution data used during the post-war trials of our sadistic captors. For readers interested in a deeper understanding of atrocities committed against individual Special Prisoners, affidavits have been condensed and included herein, as Appendix D.

Data is also presented from the criminal proceedings by United States authorities against Kempei Tai war criminals based on documents generated by the trials. A most deadly finding was contained in Lieutenant Colonel Fujino's trial documentation:

> On or about 14 August 1945, Col. Otani, commander of Tokyo Kempei Tai headquarters, ordered Fujino to execute all American prisoners.
>
> Otani feared the consequences of turning American prisoners over to liberating authorities in such poor physical condition. Colonel Fujino protested the order, disobeyed the order, and made immediate preparations for transfer of American prisoners to the eastern district's army's Omori Prison Camp, thus saving them from Kempei Tai executions.

CRIMINAL CHARGES

The following presents a summary of charges against accused Kempei Tai Headquarters staff members and resultant court findings. General charges against these inhuman, sadistic Japanese beasts were based on the death and misery suffered by American Special Prisoners held at Kempei Tai Headquarters.

1. American prisoners were deliberately murdered by poisonous injections administered by Japanese medical officers.

2. Adequate and proper quarters, hygiene, food and water, clothing, medicines, medical care, attention, and hospitalization were not provided, thereby contributing to the sicknesses, wounds, diseases, disabilities, and sufferings of American Prisoners of War.

3. Captured American airmen were detained at the Kempei Tai Headquarters for interrogation and investigation pending disposition by higher headquarters, either as Prisoners of War or as suspected war criminals.

4. Kempei Tai was responsible for and in charge of interrogation and investigation of such detainees and their maintenance, care, treatment, and physical well-being, during the period of their detention. The laws and customs of war were violated in these cases.

5. Cells in which the prisoners were incarcerated were dark, dirty, vermin-infested, unventilated, and lacking in minimum plumbing requirements.

6. During the entire period of incarceration , the prisoners were furnished no clothing whatsoever, but were compelled to wear the apparel, if any, which they were wearing at the time of their capture.

7. Food allowance, consisting mainly of rice, was insufficient to satisfy minimum human requirements for the preservation of health and life.

8. No facilities were furnished to the prisoners for personal hygiene or cleanliness nor were they given the opportunity to wash, either their bodies or their clothing, during their confinement.

9. Medical supplies and treatment were entirely inadequate, in most cases denied, in spite of the fact that numerous prisoners were suffering from serious burns, wounds, diseases, and other injuries and afflictions.

10. Necessary hospitalization, even in the most urgent cases, was denied altogether.

11. American prisoners suffered from malnutrition, personal filth, body vermin, skin eruptions and sores, untended burns, wounds, injuries and diseases.

12. American prisoners were reduced and degraded to sub-human standards of existence.

13. American prisoners died as a direct result of various physical

afflictions contracted at the time of apprehension or subsequently while in confinement.

14. Kempei Tai officers, cell guards, mess, medical personnel, and former officers of higher army headquarters were responsible for crimes perpetrated on American prisoners.

15. Confinement cells were grossly overcrowded to the extent that prisoners could not lie down without overlapping each other.

16. Japanese criminals and political prisoners shared cells with the American prisoners.

17. American prisoners could not shave or wash themselves or their clothing.

18. Food and water rations were withheld from American prisoners.

19. Shoes and socks were denied.

20. Food rations were thrown on filthy cell floors.

21. No exercise was permitted.

22. Torture was permitted by various means, such as kicking and beatings directed at wound and head areas. Forced standing at attention or kneeling in the Japanese fashion for long periods caused prisoners extreme pain and unconsciousness.

23. Guards were permitted to slap, kick, poke and hit with sticks and rifle butts, spit on, and threaten with guns and bayonets.

24. Failure to isolate seriously wounded, sick, diseased, and infected prisoners from other prisoners.

25. Medical officers administered lethal injections.

26. Prisoners were forced by threats of death and beatings to sign confessions without knowing what the Japanese script stated.

27. American prisoners were continually beaten which resulted in the death of at least sixteen prisoners.

28. American prisoners were not allowed to talk to each other. Severe beatings were administered to those caught talking. Japanese fellow prisoners told on their American cellmates, often untruthfully.

29. American prisoners were classified as accused war criminals and were designated "Special Prisoners" subject to trial and execution.

30. American prisoners were continually threatened with death.

KEMPEI TAI DEFENSE

American Prisoners of War were, at the outset, the responsibility of Japan's General Defense Command and later of the Eastern District Army headquartered in Tokyo. Eastern District Army assigned responsibility of American "Special Prisoners" to Kempei Tai Headquarters for the purpose of investigation and interrogation. It was anticipated that the period of American prisoner confinement would be of short duration since Kempei facilities were not suitable for long confinement of large numbers of men.

Kempei Tai became primarily responsible for imprisonment, feeding, clothing, care, and treatment. As the war progressed, shortages of food and clothing became increasingly acute. Rations and allowances were gradually reduced not only for the prisoners but for civilians and military alike. The Japanese Empire faced a desperate military situation. Eastern District Army Headquarters did not provide for timely prisoner transfer to other military prisons. Kempei Tai Headquarters was stuck with an overload of prisoners and did the best they could.

GENERAL STAFF — IMPERIAL JAPANESE ARMY
War Minister: General Korechika Anami
Army Chief of Staff: General Yoshijiro Umizu
Army Deputy Chief of Staff: Lt. Gen. Torashira Kawabe

EASTERN DISTRICT ARMY
Eastern District Army Commander: General Shizuichi Tanaka
Chief of the Legal Section: Lt. Gen. Tomos Aburo Shimada
Chief of the Medical Department: Maj. Gen. Shoji Kono
Staff Officer Responsible for American Flyers: Lt. Col. Kimiya Ichinoe
Medical Officers: 1/Lt. Kenji Hirano
      1/Lt. Rokuro Sonobe
      Lt. Hasabe (Office in Kempei Tai Hdqtrs.)
      Lt. Morislue (Office in Kempei Tai Hdqtrs.)
Enlisted: Sgt. Major Shoichiro Matsumoto
      Sgt. Major Goro Yamaka (Office in Kempei Tai Hdqtrs.)

KEMPEI TAI HEADQUARTERS
Kempei Tai Commander: Lt. Gen. Sanji Okido (Reports to Army Chief of Staff)
Eastern District Army Kempei Tai Commander: Col. Keijiro Otani
Deputy Commander: Lt. Col. Ranjo Fujino: Senior Staff Officer — General Affairs
Section Police Affairs Section Commander: Lt. Col. Takeo Kosaka
Medical Officers: Maj. Shinichi Morisue
      Probationary Officer: Toshitsura Hasbe
Chief Intelligence Section: Maj. Eiichi Sugihara — Overall Responsibility for Interrogations of American Prisoners
Chief Foreign Affairs Section: Maj. Eiichi Sugihara — Overall Responsibility For American Prisoners
Chief Intelligence Command Squad: Lt. Sadamu Motokawa — Responsible for Physical Care and Custody of American Prisoners
Attorneys: 1/Lt. Toshio Toyama — Responsible for Questioning of American Prisoners and Trial Decisions

1/Lt. Toshio Toyama — Responsible for Interrogations and Investigations — American Prisoners.

Foreign Affairs Section: 2/Lt. Sadamu Motokawa — Responsible for Handling of American Prisoners

2/Lt. Tsune Nemoto — Responsible for Questioning American Prisoners

Civilian Yasuo Kobayashi Also Known as "Shorty" — Responsible for Handling and Questioning American Prisoners

Warrant Officer Kenichi Yanagizawa — Handling of American Prisoners

Sgt. Maj. Masao Kuwabara — Handling of American Prisoners

Corp. Kiyoshi Tanabe — Chief Clerk

Corp. Toyokazu Himada (Canada Nisei) — Intrepretor and Interrogator

Cell Block Supervisor — Lt. Nobushige Wachi — Security, Handling, and care of American Prisoners

Intelligence Squad Leader — Lt. Tsume Nemoto — Investigations and Interrogations

WAR CRIME SENTENCES
GENERAL STAFF — IMPERIAL JAPANESE ARMY

Gen. Korechika Anami: Committed Suicide, August 1945

Gen. Yoshijiro Umezi: Signed Peace Treaty 2 Sept. 1945 on USS *Missouri*

EASTERN DISTRICT ARMY

Gen. Shizuichi Tanaka: Committed Suicide, August 1945

Lt. Gen. Tomosaburo Shimada: Committed Suicide, Sept. 1945

Lt. Gen. Goro Okido: Tried — Records show his trial delayed until facts of Osaka Kempei Tai Murder of 55 Americans Known

Maj. Gen. Shojikono: Acquitted

Lt. Gen. Kimiya Ichinoe: 20 Years at Hard Labor

1/Lt. Kenji Hirano: Life at Hard Labor

1/Lt. Rokura Sonobe: 2 Years at Hard Labor

Sgt. Maj. Shoichiro Matsumoto: Acquitted

Sgt. Maj. Goro Yamaka: Acquitted

KEMPEI TAI HEADQUARTERS

Col. Keijiro Otani: Record shows he committed suicide in 1945. Actually, he faked suicide and became a businessman in Nagasaki.

Lt. Col. Ranjo Fujino: 5 Years at Hard Labor

Lt. Col. Takeo Kosaka: In Hiding

Maj. Shinichi Morisue: Believed to have committed suicide

Maj. Eiichi Sugihara: 5 Years at Hard Labor

1/Lt. Toshio Toyama: Life at Hard Labor

2/Lt. Sadami Motokawa: Hanged, July 1948
2/Lt. Tsune Nemoto: 5½ Years at Hard Labor
Yasuo "Shorty" Kobayashi (civilian): 40 years at hard labor.
Hasabe — Probationary Medical Officer: Committed suicide, Dec. 1945
Warrant Officer Kenichi Yanagizawa: Acquitted
Sgt. Maj. Masao Kuwabara: Life at Hard Labor
Corp. Kiyoshi Tanabe: 2 ½ Years at Hard Labor
Corp. Toyokazu Himada (Canadian Nisei): 4 Years at Hard Labor
Shizuichi Tanaka: Committed Suicide, August 1945
Tomosaburo Shimada: Committed Suicide, Sept. 1945
1/Lt. Toshio Toyama: Life at Hard Labor
Lt. Nobushige Wachi: 8 Years at Hard Labor
Shoji Kono: Acquitted

After the war, Japan's Class A war criminals were imprisoned at Camp Omori. Class A war criminals were high ranking military and government officials. Camp Omori was the finest prison camp in Japan and selected for its close proximity to Yokohama where their trials were held. Before the Class A prisoners arrived at Omori, our troups cleaned, white-washed and debugged this so-called "Model Prison," which was really a deplorable camp. Among the prisoners held there during their trials were Hideki Tojo, Admiral Shigetaro Shimada, Cabinet Minister Sujuki, General Masaharu Homma, and Colonel Kingoro Yashimoto, leader of the Black Dragon Society.

In the tradition of American decency, these high-level prisoners were treated humanely and fed well.

Those Japanese war criminals sentenced to be executed, whose sentences had not been carried out, and those convicted war criminals serving prison sentences were immediately freed after MacArthur returned governmental authority back to the Japanese.

Geneva Convention (III) Rules Relative to the Treatment of Prisoners of War

The following gives a brief coverage of the Geneva Convention Rules which, in no case, were adhered to by the Japanese in their treatment of Special Prisoners.

QUARTERS, FOOD, AND CLOTHING OF POWS

Article 25: POWs shall be quartered under conditions as favourable as those for the forces of the Detaining Power who are billeted in the same area. The premises provided for the use of POWs individually or collectively, shall be entirely protected from dampness and adequately heated and lighted. All precautions must be taken against the danger of fire.

Article 26: The basic daily food rations shall be sufficient in quantity, quality, and variety to keep POWs in good health and to prevent loss of weight or the development of nutritional deficiencies. Sufficient drinking water shall be supplied to POWs.

Article 27: Clothing, underwear, and footwear shall be supplied to POWs in sufficient quantities, which shall make allowance for the climate of the region. The regular replacement and repair of the above articles shall be assured.

Article 28: Canteens shall be installed in all camps, where POWs may procure foodstuffs, soap, and tobacco and ordinary articles in daily use.

HYGIENE AND MEDICAL ATTENTION

Article 29: The Detaining Power shall be bound to take all sanitary measures necessary to ensure the cleanliness and healthfulness of camps and to prevent epidemics.

Article 30: Every camp shall have an adequate infirmary where POWs may have the attention they require, as well as an appropriate diet. POWs suffering from serious disease, or whose condition necessitated special treatment, a surgical operation or hospital care, must be admitted to any military or civil medical unit where such treatment can be given. POWs shall have the attention, preferably, of medical personnel of the powers on which they depend and, if possible, of their nationality.

Article 31: Medical inspections of POWs shall be held at least once a month. They shall include the checking and recording of the weight of each POW.

DEATH OF POWS

Article 120: Death certificates of all persons who die as POWs shall be forwarded to the POW Information Bureau. The burial or cremation of a POW shall be preceded by a medical examination of the body with a view to confirming death and a report be made. *POWs who died in captivity are to be honourably buried.*

Appendix G

Horse Stall Cell Prisoners

After the war, Scott Downing, a fellow Special Prisoner, was ordered to return to Japan to aid Special Prosecutor Robert Neptune in the tremendous task of preparing for the war crimes trials. He was able to compile lists of prisoners kept in the Horse Stall Cells. These cells were only eight by ten feet.

The following is a listing of the prisoners held in the Horse Stall Cells before WW II hostilities ceased on 15 August when American prisoners were transferred to Camp Omori.

CELL #1	CELL #2
Richard Mansfield	Melvin Uterman
Francis Jensen (died)	John C. Lamon
Harold Leavitt	Loren E Decker
John MacGuire	Robert P. Jones
Glidden C. Lurvery	William B. Strelnik
Charles J. Couchman	Wesley V. Halbert
Robert R. Michelsen	Arthur M. Shelton
William H. McClure	Scott M. Downing
Milan E. Danaway	Chaester C. Babicz
Charles W. Snell (died)	Donald E. Ryan
Stephen Spega, Jr.	Clarence P. Reams
Robert R. Ring	Thomas H. Peel
Joseph J. Deeb	Edward F. O'Mara

(CELL #1 cont.)
Harry D. Magnuson
Harry H. French
Kenneth E. Creech
Gerald Fairve
Norman D. Jorgensen

CELL #3
James P. Martin
Arthur P. O'Hara
John H. Newcomb
Delbert W. Miller
Patrick E. Pellecchia
Clarence L. Pressgrove
John W. Evans
Sylvio LaMarca
Maurice San Souci
Sherwood C. Kieman
Francis E. Reynolds
Michael J. Robertson
Dale L. Johnson
Glen B. Guyton
Theodore Fox (died)
Harold E. Halldorson (died)

CELL #5
Gordon P. Jordan
Harold J. Anderson
Michael Boyko
Joseph E. Costello
Edward Gorrie
John T. Macomb
William A. Mitchell
Wallace Moritz
Marcus E. Worde
Albert P. Lounsbury
Oliver C. Thomas
Henry W. Jones
Lloyd R. Hill
John W. Evans
Robert A. Grant
Allan C. Keniston

(CELL #2 cont.)
Orin G. Briscoe
Walter W. Branstrom
Donald D. Bloodgood
Alvin Jelggerhius
Stanley Forysteck (died)

CELL #4
John B. Boynton
Rollin Heidlebaugh
Albert S. Romoser
Robert G. Phillips
Roger J. Orzilli
Joe L. McQuade
Robert A. Franz
Robert L. Townsend
Jack G. Evans
Harvey H. Hoffman
Harry Slater, Jr.
Paul A. Trump
Robert J. Burkle
William H. McClure
Ward B. Lyons
John F. Ryan

CELL #6
Floyd F. Fielder
George L. Sheridan
Harmon H. Reeder
Robert L. Fink
Walter W. Dickerson
Abel P. Soto
Frank G. Massey
Donald R. Press
Mayner B. Hanks
David G. Farquhar
Nicholas Gazibara
Franklyn S. Green
George McGraw
Walter W. Wiermick
Dennis E. Tyring

Appendix H

Our Crew Missions

The Army Air Force rated all flights performed in the Pacific War Theater as COMBAT. However, only those missions where bombs were actually dropped on Japanese targets counted toward the required thirty-five missions needed to finish our combat assignment and return to the United States.

Our crew flew only *seven* combat missions to the Japanese homeland before being shot down. We also flew practice combat missions, Air/Sea Rescue (Super Dumbo), bombing practice, gunnery practice, and test flights. Our crew was credited in official Air Force records with the flights listed below:

16 January 1945 .... Combat Area Flight
19 January 1945 .... Combat Area Flight
21 January 1945 .... Truk (Practice)
29 January 1945 .... Iwo Jima (Practice)
11 February 1945 .... Combat Area Flight
13 February 1945 .... Combat Area Flight
16 February 1945 .... *Nagoya*
22 February 1945 .... Combat Area Flight
25 February 1945 .... *Tokyo*
2 March 1945 .... Combat Area Flight
4 March 1945 .... *Tokyo*
7 March 1945 .... Combat Area Flight

9 March 1945 .... *Tokyo* (First Blitz/Fire Raid)
16 March 1945 .... *Kobe* (Blitz/Fire Raid)
18 March 1945 .... *Nagoya* (Blitz/Fire Raid)
27 March 1945 .... *Shimonoseki Straits*

The March 9-10 fire-raid on Tokyo was history's worst bombing-raid, in regard to casualties. There were more than one-hundred-thousand Japanese killed during the raid — more casualties than from either atomic bomb mission.

The unidentifiable bodies of eight members of John A. Brown's B-29 crew were found by an American Graves Registration team, after the war. Remains of my comrades were returned to the United States and reverently buried in a common grave in Zachary Taylor National Cemetery, Louisville, Kentucky.

This beautifully landscaped cemetery is centrally located to the widely scattered home towns of these brave airmen. Our government couldn't have chosen a more fitting or lovelier final resting place for these fine, young warriors who gave their lives to preserve the world's freedom.

Buried here are my fellow crewmen — my friends. I have visited this site many times to pay my respects and offer prayers.

Bibliography

Agawa, Hiroyuki. *The Reluctant Admiral — Yamamoto and the Imperial Navy*. Kodansha Internatioal, Ltd. 1979.

Baily, Ronald H. *Prisoners of War: World War II*. Time-Life Books.

Bergamini, David. *Japan's Imperial Conspiracy*. Pocket Books, 1971.

Berry, Henry. *Semper Fi, Mac*. Berkley Books, 1982.

Blair, Clay Jr. *Silent Victory*. J. B. Lippincott Co., 1975.

Boyingtton, Col. Gregory "Pappy". *Baa Baa Black Sheep*. Bantam Books, 1958.

Braddon, Russel. *Japan Against the World: 1941-2041*. Stein & Day, 1984.

Brooks, Janice Young. *Guests of the Emperor*. Ballantine Books, 1990.

Carter, Kit C., Robert Mueller. *AAF in WWII: Combat Chronology 1941-45*. Off. AF Hist. 1973.

Castillon, Cmdr. Edmund L. *The Seabees in World War II*. Random House, 1963.

Coleman, John S. Jr. *Bataan and Beyond*. Texas A & M Press, 1978 (Jack Clayton Collection).

Congdon, Don. *Combat: The War with Japan*. Dell Books, 1962.

Cook, Haruko Taya & Theodore F. Cook. *Japan at War: An Oral History*. The New Press, 1992.

Cortesi, Lawrence. *Pacific Breakthrough*. Zebra Books, 1981.

——. *Pacific Hellfire*. Zebra Books, 1983.

——. *Valor at Okinawa*. Zebra Books, 1981.

Costello, John Wm. *The Pacific War*. Collins & Sons Ltd., 1981.

Craig, William. *The Fall of Japan*. Dial Press, 1967.

Daws, Gavan. *Prisoners of the Japanese*. Morrow, 1994.

Deacon, K. Richard. *Kempei Tai: A History of the Japanese Secret Service*. Beautfort Press, 1983.

Edoin, Hoito. *The Night Tokyo Burned: The Incendiary Campaign Against Japan, March-August 1945*. St. Martin's Press, 1987.

Enright, Capt. Joseph F. *Shinano*. St. Martin's Press, 1987.

Fakita, Frank "Foo." *Foo: A Japanese-American Prisoner of the Rising Sun*. Univ. N. Texas Press, 1993.

Farago, Ladis. *The Broken Seal*. Bantam Books, 1967.

Gibney, Frank. *Senso: The Japanese Remember the Pacific War*. Sharpe Press, England, 1995 (Jack Clayton Collection).

Goodwin, Michael J. *Shobun, A Forgotten War Crime in the Pacific*. Stackpole Books, 1995 (Jack Clayton Collection).

271

Gordon, Ernest. *Through the Valley of the Kwai*. Bantam Books, 1969.

Griffin, Marcus and Eva Jane Matson. *Heroes of Bataan*. Marcus Griffin, 1994. (Jack Clayton Collection).

Gunnison, Royal Arch. *So Sorry: No Peace*. Viking Press, 1944 (Jack Clayton Collection).

Hanley, Fiske. *504th Bomb Group History*. Olympia Sales Corp., 1992.

Hara, Capt. Tameich. *Japanese Destroyer Captain*. Ballantine Books, 1961.

Harrington, Joseph, D. *Yankee Samurai*. Pettigrew Enterprises, Inc., 1979.

Hershey, John. *Hiroshimo*. Bantam Books, 1966.

——. *Hiroshima*. Bantam Books, 1946.

Hess, Wm. N. *Pacific Sweep: The 5th & 13th Fighter Commanders*. Zebra Books, 1994.

Hicks, George. *Comfort Women*. Nortex Press, 1994 (Jack Clayton Collection).

Holbrook, Herber A. *USS Houston: Last Flagship of the Asiactic Fleet*. Pacific Ships & Shore, 1981 (Jack Clayton Collection).

Home, James. *Their Last Tenko*. Quoin Publishing, England, 1989 (Jack Clayton Collection).

Hoyt, Edwin P. *Closing the Circle: War in the Pacific 1945*. Avon Books, 1982.

——. *To the Marianas: War in the Central Pacific — 1944*. Avon Books, 1980.

——. *The Battle of Leyte Gulf*. Pinnacle Books, 1972.

——. *The Last Kamikaze: The Story of Admiral Ugaki*. Praeger Press, 1993 (Jack Clayton Collection).

Ingle, Don. *No Less A Hero*. Published by Don Ingle, 1994.

Jackson, Donald. *Torokina*. Iowa State University Press, 1989 (Jack Clayton Collection).

Jones, Betty B. *The December Ship*. McFarland Press, 1992 (Jack Clayton Collection).

Kennan, George F. *Memories*. Bantam Books, 1969.

Kerr, E., Bartlett. *Survival and Surrender: The Experience of American POW in The Pacific 1941-1945*. William Morrow & Co., 1985.

——. *Flames Over Tokyo*. Donald I. Fine Inc., 1991.

Knox, Donald. *The Death March*. Harcourt Brace, 1981 (Jack Clayton Collection).

Kuwahara, Yasuo and George T. Allred. *Kamikaze*. Ballantine Books, 1957.

LaForte, R. S. *With Only The Will to Live: Accounts of Americans in Japanese Prison Camps 1941-1945*. Scholarly Resources Inc., 1994.

Layton, Adm. Edwin T. *And I Was There*. R. Wm. Morrow & Co., 1985.

Lopez, Don. *Into the Teeth of the Tiger*. Bantam Books, 1986.

Lord, Walter. *Day of Infamy*. Bantam Books, 1957.

Lucas, Cella. *Prisoners of Santo Tomas*. David & Charles Military Books, 1957, (Jack Clayton Collection).

Manchester, Wm. *Goodbye, Darkness: A Memoir of the Pacific War*. Dell Books, 1979.

Martin, James P. bombardier of *"Sitting Pretty."* POW Experiences. James P. Martin.

Mikesh, Robert C. *Broken Wings of the Samurai: The Destruction of the Japanese Air Force*. Naval Institute Press, 1993 (H. B. Parnell Collection).

Moody, Samuel B. *Reprieve From Hell*, self published. 1961.

Mosley, Leonard. *Hirohito: Emperor of Japan*. Avon Press. 1967.

Neptune, Robert. *Collected Kempei Tai HQTR. War Crimes Trial.* US Tokyo War Crimes Prosecutor.

O'Kane, R. Adm. Richard H. *Clear the Bridge.* Bantam Books, 1977.

Pacific Research Society. *Japan's Longest Day.* 1968.

Peacock, Don. *The Emperors Guest.* Oleander Press, England, 1989 (Jack Clayton Collection).

Peck, Ira. *The Battle of Midway.* Scholastic Book Services, 1976.

Potter, E. B. *Nimitz.* Naval Institute Press, 1976.

Potter, John Deane. *Yamato.* Paperback Library, 1965.

Prange, Gordon W. *Miracle at Midway.* Penguin Books, 1982.

Reisman, W. Michaeil and Chris T. Antoniou. *The Laws of War.* Vintage Books / Random House, 1994.

Robertson, Eric. *The Japanese File.* Heinemaqnn Asia Press, 1979 (Jack Clayton Collection).

Ross, Walter & Lucille. *Courage Beyond the Blindfold.* Global Press, 1995.

Sakamaki, Kazuo. *I Attacked Pearl Harbor.* Association Press, 1949.

Sanford, Donald S. *Midway.* Bantam Books, 1976.

Schultz, Duane. *Last Battle Station.* St. Martin's Press, 1985.

Smith, Stanley W. *Prisoner of the Emperor.* Univ. Colo. Press, 1991 (Jack Clayton Collection).

Stewart, Sidney. *Give Us This Day.* Avon Books, 1956.

Tanaka, Yuki. *Hidden Horrors.* Westview Press, 1996.

Taylor, Lawrence. *A Trial of Generals: Homma/Yamashita/MacAurthur.* Icarus Press, 1981.

Thomas, Gordon & Max Morgan Witts. *Enola Gay.* Pocket Books, 1978.

Thomas, Oliver C/Flight Engineer. *Saga of the Crew of A B-29 Airplane Called "Sitting Pretty."*

Toland, John. *Rising Sun: The Decline and Fall of the Japanese Empire.* Bantam Books, 1971.

——. *Occupation.* Tom Doherty Associates, 1988.

——. *Infamy: Pearl Harbor and its Aftermath.* Berkley, 1982.

Wade, Tom Henling. *Prisoner of the Japanese.* Kangaroo Press (Jack Clayton Collection).

Warner, Denis & Peggy. *The Sacred Warriors: Japan's Suicide Legions.* Avon Books, 1982.

Weiss, Edward W. *Under the Rising Sun: War, Captivity, & Survival, 1941-1945.* Ed. W. Weiss Publisher, 1995.

Wolfert, Ira. *American Guerrilla in the Philippines.* Simon & Schuster, 1942 (Jack Clayton Collection).

Wyden, Peter. *Day One: Before Hiroshima and After.* Warner Books, 1984.

Wygle, Peter R. *Surviving A Japanese POW Camp.* Pathfinder, 1991.

Index

275

CPSIA information can be obtained
at www.ICGtesting.com
Printed in the USA
FFOW04n0630100117
31192FF